FIELDWORK TRAINING
IN SOCIAL WORK

This volume is a definitive manual for students and practitioners involved in learning and developing essential theories and models for fieldwork practicum in social work education. It addresses various functional issues in field practicum, delineates proper guidelines for students and supervisors, discusses criteria of supervision and evaluation, and explores the concerns facing South Asian field practitioners.

The volume focuses on traditional and non-traditional components and aspects of fieldwork and training, such as:

- The value and use of educational camps and skill development workshops.
- The contemporary field-level needs and strategies in social work practicum.
- Formulating alternative practice theories that will allow social work practitioners to respond to the critical social problems unique to India and South Asia.

The book provides multiple frameworks for teaching and learning fieldwork that integrate theory and practice and create an environment where students can develop intervention strategies using their knowledge, skills, and techniques.

The volume will be indispensable reading for undergraduate and post-graduate students of social work. It will also be useful for scholars of sociology, anthropology, and development studies, and practitioners engaged in various non-governmental and international organizations.

Bishnu Mohan Dash is an academician and a researcher in Social Work engaged in spearheading the movement for Bharatiyakaran of social work education in India. He is an Assistant Professor in Social Work at Bhim Rao Ambedkar College, University of Delhi, India.

Sanjoy Roy is an Associate Professor at the Department of Social Work, University of Delhi, India. He has published more than 45 articles and research papers in different journals and books, and 11 books related to women's development, fieldwork practice in social work education, and rural development.

'This book provides an interesting contribution to our understanding of the importance of the student placement during the social work education program in the Indian and South Asian contexts. The contributing authors offer culturally specific suggestions as to how the placement experience can be theorized and utilized. I would recommend this book for those interested in social work education from this region of the world.'

—**Dr Michael Wallengren Lynch,** Lecturer, Department of
Social Work, Gothenburg University, Sweden

'This book is an essential step forward towards the indigenization of field education in India. I urge administrators and faculty at the over 600 schools of social work in India to relieve field education from its place at the margins of the profession and give it the importance it deserves as the signature pedagogy of social work. I congratulate the editors and authors, who each bring a unique emphasis to the development of a field education model with a Bharatiya curriculum.'

—**Laura Gibson, PhD,** LCSW, MSW Program
Director, Brescia University, USA

'This substantial work breaks new ground in its wide-ranging account of social work theory and practice in the Indian sub-continent. Practitioners and academics will welcome the variety of content and the lively analysis of different fieldwork settings. Equally important is how this book suggests new paradigms for social work. The authors provide a timely challenge to Eurocentric pedagogical and fieldwork models; social workers and academics from across the globe will find much to learn from the important insights in this volume.'

—**Alison Higgs,** Open University, UK

FIELDWORK TRAINING IN SOCIAL WORK

Edited by Bishnu Mohan Dash and Sanjoy Roy

LONDON AND NEW YORK

First published 2020
by Routledge
2 Park Square, Milton Park, Abingdon, Oxon OX14 4RN

and by Routledge
52 Vanderbilt Avenue, New York, NY 10017

*Routledge is an imprint of the Taylor & Francis Group,
an informa business*

© 2020 selection and editorial matter, Bishnu Mohan Dash and
Sanjoy Roy; individual chapters, the contributors

The right of Bishnu Mohan Dash and Sanjoy Roy to be identified
as the authors of the editorial material, and of the authors for their
individual chapters, has been asserted in accordance with sections 77
and 78 of the Copyright, Designs and Patents Act 1988.

All rights reserved. No part of this book may be reprinted or
reproduced or utilised in any form or by any electronic, mechanical,
or other means, now known or hereafter invented, including
photocopying and recording, or in any information storage or
retrieval system, without permission in writing from the publishers.

Trademark notice: Product or corporate names may be trademarks
or registered trademarks, and are used only for identification and
explanation without intent to infringe.

British Library Cataloguing-in-Publication Data
A catalogue record for this book is available from the British Library

Library of Congress Cataloging-in-Publication Data
Names: Dash, Bishnu Mohan, editor. | Roy, Sanjoy
(Reader in social work) editor.
Title: Fieldwork training in social work / edited by Bishnu Mohan
Dash and Sanjoy Roy.
Description: First Edition. | New York : Routledge, [2020] |
Includes bibliographical references and index.
Identifiers: LCCN 2019015636 | ISBN 9781138575165 (hardback :
alk. paper) | ISBN 9780367276492 (pbk. : alk. paper) |
ISBN 9780429297120 (e-book)
Subjects: LCSH: Social work education. | Social service—
Fieldwork—Study and teaching.
Classification: LCC HV11 .F464 2020 | DDC 361.3071/5—dc23
LC record available at https://lccn.loc.gov/2019015636

ISBN: 978-1-138-57516-5 (hbk)
ISBN: 978-0-367-27649-2 (pbk)
ISBN: 978-0-429-29712-0 (ebk)

Typeset in Sabon
by Apex CoVantage, LLC

CONTENTS

List of illustrations	vii
Notes of contributors	viii
Foreword	xii
Preface	xiv
Acknowledgements	xxi

1 **Procedural aspects of fieldwork**   1
POONAM GULALIA

2 **Orientation programme to fieldwork: relevance and modalities**   43
ARCHANA KAUSHIK

3 **Fieldwork report: a pragmatic exercise**   58
SHEEBA JOSEPH

4 **Transformative learning in social work education in India: role of social work camps**   71
RAMESH B

5 **Essential guidelines for successful fieldwork supervision**   87
AKILESWARI S

6 **Essential guidelines and techniques for assessment and evaluation in fieldwork**   103
NITA KUMARI

CONTENTS

7 Contemporary field-level needs and essential strategies
in social work practicum 123
ASOK KUMAR SARKAR AND INDRANIL SARKAR

8 Strengthening 'field' in field education: structural and
functional issues in South Asian social work 138
BALA RAJU NIKKU, BISHNU MOHAN DASH,
AND ZIA ULLAH AKHUNZADA

9 Eight decades of fieldwork training in India: identifying
the gaps and missing links 151
SANJOY ROY AND BISHNU MOHAN DASH

10 Learning social work practice skills: reflections from
communities, NGOs, and universities 169
SWAPAN GARAIN

11 Non-institutional and community-based field placement
in social work: experiments with inquiry-based learning
and participatory action research 199
BIPIN JOJO AND RONALD YESUDHAS

12 Developing social work practice theories: some
alternative ideas and approaches 211
INDRAJIT GOSWAMI

13 Essential skills for fieldwork practice in social work 221
SAYANTANI GUIN

14 Using the grounded theory approach in fieldwork
education in India 229
BINOD KUMAR

15 Essence of communication skills in fieldwork 238
SAUMYA

Index 251

ILLUSTRATIONS

Figures

2.1	Pillars of social work knowledge base	44
2.2	Kolb's four-box model of learning styles	52
2.3	Levels of effectiveness of orientation programmes	56
4.1	Camp committee formation	79
4.2	Proposed social work learning transformation model through committees	80
5.1	School–agency interface for fieldwork supervision	88

Tables

1.1	Learning plan for student X	26
3.1	SMART objectives	61

vii

CONTRIBUTORS

Zia Ullah Akhunzada is a Lecturer of Social Work at the Kohat University of Science & Technology Khyber Pakhtunkhwa, Pakistan.

Ramesh B is Registrar, Karnataka State University, and former professor at the Department of Social Work, Tumkur University, Karnataka.

Bishnu Mohan Dash is an academician and a researcher in Social Work engaged in spearheading the movement for Bharatiyakaran of social work education in India. He is an Assistant Professor in Social Work at Bhim Rao Ambedkar College (University of Delhi). He is the recipient of the Academic Excellence Award, 2018. He is also an editorial board member for several national and international journals. He has also authored, co-authored, and edited eight books and published more than 30 papers in various reputed national and international journals and contributed chapters for the Post-Graduate Course in Social Work (MSW)/Social Work and Counselling of Indira Gandhi National Open University, New Delhi. His areas of interest are fieldwork, social work education, rural development, and child welfare.

Swapan Garain is a social scientist, social entrepreneur, CSR consultant, NGO strategist, career counsellor and educationist. He was Senior Fellow at Johns Hopkins University, and Professor at S P Jain Institute of Management & Research, and at Tata Institute of Social Sciences. He was a member of the Steering Committee on Voluntary Sector for VII & VIII Five Year Plans, Planning Commission, Government of India. He advises on family trusts, foundations, social business, projects, organisational restructuring, strategic impact, wealth creation and retirement planning.

Indrajit Goswami is the Professor-HR and Associate Dean (Research) of the NL Dalmia Institute of Management Studies and Research, Mumbai.

Sayantani Guin is an Assistant Professor at the School of Social Work, Indira Gandhi National Open University, New Delhi. She holds MPhil and PhD degrees in Social Sciences from Tata Institute of Social Sciences, Mumbai. She was a recipient of Junior and Senior Research Fellowship from UGC between 2004 and 2009. Prior to this, she completed a BSW from

CONTRIBUTORS

Visva-Bharati University, West Bengal, and MA in Social Work from the Tata Institute of Social Sciences, Mumbai. Her academic and research interests include casework, administration of criminal justice, and HIV in prisons. She is a lifetime member of various professional associations, namely the National Association of Professional Social Workers in India, the Indian Society of Professional Social Work, and The Indian Society of Criminology. She has published many books and articles and presented several papers in national and international seminars.

Poonam Gulalia was a practitioner for two decades before pursuing her doctoral thesis from Delhi University. She worked extensively with UNHCR, Springdales Schools, and Nehrua Yuva Kendra Sanagthan before undertaking teaching assignments at the Department of Social Work and Ambedkar College of Delhi University. For the past six years she has been working as the Fieldwork Coordinator at the School of Social Work, TISS, in Mumbai, where her work entails organizing, monitoring, and mentoring field placement for master's students of Social Work in the first year of their post-graduate programme. She also teaches a course in 'Working with Individuals.' She is passionate about her work and her contribution to the profession. She is also a visiting faculty member at the National Institute of Design, Ahmadabad, and a few state universities.

Bipin Jojo is a Professor of Social Work at the Centre for Social Justice and Governance, School of Social Work at Tata Institute of Social Sciences, India. He has been engaged with teaching, research, and outreach work with communities and organizations for the last 20 years. His area of work has been on social work with a tribal/indigenous perspective, tribal education, working with groups, development-induced displacement and resettlement and rehabilitation, mining, and participatory development.

Sheeba Joseph has been associated with BSSS since 2006. At present, along with teaching, she is also serving the institute in the capacity of IQAC Coordinator. She was the former Head of the Social Work Department and associated with national and international projects in the capacity of Faculty in Charge. She has presented papers at national and international conferences and published articles in refereed journals. She has also contributed chapters in edited books and has one authored book and two edited books to her credit. She has organized various national seminars, conferences, and workshops and been invited to deliver lectures in various training programmes and workshops. Her areas of interest are geriatric social work, women and child welfare, and social work intervention in community settings.

Archana Kaushik is a teaching faculty at the Department of Social Work, University of Delhi. She has wide experience in the field of gerontological social work. She has many books and research articles on various social issues in journals of national and international repute to her credit. She has participated in print and electronic media as writer and expert trying to raise the consciousness of citizens on socially relevant issues.

Binod Kumar is Assistant Professor at Dr Bhim Rao Ambedkar College, University of Delhi. He received a PhD from the Centre for the Study of Law and Governance (CSLG), Jawaharlal Nehru University (JNU), New Delhi. His PhD research focused on locating disaster prevention and mitigation as a subject matter of law, navigating the intersection of disaster, law, and community resilience in India. His MPhil research, at the Centre for the Study of Law and Governance, JNU, was on Governance of Non-profit Organizations in India. He is trained in different disciplines, which enables him to approach research problems from a multi-disciplinary perspective. He has been awarded the Junior Research Fellowship by the University Grants Commission and has participated in several national and international conferences.

Nita Kumari is Assistant Professor (Guest) in Social Work at Bhim Rao Ambedkar College (University of Delhi). She has an MA, MPhil, and PhD in Social Work. Prior to joining Ambedkar College, she worked as Consultant and Research and Teaching Assistant at the School of Social Work, Indira Gandhi National Open University (IGNOU), New Delhi. She was also a Research Fellow at LNJP-NICFS and Project Officer under the UNHCR-BOSCO Self-Reliance Programme, New Delhi. She has taught MA Criminology students at the National Institute of Criminology and Forensic Science and MSW students of IGNOU. She has several publications in reputed journals, as well as two articles in the *Encyclopaedia of Social Work in India* (third edition).

Bala Raju Nikku is currently with the School of Social Work and Human Service, Faculty of Education and Social Work at Thompson Rivers University, Kamloops, BC, Canada. Formerly he was with the School of Social Sciences, Universiti Sains Malaysia. He served as the founding director of the Nepal School of Social Work. He has served on the executive boards of the International Association of Schools of Social Work and the Asian and Pacific Association of Social Work Education. He is currently serving as a member of the editorial advisory boards of *International Social Work Journal, Journal of International Social Issues*, and *Practice: Social Work in Action* and as associate editor of *Social Work Education: The International Journal.*

Sanjoy Roy is an Associate Professor at the Department of Social Work, University of Delhi. He has published more than 45 articles and research papers published in different journals and books and 11 books related to women's development, fieldwork practice in social work education, rural development, etc. He is also the recipient of the prestigious Neelkanth Samaan Award and the Best Academician of the Year Award.

CONTRIBUTORS

Akileswari S is an Assistant Professor at the Department of Social Work, DG Vaishnav College, Chennai. She is one of the Indian Advisors for Catherine of Sienna Virtual College, United States, for the development of courses on violence against women. She is a peer reviewer for *Social Work Education: The International Journal* as well. She has been involved in research activities related to areas such as rehabilitation of tsunami victims, marginalization of women, and transgender and reproductive health of women.

Asok Kumar Sarkar, an alumnus of Tata Institute of Social Sciences and Jawaharlal Nehru University, is a Professor of Social Work and Principal of the Institute of Rural Reconstruction, Visva-Bharati, Sriniketan. He is also former Head of the Department of Social Work, Visva-Bharati, Sriniketan. Before joining this university, he served in the Institute of Health Management, Pachod; Department of Social Work, Assam University, Silchar; and School of Social Work, IGNOU, New Delhi, in different capacities.

Indranil Sarkar, an alumnus of Tata Institute of Social Sciences, is a research scholar in the Department of Social Work, Visva-Bharati, Sriniketan, and project coordinator for the NGO Santi Trust. Previously he has been a consultant for Action Aid India and Public Affairs Centre, Bangalore. Currently he is also engaged as guest faculty in St. Xavier's University, Kolkata.

Saumya is an Assistant Professor at the School of Social Work, Indira Gandhi National Open University (IGNOU), New Delhi, India. She was also a Lecturer at the Department of Social Work, University of Delhi. She received a Visiting Fellowship to Shanghai Open University, China, in 2014 and a Commonwealth Fellowship in 2018. She won the 2018 Young Innovator Award for her paper at the 32nd Annual Conference of the Asian Association of Open Universities (AAOU). She has published many books and articles and presented several papers in national and international seminars.

Ronald Yesudhas works as a Lecturer, Development Worker, Youth Facilitator, Researcher, Social Auditor, and Trainer. He was a faculty member at the Nirmala Niketan College of Social Work. He is currently pursuing a certificate programme in Teaching and Learning in Higher Education from Centennial College, Toronto, along with working with a couple of Canadian non-profit organizations. He is Visiting Lecturer in the field of development management, being associated with Xavier Institute of Communication and SP Jain Institute of Management Research. His current research themes include social exclusion/inclusion, urban social work, service learning, and non-profit management.

FOREWORD

Despite eight decades of professional social work education in India, it is an alarming revelation that only a few Indian social work academicians have developed the literature relating to fieldwork practice. Literature meant for fieldwork practice is a core ingredient of social work education at both the bachelor's and master's level. What calls our attention is the inadequacy of indigenous books on fieldwork practice in social work available in India. In addition, the books that are available have been very conventional in nature and have included only the basic components and contents of fieldwork training. Such books will not serve in addressing the current issues concerning fieldwork training. In light of the deepening crisis regarding the unavailability of appropriate literature concerning the latest needs of fieldwork training, this book has been prepared meticulously after selecting the relevant aspects.

The need to accommodate the indigenization of social work education and practice has been a global issue. In this regard, I appreciate the editors of the volume, Dr Bishnu Mohan Dash and Dr Sanjoy Roy, for taking the initiative to develop an excellent handbook. The book contains the procedural aspects of fieldwork practice; contemporary field-level needs in India and other South Asian countries; core components of fieldwork, particularly report writing, supervision, rural camps, orientation programmes, and fieldwork evaluation; and the various skills and ethical standards in fieldwork. The chapters have been written by senior social work educationists. What adds value to the chapters of the book is the incorporation of the real-life experiences of the authors embedded in the theories they have propounded.

The book methodically highlights and analyses important components and segments of the fieldwork report for trainees when preparing their own reports. The book analytically discusses various skills and strategies, such as rights-based approach, evidence-based practice, social network analysis, innovation, advocacy, cultural relevance or multi-cultural approach, risk and resilience perspective, and legal content or social policy perspective to fulfil the demands of the Indian social work market.

FOREWORD

Enough attention has been given to the analysis of the structural and functional issues of field practicum in various South Asian countries. The chapters thus offer novel ways to strengthen field education in South Asian social work as the authors critically review the imparting-learning continuum of social work practice skills training in the university curriculum in South Asian countries. The book on the whole has tried to document the experiments in institutional and community-based field placement through utilization of inquiry-based learning (IBL) and participatory action research (PAR). Credit is due to the authors who have paid attention to the values and ethics that play a central role in shaping the structure, function, and scope of social work education and practice. Apart from all these issues and components, the book highlights various ways to use all the methods of social work in an integrated manner.

I am sure that the book will be useful to students, teachers, researchers, practitioners, and educators of social work.

I wish Dr Bishnu Mohan Dash and Dr Sanjoy Roy all the success in their future endeavours.

Prof. Y. S. Siddegowda
Vice Chancellor, Tumkur University, Karnataka, India

PREFACE

In the global platforms of social work, there is an ongoing debate on the need for the indigenization of social work education and practice. Increasingly the Eurocentric nature of social work paradigms, theories and methodologies, and fieldwork practices are challenged, as it has become irrelevant, inadequate, and ineffective in the Indian context. In the contemporary Indian social work realm, there needs to a balance between the internationalization and Indianization of fieldwork practices. Hence, the editors felt motivated to work upon developing indigenous social work literature, particularly in fieldwork, which constitutes an important component of social work education and will surely promote the effectiveness of social work intervention in our context. We are just trying to bring Indian perspectives and Indian experiences, which will certainly be helpful to the social work students and practitioners in effectively delivering social services, as various studies suggest that fieldwork education has become marginalized and merely practised as a ritual in India. Thus, it was felt that there was an emerging need to strengthen field education in social work, particularly in Indian universities. Kaseke (1986, p. 55)[1] also observes that fieldwork is an instrument of socialization because it prepares the student for a future role as a social work practitioner. He further asserts that 'a meaningful fieldwork placement is one that enhances the students understanding of the social work profession and the nature of the problems the profession addresses itself to.' Due to the scant literature on fieldwork in social work education, particularly in an Indian context, students and practitioners have no choice except to depend on Western literature, which is not very effective and relevant in Indian situations.

After eight decades of social work education in India, very few attempts have been made to develop the literature relating to fieldwork. There are very few indigenous books on fieldwork practice in social work. Those that are available are conventional in nature and include only the basic components and contents of fieldwork training and have not addressed current issues. The most important aspects of fieldwork training, such as

PREFACE

ethical and professional standards, skills, and emerging field-level needs, have not been covered to date. Keeping in mind the latest needs in terms of fieldwork learning, the book has been carefully prepared after selecting the relevant topics. The book is divided into three sections. The first section discusses the procedural aspects of fieldwork practice. The second section presents the contemporary field-level needs in India and other South Asian countries, and the last section discusses the various skills needed and professional and ethical standards in fieldwork.

Chapter 1 is the outcome of a qualitative research study undertaken to shed light on the processes, events, and relationships useful for obtaining insights into situations and issues that arise during field placements of students in the first year of the master's programme of social work. The chapter attempts to understand the thoughts, feelings, and experiences of individuals during the journey from the personal to the professional using narrative analysis. Through these narratives, and in keeping with the learner-centred approach, it was understood that student learners construct knowledge through gathering and synthesizing information and integrating it with the general skills of inquiry, communication, critical thinking, and problem solving. It is with these essentials in mind that the emphasis lies on using and communicating knowledge effectively in order to address enduring and emerging issues and problems in real-life contexts. Moreover, teaching and assessing student learners are intertwined tasks. Supervisors as facilitators need to constantly assess if students' decisions and judgments reflect an understanding of universal truths and concepts in the humanities and to see if they can work respectfully and productively with others, including peers, para-professionals, and support staff. It also entails being part of a process wherein it is pertinent to see if students have self-regulatory qualities, like persistence and time management, that will help them reach long-term goals. Fieldwork provides the opportunity for aligning theoretical knowledge and learning with the needs of society and the market. It also provides student interns the opportunity to take responsibility for addressing peoples' problems. It is through fieldwork alone that new knowledge is developed while testing the already acquired knowledge. Therefore, fieldwork and the procedures that follow become essential tools in developing a social work curriculum that is both appropriate and responsive to social development concerns. The importance of procedures and tools for fieldwork becomes more valuable when attempting to appreciate the transferability of skills among student interns. This involves being able to explain in a coherent and comprehensive manner how practice is transformed by knowledge and by being able to apply this knowledge and learning to new situations and circumstances. Establishing a relationship between theory and practice means that both are constantly in dialogue, each informing the other in ways that illuminate different aspects of our work and the particular problem.

xv

PREFACE

Chapter 2 of the book highlights the importance and significance of the orientation programme in fieldwork education. Orientation programmes provide some understanding of the nuances of social work and the procedures and protocols of dealing with client groups in fieldwork practice. The contents of orientation programmes for different groups of social work trainees are provided, and learning outcomes in terms of student feedback are presented based on qualitative data. This chapter discusses the challenges faced in designing and implementing orientation programmes. In it, Dr Kaushik has listed various measures for improving the effectiveness of orientation programmes.

In Chapter 3 Dr Joseph has listed the nine important components of the fieldwork report for trainees when preparing their own reports. The report begins with the plan for the current day and ends with the plan of action for the next visit. The report portrays the journey of the trainee in a very comprehensive way. The second segment of the report speaks about the activities performed by the trainee or the work done by the trainee in the social welfare agency. The nature and the types of roles performed by the trainee are mentioned as the third component. Because social work is praxis oriented, the classroom learning or the underpinning theories learned as part of classroom learning are practised during the fieldwork practicum, and this is given due importance in the report. From there, the tools, techniques, and the methods of social work are included as an integral segment. It is quite possible that the trainee may confront ethical issues or dilemmas while working in the field. It must be noted as part of the experiential learning. The trainee must document the systematic observation and analysis of the work done. Competency in observing and analysing an activity, programme, situation, and individuals will add more flavour to this learning exercise. The fieldwork training experience, if not recorded or documented categorically, will not add a drop to the ocean of knowledge. Thus, this chapter shows the voyage of a trainee in the fieldwork practicum.

The social work camp known as rural camp aims to provide opportunities to experience rural life, analyse rural dynamics, and observe the functioning of local self-government and voluntary organizations. This experience aids peer participation in planning and designing activities for both their own group and for the local people. It also helps develop skills in carrying out, evaluating, and reporting the experience. Chapter 4 explores field practicum models in India. A community-based, living-learning, field practicum model is explored in the context of transformative learning theory in this chapter. Social work camp is one of the special programmes meant to indigenize social work education with a specific focus on training macro-practice in India. Although the chapter explores features and challenges of social work camps, it also narrates the social work living-learning field practicum model for social work education.

xvi

PREFACE

Chapter 4 describes the camp case studies containing innovative practices, which trace the transformative learning among the social work trainees through integrated social work

Supervision is a structured, interactive, and collaborative process that takes place within a purposeful professional relationship. Supervision requires specific competencies and functions to effectively meet its objectives. The constructive and continuous interaction between the triad – the student, faculty supervisor, and agency supervisor – regarding the field experiences is required for effective integration. During supervision, the learner moves between the two in the pursuit of competency acquisition. The better the relationship between the supervisor and supervisee, the better the supervision. In Chapter 5 Dr Akileswari has meticulously described the guidelines related to required competencies, functions, and relationships for ensuring successful supervision. This chapter provides directions for social work educators to become efficient fieldwork supervisors and enable students to bloom as professional social workers.

Fieldwork evaluation is a continuous process to assess desired changes in the personality, knowledge, skills, and behaviour of the student. A major objective of the evaluation is to help the student as well as the supervisor identify the students' strengths and weaknesses and decide where emphasis in teaching and learning should be placed. Students are evaluated on the basis of their performance in the field, adherence to the ethics and values of the social work profession, the quality of reports submitted by them, their performance in individual and group conferences, and their attendance. In the area of knowledge, the focus of evaluation is on the acquisition of theoretical concepts, principles of social work, facts gained through field experience, and various skills used in the field. Attitudinal changes are evaluated based on the development of values, beliefs, and commitments appropriate to the social work profession. The evaluation of students' performance in fieldwork is important in order to decide whether the student will be able to work as an independent professional social worker. In Chapter 6 Dr Nita has provided essential guidelines and techniques for assessment and evaluation in fieldwork. The chapter also highlights the importance of fieldwork in the grooming of students as social workers.

Sarkar and Sarkar, in Chapter 7, argue that everything discussed in the classroom cannot be taught through the practicum due to the paucity of time, old or irrelevant curriculum, or differences of specialization or an improper fieldwork setting. After completing their studies, social work students face new challenges as they cope with the working strategies of the development organization where they may begin their work. Therefore, the fieldwork practicum under its 'orientation programme for final-year students' or 'fieldwork skill development workshop' should include space for the practice of several essential strategies that are vital

PREFACE

and relevant for new social workers to become accustomed to the job. These strategies include a rights-based approach, evidence-based practice, social network analysis, innovation, advocacy, cultural relevance or multi-cultural approach, risk and resilience perspective, and legal content or social policy perspective. In this chapter, the authors have discussed these eight strategies in order to fulfil the demands of the Indian social work market.

In Chapter 8, the authors argue that many social work educators across the South Asian schools of social work do accept that the field education is a crucial element in social work training. But most often the quality of fieldwork training and the opportunities for reflective practice learning, both within the schools of social work and in the 'field,' offered to the students leaves much to be desired. Using quilting as a research method, this chapter analyses both the structural and functional issues of the field practicum in various South Asian countries and offers ways to strengthen field education in South Asian social work.

In Chapter 9 the author argues that the fieldwork training provided to students in India is poorly structured and witnesses a huge disconnect between the theoretical classroom teaching and its practice in the field. In the absence of proper fieldwork manuals and clear-cut guidelines, fieldwork training in social work education has become something of a ritual. The fieldwork training in India offered to students also differs from school to school due to the absence of a National Council for Social Work Education. The chapter identifies the various gaps and missing linkages and inherent deficiencies in fieldwork training in India and has provided various recommendations for improving this.

In Chapter 10 Professor Garain has critically reviewed the imparting-learning continuum of social work practice skills training in the university curriculum in Asian countries. The chapter also explores the perspective of field training partners, namely the communities, community-based organizations (CBOs), and non-governmental organizations (NGOs), as well as employers, about the practice skill competency of social work graduates.

In Chapter 11, Professor Jojo and Dr Yesudhas have tried to document experiments in institutional and community-based field placement through the utilization of inquiry-based learning (IBL) and participatory action research (PAR). In the IBL method, the supervisor facilitates students' learning process by helping them generate questions, investigate, construct knowledge, and reflect. PAR, on other hand, offers an action-enabled research platform where student social workers work alongside people in identifying, collecting, and analysing data to help these people take control of their lives. Though both methods seem similar, IBL and PAR are different in the orientations in terms of the students' placement and learning perspective. The two case studies provided by the authors

xviii

PREFACE

give an account of utilizing both methods in fieldwork placement to the fullest extent. Thus, the authors encourage the schools of social work in India to move towards participatory, empowering, and emancipatory methods while going for non-institutional and community-based field placement. This would increase students' interest in reading, research, and involving the community in changing their own lives through the fieldwork of students.

The pace of development and transformation in the domain of social work education and practice, including fieldwork practicum, have not yet witnessed any major breakthroughs. In Chapter 12 Professor Goswami argues that right from the beginning 'values and ethics' have been played a central role in shaping the structure, function, and scope of social work education and practice. However, it is evident that a greater amount of time and resource in social work education has been used in classroom teaching but not in field education, especially in the field training and grooming of professionals. It is also evident that almost all social work theory is constructed on the fundamental concept of 'the relationship' only. The present situation demands self-awareness of language, values, ethos, personal likes and dislikes, preferences, and the different social and cultural orientations of social workers.

Therefore, the time has come to rescue social work students and practitioners from their dichotomy of being loyal to professionalism and contributing to developmental activities. The post-modern and liberal society must appreciate an open system of ideas and diverse ideologies. We need to adapt to the changing times and transformations that affect society, culture, and behaviour. There needs to be a balance between absolute values and instrumental values; otherwise, we may fail to move ahead. It is also essential to revisit the modalities of social work education and field training. The social work educators, scholars, and practitioners shall not enjoy a monopoly in terms of determining the future of the profession. We need to incorporate a 'stakeholder approach' to redesign our curriculum, especially the fieldwork practicum, so that the profession and the professionals remain relevant to changing and emerging scenarios. This chapter will highlight the applicable social work practice theories and some alternative ideas and approaches.

In Chapter 13, Dr Guin has explored various essential skills required for fieldwork practice in social work. Through fieldwork, students can acquire important training and skills in diverse areas to effectively help individuals, families, groups, communities, and organizations deal appropriately with their problems. Certain skills are required for effective fieldwork practice. These include observation, communication, interviewing, problem solving, documentation, etc. The chapter also discusses basic communication skills like empathy, positive regard, warmth, genuineness, and various verbal and non-verbal skills. During fieldwork practice, it is essential to be sensitive to the cross-cultural differences existing among the various sections of society. The skill to work both individually and as a member of a team is important during fieldwork practice. Other skills important for fieldwork practice include the ability to act in a crisis, to plan, set priorities, mobilize resources, and implement the plan effectively. The chapter also highlights various other skills, like the ability to use all the methods of social work in an integrated manner to help people solve their problems, to develop one's own leadership style suited to the need and culture of the place. In addition, the chapter highlights skills in research, documentation viz, ability to write reports to describe events and analyse them for better understanding and for deciding on a further course of action.

Chapter 14 tries to resolve the continuous tension between classroom theory and application in the field by using grounded theory approach. It uses the qualitative analysis of narratives produced by students in their fieldwork reports, along with evaluation and feedback given by field supervisors in an academic year.

Chapter 15 discusses the importance of communication skills for trainees' self-development, as well the clients or beneficiaries with whom they engage in dialogue for critical awareness and thinking. The three-year bachelor's programme or two-year master's programme in social work aims towards development of these skills for direct practice, planning, use of supervision, and helping the client help themselves. This chapter discusses the patterns, characteristics, and styles of communication along with various theories of communication. The author argues that there should greater attention paid to skills training in all social work course curricula. It must be taught, and students must be given opportunity in fieldwork to practice and test it.

This book will not only be useful to students of social work at the bachelor's, master's, and MPhil and PhD levels but also for the MA students in disability studies, human rights, counselling and social work, and other allied disciplines. The book will be extremely useful to the students, teachers, researchers, and development practitioners engaged in various non-governmental and international organizations.

Note

1 Kaseke, E. (1986). *The role of fieldwork in social work training*. Social development and rural fieldwork, proceedings of a workshop held in Harare, Harare, *Journal of Social Development in Africa*, pp. 52–62.

ACKNOWLEDGEMENTS

We are grateful to Routledge for their interest in and support for our edited volume, *Fieldwork Training in Social Work*. We are deeply thankful for the cooperation and professionalism of the entire team of Routledge for helping to improve the quality of the book. We are also thankful to the contributors for writing chapters of the book that we are sure will be immensely valuable for students.

1

PROCEDURAL ASPECTS OF FIELDWORK

Poonam Gulalia

Introduction

The International Federation of Social Workers (2013) in the Global Definition of social work defines it as

> A practice-based profession and an academic discipline that promotes social change and development, social cohesion, and the empowerment and liberation of people. Principles of social justice, human rights, collective responsibility and respect for diversities are central to social work. Underpinned by theories of social work, social sciences, humanities and indigenous knowledge, social work engages people and structures to address life challenges and enhance wellbeing. Underpinned by theories of social work, social sciences, humanities and indigenous knowledge, social work engages people and structures to address life challenges and enhance wellbeing.
>
> (p. 1)

This definition explains social work as a 'practice-based profession' as well as an 'academic discipline.' In other explanations of social work the two concepts of theory and practice appear. Professional social workers are required to develop and practice ongoing social work knowledge, values, and skills in order to be competent social workers. Along with a commitment to continue to learn and grow, the social work professional needs to be able to handle ambiguity. It is a reality that many situations do not fit into a neat package; "people making it somehow day to day, hour to hour, not without pain, struggle and suffering but with capabilities and resources that can be built upon and supported by our alliance with these possibilities" (Saleebey, 2013, p. 43).

In India, because there is no accreditation/licensing process for social workers and there are no regulatory mechanisms for screening ethical/

unethical practices, there is no universal acceptance of social work ethics for the profession in the country. One of the major factors for this is the diversity of cultures and social realities, which make it difficult to implement one set of values for all. However, this does not mean that professional practice should not have guidelines. Two documents are used in social education in India that provide the value base for social work, and guidelines for ethical practice. These are the Declaration of Ethics for Professional Social Workers, accepted by the Bombay Association of Trained Social Workers (BATSW, 2002), Mumbai, and the principles stated in the International Federation of Social Workers (IFSW) and International Association of Schools of Social Work (IASSW, 2014).

Social Work started with charity-based orientation. After Independence, there was a shift towards welfare-oriented approach in Social Work, which later shifted to a development-oriented approach and then towards justice and empowerment (Desai, 1994). Over the years there has been paradigm shift to address social issues relevant to the Indian context. This has been emphasized by many social work educators since the mid-1980s, who have since advocated for a greater focus on macro-level social work practice rather than individualized social work practice (Desai, 1994; Nanavatty, 1997; Ramachandran, 1988).[1]

Contemporary social work education in India, while drawing from the deep-rooted Western ideology of 'social work' has undergone a reorientation in terms of curriculum, structure, and pedagogy. It has positioned itself to train students with a knowledge base and skill set to be able to address the complex relevant issues and realities of Indian society. Literature on the social work profession lends support to this shift and states that the holistic focus of social work is universal, but the priorities of social work practice will vary from country to country and from time to time, depending on cultural, historical, and socio-economic conditions (International Federation of Social Workers, 2005).[2] In India, with a changing polity and shifts in focus from structure to culture and the emergence of subaltern positions and voices (of caste, class, gender, sexuality, ethnicity, age, and ability) social work education has visualized landmark moves towards empowerment developmental, radical anti-oppressive, and post-modern stances.[3] The current social work education in India reflects priorities on globalization and is designed to address relevant social issues with an increased focus on the community context (Weiss-Gal and Welbourne, 2008).[4]

In India, there is very limited evidence or literature to review student learning trends; however, a wider literature search reveals empirical evidence that in the United States many students enrolling in social work programmes have a consumer-oriented approach to the educational experience and make known the outcomes that they expect (Lager & Robbins, 2004). Some present with a sense of entitlement that is not related to the level of performance they demonstrate either in the classroom or in the field, expecting a good grade because they have tried (Tsang, 2011). More and more students are entering the field with their own psychosocial histories such as mental illness, childhood trauma, and addiction histories, and although many are able to manage the academic rigours of the programme, problems emerge when vulnerable students are in the field (Bogo, Regehr, Power, & Regehr, 2007; Lager & Robbins, 2004; Pooler, Doolittle, Faul, Barbee, & Fuller, 2012).[5]

Social work: a generalist perspective

The social work profession provides opportunities to work in different practice settings and with people, individually and collectively, whose diverse problems, issues, and needs interfere with their personal and social functioning. Generalist practice is both a way of thinking and a way of doing. Social workers, as generalists, view problems through a wide-angle lens rather than a microscope to understand problems in the broadest context possible. This wide-angle lens stimulates the planning of multi-faceted interventions that address both the individual and societal dimensions of any given problem. Generalist practitioners work with many social system levels simultaneously: individuals, groups, families, organizations, and communities. Moreover, generalist social work practice is an art that involves a skill that results from experience and training. It also involves the knowledge of human behaviour and is based on client involvement in developing options designed to resolve problems. It emphasizes students learning to use the client's resources (psychological and physical), as well as those extant in the community in the problem-solving process. It is based on an orderly helping process, on planned change efforts, and focuses on solutions (Heffernan, Shuttlesworth, & Ambrosino, 1998, pp. 275–276).

Generalist practitioners work in a variety of practice settings with diverse population groups that present an array of problems. Social workers focus their professional practice on working with a population, such as people with disabilities, the elderly, unemployed, marginalized, Dalits, or tribals. They may develop expertise in utilizing intervention techniques such as crisis intervention, family therapy, social planning, locality development, or social research. Social workers also develop specializations in a field of practice such as public health, mental health, community planning, gerontology, family and child equity, Dalit and tribal welfare, community organization, and development practice.

Additional specialties are grouped according to practice roles, such as direct service practitioners, community organizers, policy analysts, family life educators, and administrators, among others. Even when social workers develop specialties, the wide-angle lens of the generalist is applicable, as problems need to be understood in their context and interventions developed with an eye on the implications at all system levels. Social workers are described as professional 'helpers' – helping others resolve problems, assisting in obtaining resources, supporting in times of crisis, and facilitating social responses to needs.

Professionalism in social work

Professionalism in social work is reflected in the degree to which an individual has the requisite knowledge and skills and adheres to professional values and ethics when attending to clients and client populations. The helping profession values working with others in a partnership. Effective social work practice involves empowering persons and enabling change. It appreciates differences and celebrates diversity based on the ideal of social justice.

Problems, issues, and needs

Social workers have been described as 'professional helpers' designated by society to aid people who are distressed, disadvantaged, disabled, deviant, defeated, or dependent. They are in the process of enabling people to lessen the chances of being poor, inept, neglected, abused, divorced, delinquent, and criminal or alienated (Siporin, 1975, p. 4). Rather than applying labels that denote pathology, it is more appropriate to focus on the strengths of social systems, thereby promoting personal and societal competence. Problems, issues, and needs that arise result from the interaction between persons and their social environment. Problems are basically defined as difficulties in human conduct or in the performance of social relationships that require resolution. Additionally, when concern arises about a societal condition, it is defined as a social problem, which causes discomfort for individuals and malfunctioning in society. Issues are disputes, controversies, or disagreements that occur within or between social systems. When any of these occurs, it can precipitate a need or opportunity for change.

Failures or breakdowns in the social institutions of a society and gaps and barriers create needs for people of that community/society which need to be addressed through social change. Programmes and services are then developed in the social delivery system as residual supports.

Social work goals and service delivery

The goals and objectives of social work are achieved through the delivery of social service programmes. Four interrelated goals, which describe social work activities, reflect the profession's purpose to better the human condition and to strengthen the relationships between people and the institutions of society (NASW, 1981a).[6] These include:

- To enable adaptive social functioning, including the developmental capacity to solve problems and cope and deal with life tasks.
- To improve the operation of the social service delivery network.
- To link client systems with needed resources.
- To promote social justice through the development of social policy.

As far back as 1978, Baer and Federico established that entry-level social workers must be able to:

- Identify and assess situations where the relationship between people and social institutions needs to be initiated, enhanced, restored, protected, or terminated.
- Develop and implement a plan for improving the wellbeing of people based on problem assessment and the exploration of obtainable goals and available options.
- Enhance problem-solving, coping, and developmental capacities of people.
- Link people with systems that provide them with resources, services, and opportunities.
- Intervene effectively on behalf of populations that are most vulnerable and discriminated against.
- Promote the effective functioning and human orientation of the systems that provide people with services, resources, and opportunities.
- Actively participate with others in creating new, modified, and/or improved service, resource, and opportunity systems that are more equitable, just, responsive to consumers of services, and work with others to eliminate these systems that are unjust.
- Evaluate the extent to which the objectives of the interventions have been achieved.
- Continually evaluate one's own professional growth and development through assessment of practice, behaviour, and skills.
- Contribute to the implementation of service delivery by adding to the knowledge base of the profession as appropriate and by supporting and upholding the standards and ethics of the profession.

What is fieldwork?

Fieldwork placement is a critical method and phase of social work instruction that provides the student with an opportunity to integrate classroom knowledge with experiential learning[7] in a relevant social work setting. During placement, a student is supervised by professional social workers of the organization and/or by supervisors from the academic institution.

Social work as a practice-based professional discipline is anchored on a unified curriculum consisting of both theory and practice components. During fieldwork, students have the opportunity to link and test the acquired theory with the professional aspects of the workplace (Tsui, 2005). Field placement represents a laboratory where theories taught at the university level are tested and practised under the supervision[8] of a qualified practitioner so the student can acquire skills. Fieldwork is therefore intended to help students translate theoretical content covered in the classroom to real-life situations as part of a student's preparation to become a professional social worker.

It is through the varied opportunities to practice that students assimilate the social work principles, values, and ethics of the profession. It takes academic acumen, evidence-based knowledge, field-related skills, and hands-on experience to become a fully backed social worker (Dhemba, 2012).

Fieldwork curriculum

Certain prominent advantages have been cited by researchers as being the advantages of having a fieldwork curriculum[9] as an integral part of the programme:

- The requirements of social work practice can shape the content of what is learned by students through a fieldwork practice curriculum.
- Students are empowered through the existence of a written fieldwork curriculum.
- Students can understand at the beginning of the fieldwork what learning is expected of them in the context of the stated objectives.
- Supervisors and faculty advisors are empowered through the development of the curriculum.

There is need to move from an implicit curriculum to an explicit one. In doing so, it is possible to provide a common curriculum for students in one programme. This provides a shared language for supervisors/teachers and students of social work practice. Practice teachers/supervisors tend to share a lot of practice material that they have developed over the years they have been practitioners/mentors.

The curriculum statement should clearly state what is required of each of the three partners – universities, workplace organizations, and students. The courses should be clearly designed with clear details about who has responsibility for organizing, coordinating, and assessing students to ensure that the interaction between the three participants functions as smoothly as possible.

Well-organized partnerships allow students to seek the support they need when required. The curriculum needs to be able to provide opportunities for the student to apply what they have already learned and encourage them to become autonomous in their own learning. The field placement must demand that students engage in deeper learning as they further develop skills and abilities learned in more theoretical courses and then confront them with the reality of taking responsibility in the world of work (Bates, 2003). The curriculum should be a deliberately constructed experience which requires statements of its intent to work from practical and transactional goals towards emancipatory and transformational activity.

It is possible with a practice curriculum to know when learning has been achieved in given areas and then to move on to other components of the curriculum or to find ways to compensate for deficiencies in the learning environment. The curriculum allows for a range of different learning opportunities and learning methods to be used. Moreover, the examination of practice competence can be structured and harmonized to fit with the pace of learning.

The first two years of the master's programme covers the core knowledge, values, and skills which are identified as necessary for successful social work practice. As a foundation to practice, the curriculum is not specific to any particular setting or any client group, but rather is generic in nature. The second year helps students build on the learning that has taken place during the first-year placement. It enables students to learn a focused area of practice based on their specialization or thematic area.

Schools/departments of social work

Through the director, fieldwork coordinator, and the academic coordinators the department/school of social work has the overall responsibility to ensure that fieldwork is conducted in a manner that is both professional and practical. It should ensure that:

1 Students are placed in appropriate fieldwork settings and/or agencies/ placements.
2 Specific areas of social work interventions that students must be exposed to and actively involved in during placement are included.
3 Students are helped to develop learning plans that outline learning goals.
4 Supervisors and agencies are provided guidelines to help them supervise students. Where resources allow, meetings with agency/placement

supervisors are arranged from time to time to ensure that agencies understand and appreciate their roles and that they give their best to the students.

5   Students and agency supervisors are supported in working together.

Learning objectives during fieldwork need to be aligned to the course content that was expected to be covered by the end of each academic year and the associated exposure to appropriate theories and concepts. It needs to be reiterated that fieldwork is one of the most discussed components in social work education. It is the interface of education and practice, and it is here that the college/school/department makes choices about its goals, resource allocation, agencies, and practitioners, and it is here that the hopes and aspirations of students intersect and sometimes conflict.

Based on the goals of the social work profession, the overall knowledge, skills, and attitude of social work can be stated in the following objectives.

Overall knowledge objectives

These critically evaluate multi-disciplinary knowledge through a value-based examination of various viewpoints:

- Dynamics of human behaviour
- Roles played by the social systems of groups, family, communities, and organizations
- Political economy of the state, political, legal, judicial systems, and the market from local to national and international levels

Overall attitude objectives

This includes developing critical self-awareness in relation to ideological and ethical dimensions of the profession:

- Attributes such as honesty, integrity, creativity, and optimism
- Values of social equity, people's participation, self-determination, peace, and collaborative social relationships
- Sensitivity to marginalized and vulnerable groups

Overall skill objectives

- Develop life skills for self-awareness, self-esteem, self-responsibility, inter-personal communication, and social interactions and relationships.
- Garner and enhance people-centred skills.

- Though most research on student experiences has been conducted in Western countries, case studies and evidence help in gaining a wider understanding of critical issues. One such study within the Western context on reflective learning experiences in social work education conducted with students in a post-graduate programme in social work provides insight into experiences from the lives of students:[10]

> *Undergrad was about taking in info in and reeling it back out. Here there has been much more of a 'process' around learning. To be encouraged to look back on previous experience and examine what you did, why you did it and what you might do differently or indeed the same in the future has allowed me to learn a great deal.*
>
> *My own capacity for critical thinking has developed greatly over the two years and I found many things I took for granted and believed, fundamentally challenged.*

Structure of concurrent fieldwork

Fieldwork in the first year of the master's programme is concurrent, which means that it runs parallel to coursework. Agencies providing field education opportunities include non-governmental, governmental/municipal organizations, and people's movements and community-based organizations in rural and/or urban settings. During the field placements, students are expected to be involved in the ongoing work of the agency. Depending upon the setting, students are provided opportunities to work with different populations, such as children, women, adults, the elderly, persons with disabilities, and the chronically ill. Wherever opportunities arise, students are also engaged in the process of programme planning and development.

The rationale for using concurrent field placements initially and then block fieldwork at a higher level is to offer students an opportunity to gradually acquaint themselves with the profession. The fact of the matter is that initially, in the first year, course expectations are not as high and fieldwork is generic. Students are expected to model their supervisor, undertake basic tasks/activities at the agency, engage with people, observe, practice listening, and undertake effective communication besides performing tasks under the guidance of their field contacts/supervisors. Placements at this level are largely of an exploratory nature, with the student undertaking tasks that are not too complex. However, in the second year, the student is expected to be active at a practical level, carrying out tasks that have considerable scope for increasing the independent execution of skills and duties.

Block placement, on the other hand, allows students to immerse themselves in the work of an agency/placement and is much more conducive and in tune with the pursuit of intellectually and professionally stimulating tasks. But one of the disadvantages of the block placement is that it results in postponement of application of theory into practice until some basic level of theoretical knowledge has been attained. The choice of the most appropriate combination or selection of the form of fieldwork is based on the demands of the classroom curriculum in terms of the course configuration and the amount of time for each course/subject. Even if these decisions are taken by individual colleges and institutes, it is necessary to keep the underlying principle in mind (i.e., guaranteeing professional growth and student learning).

Social work training institutions generally follow four forms of fieldwork, namely, concurrent, block, a combination of both concurrent and block, and in-service placements. Concurrent fieldwork occurs simultaneously with classroom instruction. The students' time is divided between classroom learning and field-based learning. Typically, students spend two days a week in the field and they take classes the remaining four days. A major strength of the concurrent fieldwork arrangement lies in the simultaneous and immediate application of theory learned in the classroom into practice. Students can also share and readily discuss their placements while at placement, and this can contribute to effective integration of theory and practice. The disadvantage, as stated by Hall (1990, p. 31), is "the possibility that the fieldwork experience becomes more fragmented and students are unable to do justice to either theory or practice because of the overlapping expectations of workplace and school."

It has been reported that the rationale for using concurrent placements initially at the first or second year or at both levels and then block placement later is to offer students an opportunity to acquaint themselves with the profession. Placements at this level are of an exploratory character, with the student carrying out tasks that are not too complex. However, at later levels, the student is expected to be active at a practical level, carrying out tasks that have considerable scope for increasingly independent execution of duties and skills.

Block placement allows students to immerse themselves in the work of an agency and is more conducive to the pursuit of professional stimulating tasks. However, it has a clear separation of the timing and context in which theory and practice take place, as students are away from the training institution for a prolonged period.

The choice of the most appropriate form or combination is based on the demands of the classroom instruction in terms of course configuration and the time required for each subject. Each institution is unique in terms of prevailing circumstances and conditions, and it is essential to settle for the most effective form of fieldwork that guarantees professional growth and development of the student.

Briefing about fieldwork

Students embark on fieldwork with a half-day briefing and presentation about fieldwork as an integral component of the programme. They are oriented by the fieldwork secretariat about the structure and elements in the field practicum. Visits are organized to governmental and/or non-governmental agencies in urban and semi-rural areas. The organizations are identified thematically. The objectives of these visits are:

- To expose students to organizations working in the area of education, health, and livelihood.
- To help students get acquainted with the objectives, structure, functioning, management process, programmes, and activities of the organization in the given sector, including understanding the role of professional social workers and others in the organization, viz. technical staff, voluntary workers, and grassroots workers.
- Also, getting exposure to direct interaction with the constituencies that agencies work with, if possible, and to help students get a broader perspective of social work practice and the roles of social workers, para-professionals, and others in a variety of settings.

Following the visits, the students meet to discuss the visits in a group discussion that is facilitated by the staff member who accompanied the group. They are then required to write individual reports. After three visits, students make thematic presentations before the whole batch of first-year students so peers can share and learn from each other.

Group laboratory sessions

'Group labs' are experiential training sessions conducted through structured exercises. These exercises are simulated situations that participants undergo. The exercises involve not only intellect but also body and emotions and sensitize students to areas they are not always conscious of. These sessions initiate students into structured experiential learning to facilitate understanding of the self and the field. It is conducted in the first week of the semester and takes place through two-hour sessions once a week for five weeks. The labs comprise structured exercises conducted in small groups facilitated by faculty members of the fieldwork secretariat. Using these skills, a social worker displays his or her capacities to use interventions towards a goal-directed purpose. Skills are developed and refined through exposure and experience. This involves conscious use of own self and one's capabilities. The skill laboratory is a platform on which these principles are translated into practice skills. It helps students learn through simulated situations and reflections carried out in a relatively safe environment. Group learning and peer support enable students in such a way that it facilitates the process of self-introspection. Exercises on sensitivity and perception are designed so that students develop an ability to understand and empathize with persons in need. The workshops on self-awareness and sensitivity are a prerequisite for any skill training when working with people.

Fieldwork placements

Shortly after the orientation to the field, students are required to furnish the fieldwork secretariat with information about themselves, such as their educational background, language capabilities, and work experience and interest areas. Based on this information, the secretariat proceeds to match students with agencies to provide students with the most conducive learning environment. Agencies are identified as an ongoing process. However, the selection of an agency is contingent on the extent to which the fieldwork experience provided will meet with the objectives and goals of first-year fieldwork. The agency placement needs to be one wherein students will get broad-based exposure to social realities and an opportunity to engage with individuals, groups, and communities and thus develop the basic skills of working with people.

The broad themes around which the fieldwork agencies/placements are identified include health, disability, education, livelihood, governance, and social exclusion. Each selected agency/placement is then anchored by the school of social work. The number of student placements per agency is decided according to the need and the willingness of the agency to host that number, the scope of work of the organization, and the availability of a qualified supervisor. The number of students placed per agency ranges from two to eight, depending on the reach of the agency, but it is most often two students per agency/placement. Announcements regarding fieldwork placements are done a week prior to the commencement of fieldwork. Students are expected to contact and meet their respective supervisors prior to commencing fieldwork.

Fieldwork secretariat

This is a team that plans, organizes, and facilitates fieldwork. It consists of a full-time fieldwork coordinator, two full-time fieldwork supervisors, and centre-based representatives from the school of social work. The fieldwork coordinator is responsible for coordinating the overall functioning of the fieldwork programme. She or he, along with the two full-time supervisors, plans and organizes the fieldwork programme, which includes orientation, placement, contact, and communication with fieldwork agencies. It also involves capacity building of supervisors and contact persons, provision of inputs, and collaboration among various stakeholders. Additionally, it involves identification and exploration of fieldwork agencies, monitoring attendance at individual conferences, group conferences, addressing challenges during fieldwork, and facilitating its functioning and completion.

The fieldwork secretariat is responsible for the overall planning, organizing, coordinating, and monitoring of the fieldwork programme during the first year. The specific responsibilities of the fieldwork secretariat are:

- Coordinating and networking with field agencies and field instructors with the purpose of facilitating the administration and deliverance of the first-year fieldwork programme.
- Organizing the different components related to field orientation to facilitate students' incremental learning of and from the field.
- Purposefully distributing students across field settings based on the students' background, previous experience, areas of interest, and specifics of the field setting besides identifying areas of supervisor expertise.
- Troubleshooting and facilitating student learning through interactions with field instructors, faculty advisors, and agency personnel.
- Monitoring first-year fieldwork through a regular review of students' progress and learning.
- Facilitating feedback meetings with students and field instructors for ongoing and end-of-placement review and evaluation.
- Developing fieldwork curriculum, standards, and evaluation mechanisms and resources for enhancing field instruction.
- Creating and sharing learning opportunities for field instructors to enhance their knowledge and skills in field instruction in the profession.

Student learning

For the student intern, it is essential that she or he fully utilizes this unique learning situation where they have the right to feel and to express uncertainty. They also have the opportunity and the license to query and to investigate. Constant reflection upon experiences gained gives an opportune chance that the field placement will be an instructive period.

For many students, the field placement and the associated learning can be challenging and may sometimes be a revolutionary experience, especially if exchange students come away from the developed world into the not-so-developed Asian countries, as they often do.

It is during these placement periods, which last anywhere between two and four months or more, that they come face to face with the concrete daily challenges of a wide professional field. It is here that they tend to draw parallels or question how and where theory and practice are aligned and whether their learning and experiences in the field would suffice them in the world of work.

The experience of mentors and professionals has been that the student must acquire the information necessary to be able to describe and relate to the practice workplace, its goals, function, and work methods. The student must also train and develop self-knowledge, the ability to show empathy and a professional approach towards clients and client populations, which together contribute to self-assurance and respectfulness towards future target groups and beneficiaries.

An important part of the supervised fieldwork is that students get to be responsible for work tasks that social workers conduct within the organization. A model that structures one way of gradually giving the student more responsibility is the following (developed by Calvert, 2014):

1   Student observes the work of the supervisor. What does the supervisor do? What does the supervisor say to target groups of the organization, colleagues, and other professional actors? What methods are used by the supervisor? These observations form the basis for the observation summary the student does during the field placement.
2   Shared work. The student and the supervisor both take part in meetings and in different work tasks.
3   Student in action. The student carries the main responsibility for the actions taken, but the supervisor observes, supports and assists.
4   The student carries out the work independently. This work is the basis for the process summary the student writes as part of the course requirements.

It is well established that the learning objectives for first-year social work students are as follows:

Students should grasp the nature of the field placement/agency and the particular social problems that the organization attempts to address. The following can provide a guide to the learning outcomes:

a)   Articulate how the organization was established, the vision, the mission, the programmes, operations, goals, and objectives of the organization's social service delivery system

b) Organizational structure, types of personnel employed, their job descriptions and professional qualifications, authority relationships
c) Identify the strengths and needs of the client system being served by the agency; problems handled, agency programmes and services, methods of helping and procedures of admitting clients to client status
d) Source of funding

Learning styles

Kolb (1984) described learning styles as the way students prefer to process new information, including strategies that are consistently adopted to learn. It is largely accepted that students learn in different ways.

Fleming (2001): The VARK model was proposed by Fleming (2001). VARK is a questionnaire that provides users with a profile of their learning preferences. The ultimate goal of the study is to investigate the impact of undergraduate students learning preferences (VARK model) on the language achievement

Gaiptman and Anthony (1989): Self-directed learning is implemented during fieldwork placements, enabling students to become active in the learning process and integrating the individual's previous experiences, application of knowledge and present learning needs.

Howard and Howard (1993): Human potential can be tied to one's preferences to learning. Gardner's focus on human potential lies in the fact that people have varied capabilities and skills. This model is used to understand overall personality, preferences and strengths of individuals.

Schulz (1993): It is believed that students will learn more quickly and easily if they are able to utilize their preferred style

Brown, Cosgriff, and French (2008): Learning styles also influence how the learner interacts with their environment, how they internalize experiences, and how they best express themselves

DiBartola (2006) discusses the learning-style inventory challenge and enumerates "satisfied/totally satisfied", "achieved/totally achieved", or "improved/totally improved" as questions of the Healthy Living Questionnaire to be administered to participants to evaluate the same.

Forrest (2004): There is value in developing awareness of learning styles which can help students to recognize their strengths, acknowledge limitations and work collaboratively in relationships with others

Titiloye and Scott (2001): The value of developing awareness of learning styles can help students recognize their strengths, acknowledge limitations, work more efficiently when self-directed, and develop effective collaborative relationships with others.

Provident, Leibold, Dolhi & Jeffcoat (2009). Poor understanding of learning styles can lead to misunderstandings about the students' motivation and ability to take responsibility for their learning.

Student reflections

Students need to learn to analyze their own learning preferences. With this purpose they need to develop an awareness of the impact of learning styles on professional development.

Feedback

According to Mohit, an important aspect of learning is the support provided through feedback:

During fieldwork, I have valued structured and specific feedback received during supervision. A prolific note-taker, I always prefer taking notes to refer to later – although this is not always practical or appropriate. If a supervisor prefers to provide feedback verbally, I will record comments for later reference.

Anita echoed these sentiments:

> When receiving feedback, I need to write down the feedback as I hear it, this also enables me to reflect at a later date, and learn from the feedback. An optimal fieldwork environment is when I am able to retreat to a quiet office or library, if available, to read and make notes.

Another student, E, said,

> I am a kinaesthetic learner and show preference for detailed and descriptive feedback. In past fieldwork situations, I have sought immediate feedback from my supervisor following a learning situation. Within this feedback, I request that my supervisor details two things that went well and one thing to improve on next time. This has proved useful in allowing me to identify specific areas of performance that need refining. During one fieldwork placement, my supervisor found it challenging to provide specific, constructive feedback. To resolve this I asked specific questions regarding my performance following home visits to determine what areas to improve on next time.

As a method of reflection, verbal discussion proves more beneficial than keeping a written journal. This preference is supported by Fleming (2001), who suggests that kinaesthetic learners find journaling challenging. E explained that during fieldwork five, a three-week fieldwork experience based on learning contracts

Learning contracts

About learning contracts, B indicated she felt they were somewhat restrictive during fieldwork:

> Although I enjoyed using knowledge-based learning contracts related to migrant population[s], I attribute success with this particular learning contract to the fact it was based on concrete knowledge that could be related to through my knowledge base. Academically, I rely heavily on literature and research when formulating ideas and this was reflected in my use of this specific learning contract. During fieldwork, endeavour to ensure that learning plans are not overly specific so that they do not detract from the overall learning experience. In order to maximize my learning, I would prefer to write down evidence of my learning objectives for my supervisor to read.

Invariably, students find some fieldwork placements do not suit their learning style. S reported the first of two examples of such situations:

> In considering the match between my learning style and the learning environment available in a community, I initially found the laissez faire approach of my supervisor quite intimidating as I prefer a structured, organized approach. Her preference was for me to shadow her for the first few days, which I found uncomfortable as I felt pressurized to begin working towards meeting my learning objectives and could not readily identify opportunities to do so. My initial concern at the amount of observation in this setting dissipated by week two when I began to appreciate the value of observation in the agency meetings in order to grasp the process. As much as a strict schedule is in place, meetings are largely abstract with para-professionals and staff raising and responding to issues and articulating why they feel the way moments during these meetings, which I initially found a waste of valuable time, were actually necessary so that staff and patients (and students) could consider and reflect upon what was being said.
>
> A specific example of when my learning/thinking styles have contributed to difficulties in placement includes a situation where

I consistently felt that I was being pumped with too much information by the field contact and the para-professionals. After I [saw] a client with my field contact I was asked a series of questions usually relating to the client's condition and frame of mind and what I considered to be the next step as a follow up. The supervisor would then supplement my response with large tracts of detailed information in a monologue. I felt quite overawed by this flood of information and when I attempted to jot down notes my supervisor would say "You don't need to write this down". Past experience has shown that I tend to process information more efficiently if I am able to make notes as I hear it.

Discussion

These stories clearly show that learning styles have a profound impact on learning. Personal awareness of learning styles and confidence in communicating this are first steps towards achieving an optimal learning environment (Alsop & Ryan, 1996).

The three students documenting their experience in this chapter stressed the need for a conversation about learning styles at the beginning of a placement. This would help ensure that learning preferences are taken into consideration while opening the way for ongoing dialogue about learning outcomes. There will often be differences in student and fieldwork supervisor learning styles. Although it may be tempting to assume that similarity in learning styles is necessary to an effective learning experience, students report that differences in style can be complementary and may extend their learning strategies.

Becoming multi-modal has its advantages in that the learner is able to adapt to each learning situation. According to student S:

Possibly, the greatest shift in my approach to future learning has been that I am capable of utilizing other learning styles/thinking styles effectively. This is evidenced in my ability to now combine observation (aural and visual) with effective reflective journaling (reader/writer) and has assisted me metacognitively in that I am now more able to monitor my state of learning as suggested by Moon (2006).

Student S's observations support the contention that self-awareness is an important first step in utilizing learning styles effectively.

This account has focused on the stories of students and has conveyed their perspective of the value of knowing about learning styles. It suggests that taking time to consider learning styles will have an impact on learning. To provide a balanced view, it would be valuable to explore the experiences of fieldwork supervisors. For instance, do we as supervisors know the students' learning style? Do they recognize the impact of learning preferences? How does an exchange of information about learning styles impact on supervisors' experiences of fieldwork placements?

From the perspective of students, being able to recognize their predominant style of learning provides an understanding of strengths and weaknesses in relation to learning opportunities in fieldwork. Personal awareness can enhance the management of self-directed learning in fieldwork. During a fieldwork placement, a collaborative approach to learning is essential. Setting up the learning environment by sharing information about learning styles is a constructive strategy that helps clarify expectations of all stakeholders. A fuller understanding of this fundamental aspect of learning has the potential to enhance educational experiences.

Partnerships and collaborations

Field practice has always been an integral part of social work education both in India and elsewhere. Although the training period and status vary in various social work colleges and universities, the fact remains that it has been considered vital on account of the job-related focus of the education, making it essential to combine theory and practice within the framework of the curriculum.

Course supervisors and practitioners who double up as mentors have the important task of contributing to students' learning. The question arises as to how we become more accountable to the learning of our students by working on learning goals which are in consonance with the emancipatory models of the curriculum. A quick survey of the manuals and handbooks used by schools of social work in India and elsewhere reveal that the field placement courses designed to enable student interns to gain practical skills in the workplace are increasing. These courses are designed to provide students an experience of the workplace culture. They also provide a pre-induction experience besides enabling a student to test theoretical learnings with practical experiences. The production of knowledge for practice has long been the subject of debate in professional education. Work-integrated learning is seen as an opportunity for students to put theory into practice.

Host organizations address students on fieldwork placements with the following in mind:

- They bring in new ideas/look at 'old' problems with 'fresh eyes'
- They possess good problem-solving/analytical skills
- They are up-to-date on new technologies, theories, and concepts
- They are ideal to tackle one-off projects which might otherwise be put to one side
- It builds closer links to the university/college

When host organizations participate in the work placement programme, they agree to ensure the following:

- To provide a safe workplace for the student.
- That the student is briefed or given a short induction course on organization practices upon commencing work.
- To assign a member of the staff to act as a work placement supervisor to the student.
- To draw up an outline programme of the jobs, activities, and training that the student is expected to complete.
- To provide work experience compatible with the student's level of knowledge, experience, and expectations.
- To approve and sign the learning log/time diary during placement and the supervisor's assessment report and the final written report at the end of the placement.
- To report to the academic mentor or placement coordinator, any aspects of the student's approach to the placement with which they are not satisfied.

Roles of each party

Student role

- Attend supervision sessions and meetings when arranged.
- Act within the procedures of the work placement organization regarding punctuality, health and safety, confidentiality, equal opportunities, and other relevant procedures.
- Carry out the placement requirements, including the production of regular recordings and a final report.
- Collect evidence demonstrating her or his progress in terms of the learning outcomes agreed to in the placement contract and share this with the work placement supervisor.
- Contact the academic mentor or work placement coordinator if the placement is breaking down.
- Inform the work placement organization and college if there is any absence from placement.

Work placement/fieldwork supervisor

Supervisors play key roles in supervising students while on placement. These roles include:

- Liaison with the college/department in the operation and review of the placement.

PROCEDURAL ASPECTS OF FIELDWORK

- Provide support, guidance, and appraisal to the student during the placement period.
- Provide regular and agreed times to meet with the student to discuss their progress and learning throughout the placement.
- Encourage the student to demonstrate their progress on placement through the collection of evidence, including reflective recordings and other material.
- In consultation with the student and the academic mentor, prepare and submit an evaluation of the student's progress and performance on placement.

Clearly the specific roles of the supervisor will vary according to the nature of the placement, the needs of the students, and the normal routine of the organization.

Academic mentor/faculty advisor

An academic mentor is specifically allocated to each student for the purpose of supervising the student during the placement. The roles include:

- Provide a key contact point for students while they are on placement.
- Regularly convene a three-way meeting between the student, supervisor, and mentor during the period of the placement to discuss the recordings, supervision, progress of the placement, and final reports.
- Be involved in preparatory and briefing meetings before and after the placement.
- Provide ongoing personal support to students on placement.
- Offer critical dimensions to students in relating their practical involvement to the course generally.
- Provide guidance where required to students in writing key placement documents (i.e., learning log/time diary).
- Guide analysis and evaluation of the placement experience.
- Ensure that students and supervisors are adequately briefed on the roles and experience of placements.

Placement/fieldwork coordinator

The placement coordinator is responsible for the establishment of placements and supporting students on the degree programme. The role includes:

- Brief students on college expectations for placement.
- Work with students and faculty in liaising with organizations and setting up placements.

- Assess the suitability of placement organizations based on pre-defined criteria.
- Formally confirm the placements.
- Maintain a database of current and future placement organizations.
- Be involved in the provision of training and support to work placement supervisors.
- Provide administrative support to the fieldwork programme.
- Produce and update a placement handbook/manual.
- Support and advise during the placement and assessment process.
- Provide a backup point of contact for administrative issues which may arise during placement.
- Monitor the quality of students' placement experience.
- Gather and collate feedback from placement organizations.
- Advise students in relation to health issues.

Supervisory structure

The primary task of the supervisor is to maximize opportunities for the students to learn for themselves within the context of the placement setting. The individual mentors who provide the guidance, protection, and control are called supervisors. Essentially, there are direct supervisors who interact with the students regularly and meet them in the field frequently. There are faculty supervisors/faculty advisors and academic supervisors who are appointed by the school and have the overall responsibility of supervising and reporting on students' learning and progress. Supervisors, whether from the school or the agency, are preferably and invariably social workers who are themselves allowed to undertake the responsibility because they are qualified by training, expertise, preparation, and endorsement by the school and the agency.

Ideally it is expected that students will receive at least one hour a week of one-to-one supervision from the supervisor. The supervision meeting is a time for the student to review his or her work, obtain constructive feedback, and identify areas that require additional support or attention. The student needs to assume increasing responsibility for the focus and content of the supervision meetings. This includes drafting an agenda, providing discussion points prior to the meeting, and coordinating with stakeholders to provide a holistic view of the issue.

The supervisors need to ask themselves whether they are actually ready to supervise. This is an additional responsibility, and the supervisor needs to be sufficiently secure in their knowledge and social work practice and feel that they have enough to offer to students. Supervisors also need a good understanding of the theory that supports intervention methods so that experience and knowledge can be brought together in an understandable way for the student.

There are certain qualities which a supervisor is expected to possess, viz.:

a) A similar orientation to practice as a student.
b) Should be an experienced practitioner.
c) Should have the ability to boost confidence and acknowledge competence.
d) Should be open to a different point of view coming from the student.
e) Should have the ability to maximize the student's learning.
f) Should have a willingness to be an active participant and the capacity to enjoy supervising.
g) Should have a willingness to appraise the student openly, providing a different point of view, with evidence to support it when necessary. The supervisor needs to be open, accepting, supporting, and able to create an environment where the teaching-learning relationship can be established and developed. It is necessary to create a favourable learning climate for the student.
h) Ability to help students with personal feelings of a more stressful kind, which may be aroused through the process of involvement in work.
i) To provide healthy criticism which is non-threatening.

Field contacts

All students must have field contacts,[11] also known as para-professionals, to guide them during their placement. These field contacts oversee the learning tasks of the students, assist the students with any concerns or dilemmas, evaluate the students, and provide guidance.

Para-professionals are given a variety of titles, including caseworker aides, mental health workers, and service coordinators, among others. Largely, the function is task oriented but sometimes it is clerical or routine in nature. In either case, the para-professional works under the direction of a professional staff member. Regular supervision and ongoing training opportunities are important for ensuring a high level of quality performance from the para-professional.

Para-professionals are a link in the human service continuum, but the significance of their contribution is debated. Quite often, para-professionals have opted for traditional methods of intervention, rather than provide innovative grassroots services as originally intended. A second issue relates to the impact of the use of para-professionals on professional classifications. Declassification of professional social work positions and an overlap of function between social workers and para-professionals create tension between them regarding the domain of professional activity.

- The student is expected to periodically brief the supervisor and field contact on his or her progress and seek advice when necessary in time of any change, alteration, or amendment impacting fieldwork.

- The student is expected to terminate the helping relationships with clients and client populations in a professional way. They are required to make detailed reports on the cases they were working on, what was left to do, and similar information, thus handing over responsibility to the supervisor/field contact, who will take appropriate follow-up action.
- Students are required to write and submit a summary report to the faculty advisor, agency, and fieldwork coordinator at the end of the placement period.

Fieldwork as a guided process

During individual conferences, which are an integral part of supervision, the fieldwork supervisor facilitates self-directed learning by the student. The student is required to plan individual conferences with his or her supervisor such on a regular basis – preferably weekly – keeping in mind that structure and consistency are lent to the process of field instruction. The field recordings of students serve as an effective tool for purposeful discussions during these conferences. Students are expected to incorporate the suggestions of the supervisor in the fieldwork process and recordings.

Group conferences too are a method of learning within the group. These are organized at regular intervals. They are organized in the form of discussion groups gathering students in a common setting, students across settings, and with key persons involved with students. Group conferences may be conducted to discuss issues, review work and professional growth, share field experiences, and obtain feedback from peers or for any other reason that the supervisor, student, agency personnel, or faculty advisor sees as being facilitative of learning.

Learnings from case studies

Case study 1 of an exchange student X on field placement at TISS, Mumbai

A. COURSE GOALS

Knowledge and understanding
- Describe how the different types of knowledge (theoretical and experience based) are used and integrated in social work.
- Describe, explain, and analyse the relevance of contextual and organizational conditions for the social worker's space to act and professional role.

PROCEDURAL ASPECTS OF FIELDWORK

Competence and skills
- Identify, motivate, and autonomously apply different theories and methods in social work, with consideration for age, gender, ethnicity, and class.
- Identify and analyse problems and resources, and where applicable, propose decisions and interventions.
- Establish, maintain, and end relationships and demonstrate an understanding for processes in social work.
- Identify important cooperation partners and give examples of cooperating with them.

Judgment and approach
- Problematize social work based on the practical experiences gained through the course 'Supervised Fieldwork' and demonstrate an understanding for the client's experiences of the provided social work with consideration for class, gender, ethnicity, and age.
- Reflect on and critically assess ethical dilemmas, conflicts, and power configurations in social work.
- Analyse and critically assess how organizational, professional, and one's own norms, values, and attitudes affect the interaction and relations with the target group and cooperation with other professional groups.
- Demonstrate a capacity for empathy and critically reflect on how one's self affects and is affected by the social work.
- Identify and evaluate the ability to put theoretical knowledge and skills to practical use, and identify the need for further knowledge within social work.

Discussion

The overall aim of field practice is for the student to achieve an in-depth understanding of social issues and processes at various levels, to enable them to work methodically with the aim of learning independent working with reflectivity in the profession. It also entails learning the ability to develop self-reflection and self-awareness.

The learning plan prepared by the student is a document which the supervisor and the student formulate together and which serves as a guide during the fieldwork education course. The learning plan has the goals of the course enumerated (Table 1.1) and needs to be specific to the workplace conditions at the placement. The learning plan was continuously discussed and/or revised as per the progress of the student. The purpose of the learning plan needs to be reiterated here, viz. that it serves as a tool to enable the student to reach the formulated goals by providing structure. By enabling the student to monitor his or her

Table 1.1 Learning plan for student X

Sr No	Learning Tasks	Date	Supervisor
1	Developing a brochure for ABC centre. **Subtasks** • Study last few years' annual reports and read activities conducted at the centre. • Take reference from previous brochures.	3–12 Feb	A, P
2	Writing report on Diploma in Youth Development and Social Change Course, include interviewing students. **Subtasks** Attend one class on Saturday (6 Feb) • Attend field visits with them. • Meet the students to discuss the programme with them and how their perspective about social work has changed and any personal development they have seen in due course. Document my observations in a report format.	6–19 Feb	A, P
3	Study CSR policies of corporate organizations in India and create a database **Subtasks** • Understand the current collaboration with CSR. • Conduct secondary research on different corporate social responsibility policies in India and see if they match with ABC's values – which ones might be the next investors or where could ABC start to look for funds. • Document in an Excel sheet format.	22 Feb–4 Mar	A, P

| 4 | Create archives of ABC – Child learning centre – Zilla Parishad programme (a local non-formal education support programme for public schools). | 7 Mar–6 Apr | A, P |

Subtasks

Read about the project.

- Meet persons involved with the programme; ask them about their view and the impact it created.
- Document my observations in a report format.

| 5 | Review and study 'national-level smart city' programme regarding building a perspective for Mumbai | 11–22 Apr | A, P |

Subtasks

- Read about the project, go out and meet locals, get their opinion on the matter, do they know how it affects them, what do they think about it, understand its connection with Mumbai.
- Write a small report about it all.

| 6 | Participate and interact with people in Mumbai's slum programmes regarding children and migrant workers. | 22 Apr–8 May | A, P |

Subtasks

- Meet the women and migrant workers who are involved with the ABC programmes and interact; try to understand their situation and build perspective towards the issue of migration in India.

Source: Developed by Author in consultation with student

own progress, it also enables the mentor to monitor the progress of the student and serves as a basis for evaluation. The assessment of the learning tasks revealed that the student was able to acquire the skills and abilities required while carrying out social work at different levels and in collaboration with the para-professionals in the fieldwork setting. With the growing complexity of social problems, there has been a shift of emphasis from competence-based approaches to a reflective practice paradigm. In doing so, the student was able to appreciate that the fieldwork curriculum served as an 'emancipatory interest,' as the learner was able to stand alone and take charge of her or his own learning. Ongoing learning was thus directed by the learner which assumed a process of meaning-making, recognizing that meaning is a social construction in the fields of practice.

There were spaces, of course, where the student felt a great deal of uncertainty in field practice but had the space in supervisory conferences to query and to investigate. Constant reflection related to day-to-day experiences gained by the student gave her or him the opportune chance to use field placement as an instructive phase. On some occasions the associated learning from the field was a revolutionary experience, especially since the exchange student was from one part of the developed world and was on placement in a not-so-developed Asian context. It is these experiences which helped her or him draw parallels and which provoked her or him to question how and where theory and practice are aligned and whether the learnings and experiences in the field placement would suffice for them in the world of work.

This week's key learning experiences – what was the most interesting and/or most useful skill, idea and/or concept I learned this week.

The skills I utilized most this week was self-reliance and independence. I developed these skills when trying to set up meetings with relevant programme coordinators to discuss our work plans. I assigned myself research work, when there was no other work available, in order to utilize my time wisely. I also used my own innovative when suggesting that I could write a report on my observation from the workshop.

D. W. Johnson (1986, cited in Mallick, 2007) suggests that experiential learning is based on three assumptions:

1   People learn best when they are personally involved in the learning experience.
2   Knowledge must be discovered if it is to mean anything or make a difference in behaviour.
3   Commitment to learning is highest when people are free to set their own learning goals and actively pursue them within a given framework.

Charlotte Towle (cited in Price 1976) was concerned about problems in helping students maintain a balance between creativity (experimentation) and responsibility, and how to help students incorporate and have integrated learning of values, knowledge, and content. Learning and developing learning through experience addresses some of Towle's concerns.

Experiential learning is learning through experience. Such learning is important because it is unique to the learner and has a lasting impression. In order to learn experientially, among other things, the learner must participate in the learning process and be open to learning. An activity offers scope for experiential learning, but an activity does not necessarily mean that learning is taking place. Critical reflection is crucial to experiential learning. Experiential learning involves learning of knowledge, attitudes, skills, and perspectives. In social work education, such learning is acquired during fieldwork. Fieldwork offers the ability to integrate classroom learning with learning in the field. Crucial elements in experiential learning include concrete experience, observation and reflection, abstract conceptualization, and active experimentation. Experiential learning requires intrinsic motivation, social interaction, and engagement in the field. It facilitates continuity – that is, learning leads to further learning. Finally, key processes in experiential learning are doing, thinking, interacting, engaging, discovering, learning, assessing, applying, experimenting, and critically reflecting.

Case study 2

Referring to the customized International Study and Field Placement at the Tata Institute of Social Sciences in Mumbai, India, one would need to mention the Social Service Worker Programme of certain international placements. These help students with the skills, knowledge, and attitudes required to work in the diverse and complex field of social services. The purpose of the Social Service Worker Programme is to train individuals seeking employment as social service workers in the field of social services and to provide further training to those already employed in the field. The programme is based on a philosophy of self-directed learning, personal growth, and enhanced awareness while developing skills and knowledge relevant to social services and the clients served. Students in the Social Service Worker Programme come from a wide variety of backgrounds and range in age from 18 to 60. Some have Bachelor of Arts degrees and are looking for specific social service skills, whereas others are secondary school graduates or mature students with extensive life experience.

The Community Worker Programme prepares students to work in solidarity with communities, from a rights-based and empowerment approach, towards lasting social change. Students are taught to understand

and analyse the historical, social, political, economic, and systematic ways in which current issues, needs, and injustices have developed and how these continue to be experienced by marginalized communities. The programme's multi-level approach to community work (individual, community, civil society, governmental, and global) enables graduates to work in a variety of different roles and in a number of different settings, that is, issue-based organizations, resident/tenant associations, community centres, self-help organizations, advocacy groups, and in the many social services agencies found throughout a multi-cultural city. In keeping with a tradition of attracting diverse, talented, and dedicated student populations, the Community Worker Programme requires a high level of maturity, personal and social responsibility, and a commitment to principles of social justice. When selecting students for international placement, students must be prepared to examine their own behaviour and ideas critically and must be able to work with others, across all differences, in a respectful and supportive manner.

The goals of field placement for this programme

Goal #1 Have students spent time in the field of social services and community work at TISS's partner agencies to observe and assist with programmes.

Goal #2 Have the students and faculty experience, observe, and explore what it means to be marginalized in India and bring back this knowledge to students and faculty in their own home country.

Goal #3 Involve the students with other TISS students by attending campus classroom visits and discuss school, culture, and social issues that impact the delivery of social services in India.

Goal #4 Experience and explore Indian culture and reflect on anti-oppressive practices in an international context.

Student's reflections on placement

I am very grateful for the opportunity to come to learn, observe and participate in activities offered by H and TISS. This life changing experience has equipped me with skills and knowledge for the present and the future. It was great to live on campus and have interactions with the students to share ideas and learning from each other. The community outreach provided an in-depth learning and understanding of the community life and culture. Here are the main points I would like to make.

1   My placement with the Agency H has the strategy of "Changing of the mindset from Victimhood to Change

PROCEDURAL ASPECTS OF FIELDWORK

Maker". H has achieved this through building community leaders, focusing on gender education and empowering women. Hs approach is to enable, break and change social norms by changing attitudes without breaking community cohesion. Through self-help groups (SHG), women have received training to handle their issues, including tailoring, catering, small savings and health. Women members are witness to their own success (Farida' story of the SHG in S Nagar). I learned and understood that the GEMS programme was very effective, because it teaches and instils gender education to the young people. This translates to a better future for the next generation regarding changes to social norms that will reduce violence against women and balance gender awareness.

2   H also empowers communities to address their own issues by training leaders This was evidenced on how H has evolved from its founding and leadership by the upper caste to a fully grassroots organization lead by members of different castes. To date there are H trained Advanced Quest Fellows, Mentors, and Fellows who are spearheading community programmes and organizations. This approach helps to decentralise the activities.

3   H has been involved in advocating, organizing people and focusing on interventions (gender, violence against women, women's sexual & reproductive health, education, saving, self-help groups and basic amenities). This approach is based on Dr Ambedkar's motto "Agitate, organize and educate". Community members, especially women, have benefitted through their participation in groups to address women's lack of recognition in society. The future focus of H is quite appropriate as they establish a Federation of SHG to achieve long-term goals in the coming three years, such as:

1   Develop women entrepreneurship;
2   Create platforms for market linkages to SHG products;
3   Initiate microfinance schemes to provide immediate loans and subsidy; and
4   Establish women's cooperative.

These future projections bring hope and relief to the plight of the rural single women, who suffer social exclusion, isolation and other forms of oppression. My learnings in India enhanced my adaptability and further enhanced my learning.

I hope to review and refine my new learnings and integrate them into my ongoing learnings and my future work practise in Toronto and abroad. I hope to work very closely with my employment supervisors to share the new learnings and approaches, and integrate them in the organization's programmes, or implement the new strategy for a new programme, I will develop for the organization.

I will share my learning experiences on my return with my fellow programme students in both first and second year, through the Student Success programme. As a peer leader, I will organize with the Student Success specialist for an opportunity to share this marvellous and life changing experience.

Student 2 at the same agency

There were countless lessons learned as a result of doing my International Placement with H. I am impressed that H is a grassroots leadership agency that seeks to empower leaders and agencies. It is a testament to the empowerment and self-sustaining success of the organization that the founding leadership was once upper caste persons, but now the leadership team includes persons from marginalized lower caste communities. Although empowerment is a focal point in the teachings of the Community Worker Programme in Toronto, and rightly so, the reality is that most social workers in Toronto are anything but empowering. In Toronto I sense there is an arrogance and false superiority complex with most of the 'professionals' that greatly impedes the work being done.

I was extremely marginalized in my formative years – perhaps in the bottom one percent, and the affiliation with most social workers was paradoxically disempowering or counterproductive. I realize now that I succeeded through the many hurdles of life, as a result of mentors and leaders comparable to those at agency H. It is very validating and reassuring to see that empowerment does in fact also work in the community and social fields when there is a sense of inclusiveness, equality, mutual respect, warmth, authenticity and unity.

Reflective diaries are a private record of experiences throughout placement and so it is important to use them to report thoughts, feelings and opinions rather than merely the factual events of the day. Only by reporting personal feelings following an event can experiences be built upon and improved. It is important to use your reflective diary to record positive experiences and achievements as well as the not so positive ones. A balanced view of what has taken place is essential.

In actual fact, making [15] minutes available to note a few things that have happened throughout the day is very therapeutic. I found that taking a little time out every evening to complete my reflective diary helped me to get the day's events in perspective. I found that using a reflective diary was an excellent way to clear my mind and ensure a positive, fresh start the following day.

Everyone feels under pressure at some point while on placement, especially if you are the only student at a placement centre and in an entirely different location from one you have been used to. At the end of a stressful and demanding day it is a relief to be able to unload the burdens of the day onto your reflective diary before they build up and become blown out of proportion. When I look back I realize that they have provided a release for pent up anxiety and stress, and perhaps improved my performance throughout placement.

Earlier I had considered myself to be a quiet student, often unaware of my achievements and always lacking the confidence to express these in the hope of gaining recognition. This is where keeping a reflective diary was of greatest benefit to me; by noting my capabilities, strengths and daily accomplishments every day in my reflective diary

I had the evidence I needed to chart a definite upward progression in skills throughout the placement. Although my practice educators never asked to see my reflective diary, I often took it to supervision and allowed them to read entries I thought to be important. By doing so, I not only boosted my own self-esteem and confidence, but I also provided my practice educator with evidence of my acquiring competence skills.

Experiential learning offers us a sense of ownership over the knowledge, skills, attitude and perspectives that we acquire, because we have interacted with our external world and our learning that is likely to be unique. Experiential learning helps us to internalize our learning in a way that we are able to make social work responses to diverse situations and not just the particular ones in which learning happened. Further, experiential learning helps the learner to participate in the planning the learning goals, as the same is developed according to how much and where the learner is at a given point in time. Thus, experiential learning through fieldwork practicum results in personal theories about effective intervention and continuously recurs as a person tests out and confirms or modifies his or her personal theories (Johnson, 1986, cited *ibid.*).

Anupriyo Mallick (2007) suggests that the learning experience in social work includes broadly four areas: Knowledge, Attitudes, Skills and Perspective. Knowledge includes the information we receive, discover and explore in regard to the social, economic, political and cultural context of the people we work with and their challenges, knowledge about ourselves, knowledge about responses (from State, non-state social work agencies, lawyers, doctors, *anganwadi* workers, teachers, etc.) to address problems and vulnerable populations. Skills include verbal and non-verbal communication skills while engaging with people during fieldwork, and analytical and reflective skills.

Skills are developed from the knowledge we gain about the field context and ourselves. Learning of skills is at various levels. It includes skills when working with individuals, groups, communities. Skills are also developed to work with people in various government and non-government systems, and to record, assess and analyse intervention. Learning of skills can happen only during field practice. Developing skills to work with people is a complex task sometimes and one can face difficulties. We must remember once again, that our experiences must be shared with our supervisor and field contacts. We can then work together to develop skills. We must also remember *to recognize the uniqueness of our own skills of social work, reflect on them, and work towards developing them.*

Case study 3

If I am being completely honest, I would have to admit that before I went on my first fieldwork practice placement I could not see what the benefit of keeping a reflective diary would be. However, I did keep a diary from day one. The first couple of days were really reflections of how I was feeling, what I thought of the place, the people, the events. As time progressed I started to reflect more on practice – what had gone well and what had not. It is strange but when I started to write down what had happened each day I was able to analyse the events more clearly. I was able to pinpoint possible factors that had contributed to the outcomes in intervention that had been achieved. in the field with the help of my co-workers and the para-professionals. One of the benefits of cataloguing events in the diary was that I could look back over the previous weeks and see how I had improved.

The role of the mentor might include undertaking the following roles and tasks:

- An advisor: offering support and guidance
- Providing an objective viewpoint
- An observer: of treatment sessions, preparation
- A sounding board: someone to generate new ideas
- Providing an opportunity to reflect
- A counsellor: a sympathetic, non-judgemental ear
- A problem solver: to discuss and consider problems
- A questioner: someone who will challenge ideas
- A supporter: providing encouragement, reassurance, motivation and building confidence
- Providing feedback
- A networker, friend and ally.

Mid-placement review

Towards the close of the first semester, a formal mid-placement review session is required to be conducted through an open dialogue between the student and fieldwork supervisor, with the latter taking an active role in drawing out and discussing the learning opportunities, the student's ability and interest in actively learning from the field, and critically analysing one's own engagement in the learning process. The mid-placement review pertains to the following areas:

- Areas of learning can be in terms of both knowledge gained and skills acquired. Prior to this review, a summary could be made of the tasks undertaken by the student, identifying what has been learned through each task in terms of knowledge, skills, use of self, examination of one's own attitudes and feelings, relating theory to practice, values, and so on.
- Areas of strength. The student needs to identify areas in which he or she has confidence and has demonstrated some competence. The idea is to help students realize their own strengths in the learning–doing praxis and thereby develop better confidence in dealing with various aspects of practice.
- Areas for future learning. These are aspects in which the student has been able to demonstrate some competence which he or she needs to develop for effective practice. These include areas in which the student has not had the opportunity to develop either confidence or competence, areas in which the student is struggling, and/or areas in which other extraneous factors played a significant role and the student has been unable to deal with such issues or contexts.

Evaluation of fieldwork

Evaluation is the more formal aspect of feedback in the guided learning process. It is a continuous process in field education. A structured review and evaluation process is put in place with a mid-placement comprehensive review at the end of the first semester and a final end-of-placement evaluation. Like feedback, evaluation is a participatory process, and the fieldwork supervisor needs to explain the evaluation process to the student at the beginning of the placement. Evaluation needs to concentrate not merely on inputs made by the student in terms of willingness, enthusiasm, and energy but, more importantly, on the process and outcome of the students' efforts.

Each student's professional growth as a social worker is evaluated by examining several discrete areas. Broadly speaking they are:

- Overall consistency of progress in fieldwork performance throughout the year.
- Ability to analyse social situations, individual needs and resources, skills in problem identification, case planning, and evaluation.
- Ability to conceptualize and integrate theory and apply it appropriately in practice.
- Identification with the social work profession and internalization of values and goals of the profession as reflected in role performance.
- Motivation to help others instead of being preoccupied with one's needs and problems.
- Ability to approach work with professional zeal and responsibility and commitment towards the client system/constituency, agency, colleagues, and the fieldwork supervisor.
- Capacity to relate purposefully, empathize, and respond appropriately while working with individuals, groups, and communities. Capacity for sustained work and ability to involve clients in the process of engagement.
- Aptitude to utilize methods of social work, capacity to use skills and techniques for enhancement of the process, interaction, thinking, and reflection and action in the client system and social context.
- Capacity for self-direction, independence, and resourcefulness in work, including management of time and workload.
- Extent of openness to learning, accepting constructive criticism and supervision, and adopting appropriate attitudes.

This encapsulates the impact the placement experience has on the student, the attitude towards field instruction, and the appraisal of performance. The reflection can also examine how the student's ideological stance is reflected in the way he or she works. It is inclusive of the student's openness to learn; capacity to change and grow as demonstrated in the placement; capacity to use supervision effectively; and identify, locate, and use community resources.

Guidelines for resolution of problems in meeting competency expectations

The field practicum is distinct from most other course curriculum of the department/school of social work in that it entails not only educational objectives but also professional responsibilities to clients, organizations, and the community. When students engage with clients and client populations and assume service responsibilities, there are ongoing professional, educational, and ethical responsibilities to be kept in mind. Various kinds of issues and limitations and external stressors may impede the performance of some students. When personal issues impact field performance and professional behaviour and obligations and agency expectations are not being met appropriately, faculty and field instructors have the responsibility to intervene.

When performance is marked by inappropriate or unethical behaviour, excessive absences, non-compliance with the organization's mandate, or competence and skill deficits, a Stage 1 Review will be convened. Early recognition and feedback regarding serious performance issues are especially relevant. Students and clients are better served by early recognition of significant performance difficulties.

It is the responsibility of the student and field instructor to identify any problematic behaviour pattern or major issue in the practicum which impacts student learning. The student and field instructor are to document their attempts in the teaching/learning experience to address these difficulties. In practicum settings, where there is an educational or fieldwork coordinator, their role is to become involved when the student and field instructor/supervisor cannot resolve the issues at hand. It is anticipated that most of the issues will be dealt with through identification and discussion. However, if the issues remain unresolved through this process, a Stage 1 Review Meeting is to be arranged.

The Stage I Review Meeting will cover the following:

a) A clear identification of problems in learning and teaching-learning, whether there is sufficient evidence of the student's practice to arrive at an evaluation have regular procedures been followed in field instruction as specified in the work plan/learning plan (e.g., nature of assignments, field instruction sessions, nature of feedback given to the student)?
b) Specification of learning objectives to be achieved and behaviour changes expected

c) Any necessary actions and procedures to be taken in field instruction
d) A time frame for review meeting and a schedule stating when a sample of the student's practice is to be reviewed by the liaison
e) A review of the procedures involved, including grading

The process and outcome of the Stage 1 Review Meeting will be documented. A copy will be given to the student, field instructor, and fieldwork coordinator's office. Should the practicum concerns not be resolved through this procedure, a Stage 2 Review Meeting will be convened. For a Stage 2 Review Meeting networking with the assistant dean, field educator/instructor or fieldwork director, fieldwork may be necessary due to the serious nature of the concerns in the practicum. The assistant dean or programme convenor notifies the dean and/or academic council and convenes a meeting with the student and appropriate field and faculty personnel.

The Stage 2 Review Meeting will basically assess the degree to which the student has met the objectives set out in the previous meeting, the extent to which any activities in the field instruction have been useful, and any other relevant issues.

As Shardlow and Doel (1996, p. 4) observe, "learning, for a student on placement, does not just happen by osmosis; it requires effort and planning by both student and practice teacher."

Conclusion

Varied situations arise during field placement wherein students are provided ample opportunities to work on their own reactions and experiences and, in the process, develop self-awareness of their personal values, attitudes, feelings, and reactions which can impact their relationships and work with client populations. To achieve the intended learning outcomes of fieldwork, students are expected to use the help of mentors, who help develop and train the ability both for self-reflection and for objective analysis to communicate experiences, knowledge gained, and personal reflections. Many host organizations and field placements remain committed to the process of work-integrated learning and the ongoing viability of all social contexts to which contribution can be made.

While engaging with field placement and student learning, it becomes essential to appreciate that these are partnerships which are mutually respectful of the capabilities and development potential of partner organizations and the student body (Humphries & Camilleri 2005). The student's adaptability to the work environment ensures that transformative learning, both by students and agencies/organizations, can be by newer kinds of partner/stakeholder relations. This can be enhanced by developing a learning community such that students are able to develop their own self-supporting groups, become more actively involved in learning, and have a greater sense of responsibility for their fellow students (Tinto, 2003). It is this learning community which becomes the social learning support network that students rely on when things get tough (Harris, 2005). Finally, induction into a profession takes time and enabling students to gather experiences that proactively assist them with social integration so that they begin 'identifying' with the profession.

Notes

1 Chapter 2 Social Work education: Curriculum, Pedagogy, and Evaluation. Retrieved February 14, 2017, from shodhganga.inflibnet.ac.in
2 Professional Social Work education and practice in India – Strengthening inclusive perspectives and Approach. G. Sathiyan and P. Ilango.
3 Ibid.
4 Singh, S., Gumz, J. E., & Crawley, C. B. (2011). Predicting India's future: Does it justify the exportation of US social work education. *Social Work Education*, 30(7), 861–873.
5 Buck, W. P., Fletcher, P., & Bradley, J. (2016). Decision-making in social work field education: A 'good enough' framework. *Social Work Education*, 35(4), 402–413.
6 The NASW Code of Ethics is intended to serve as a guide to the everyday professional conduct of social workers. This Code includes four sections. The first section, "Preamble," summarizes the social work profession's mission and core values.
7 Stephen Hamilton (1980) suggests that experiential learning refers to "educational programmes functioning outside of conventional school classrooms that place participants in responsible roles and engage them in cooperative, goal-directed activities with other youth, with adults, or both" (p. 180).
8 Supervision refers to those planned regular periods of time that the student and supervisor spend together discussing the student's work in the placement and reviewing the learning process (Ford & Jones, 1987).
9 The fieldwork curriculum covers the core knowledge, values, and skills that have been identified by the school/department as necessary to successful social work practice.
10 Halton, C., Murphy, M., & Dempsey, M. (2007). Reflective learning in social work education: Researching student experiences. *Reflective Practice*, 8(4), 511–523.
11 The para-professional of the agency with whom the student remains in daily contact in the field who also facilitates student learning.

References

Alsop, A., & Ryan, S. (1996). *Making the most of fieldwork education: A practical approach*. London: Chapman & Hall
Baer, B. L., & Federico, R. (Eds.). (1978). *Educating the baccalaureate social worker* (Vol. 1). Cambridge, MA: Ballinger.

Baer, B. L., & Federico, R. (1978). *West Virginia undergraduate social worker curriculum development project: Educating the baccalaureate social worker.* Cambridge, MA: Ballinger.

Bates, M. (2003). The assessment of work integrated learning: Symptoms of personal change. *Journal of Criminal Justice Education, 14*(2), 303–326.

Biddle, B. J. (1979). *Role theory: Expectations, identities and behaviours.* New York, NY: Academic Press.

Bombay Association of Trained Social Workers. (2002). *Declaration of ethics for professional social workers.* Mumbai: BATSW.

Bogo, Marion & Regehr, Cheryl & Power, Roxanne & Regehr, Glenn. (2007). *When Values Collide. The Clinical Supervisor, 26,* 99–117. doi:10.1300/J001v26n01_08.

Brown, T., Cosgriff, T., & French, G. (2008). Learning style preferences of occupational therapy, physiotherapy and speech pathology students: A comparative study. *Internet Journal of Allied Health Sciences & Practice, 6*(3), 12.

Calvert, F. (2014). Competency-based models of supervision: Principles and applications, promises and challenges. *Australian Psychologist, 49,* 200–208.

Datar, S., Bawikar, R., Rao, G., Rao, N., & Masdekar, U. (Eds.). (2010). *Skill training for social workers: A manual.* London: Sage Publication.

Dhemba, J. (2012). Fieldwork in social work education and training: Issues and challenges in the case of eastern and southern Africa, social work & society. *International Online Journal, 10*(1).

DiBartola, L. M. (2006). The learning style Inventory challenge: Teaching about teaching by learning about learning. *Journal of Allied Health, 35*(4), 238–245.

Fleming, N. (2001). *How do I learn best? A student guide to improved learning: VARK – visual, aural, read/write, kinaesthetic.* Chch, NZ: Fleming. Supplementary web site. Retrieved April 24, 2017, from www.vark-learn.com

Fleming, N., & Baume, D. (2006, November). *Learning styles again: Varking up the right tree!* P4-7. Educational Developments, SEDA Ltd. Vol 7. No 4.

Ford, K., & Jones, A. (1987). *Student Supervision.* London: BASW, Palgrave Macmillan.

Forrest, S. (2004). Learning and teaching: The reciprocal link. *Journal of Continuing Education in Nursing, 35*(2), 74–79.

Gaiptman, B., & Anthony, A. (1989). Contracting in fieldwork education: The model of self-directed learning. *Canadian Journal of Occupational Therapy, 56*(1), 40–44.

Hall, E.T. (1990). *The Hidden Dimension.* New York: Double day.

Hamilton, S. F. (1980). Experiential learning programs for youth. *American Journal of Education, 88*(2), 179–215.

Heffernan, W. J., Shuttlesworth, G., & Ambrosino, R. (1988). *Social work and social welfare: An introduction.* St. Paul: West Pub.

Howard, D. C., & Howard, P. A. (1993). Learning technology: Implications for practice. In D. Carey, R. Carey, A. Willis, & J. Willis (Eds.), *Technology and teacher education annual.* Charlottesville, VA: Association for the Advancement of Computing in Education.

Humpries, P., & Camilleri, P. (2003). Social work and technology: challenges for social workers in practice: A case study. *Australian Social Work, 55*(4), 251–259.

IASSW. (2014). *What is social work?* Retrieved from https://www.ifsw.org/what-is-social-work/global-definition-of-social-work/

Ingrid Mary Provident, M.L. Leibold, C. Dolhi & J. Jeffcoat (2009). *Becoming a Fieldwork 'educator' enhancing your teaching skills, OT Practice,* 14(19): CE1–CE8

International Association of Schools of Social Work and International Federation of Social Workers (2005). *Global standards for the education and training of the social work profession.* http://www.ifsw.org./en/p38000868.html (Accessed on 26 March 2014).

International Federation of Social Workers/International Association of Schools of Social Work (IFSW). (2013, March). *Global definition of social work.* Retrieved May 3, 2013, from www.ifsw.org: http://ifsw.org/get-involved/global-definition-of-social-work/

Johnson, D. W. (1986). *Reading out: Interpersonal effectiveness and self-actualisation.* Upper Saddle River, NJ: Prentice-Hall.

Kolb, D. (1984). *Experiential learning: Experience as the source of learning and development.* Upper Saddle River, NJ: Prentice-Hall.

Lager, P. & Robbins, V. C. (2004): Field education: Exploring the future, expanding the vision. *Journal of Social Work Education,* 40, 3–11.

Mallick, A. (2007). Field work training in social work curriculum: Reflections on learning and teaching. *The Indian Journal of Social Work,* 8(4), 573–580.

Moon, J. A. (2006). *Learning journals: A handbook for reflective practice and professional development* (2nd ed.). London and New York, NY: Routledge.

Nanavatty, M. C. (1997). Professional associations of social work: An analysis of literature. *The Indian Journal of Social Work,* 58(2), 287–300.

National Association of Social Workers. (1981a). *Standards for the classification of social work practice, policy statement 4.* Silver Spring, MD: Author.

Pooler, D. K., Doolittle, A., Faul, A. C., Barbee, A., & Fuller, M. (2012). An exploration of MSW Field Education & impairment prevention: What do we need to know? *Journal of Human Behaviour in the Social Environment,* 22(7), 916–927.

Provident, I., Leibold, M. L., Dolhi, C., & Jeffcoat, J. (2009). Becoming a fieldwork "educator": Enhancing your teaching skills. *OT Practice, 14*(19) (Suppl), 2, CE1–8.

Ramachandran, P. 'Perspective for Social Work Training – 2000 A.D.,' *The Indian Journal of Social Work,* 49(1): 11–20.

Saleebey, D. (2013). *The strengths perspective in social work practice* (6th ed.). Advancing Core Competencies, University of Kansas. Boston: Pearson Educational Inc.

Saleebey, D. (2016). *Host organisation's guide to work placement 2016.* Ireland: University College Cork.

Schulz, C. D. (1993). Accommodating students' learning styles with microcomputer software. In D. Carey, R. Carey, A. Willis, & J. Willis (Eds.), *Technology and teacher education annual.* Charlottesville, VA: Association for the Advancement of Computing in Education.

Shardlow, S., & Doel, M. (1996). *Practice learning and teaching.* London: Macmillan Press Ltd.

Sharma, S. (2015). Fieldwork supervision meeting requirements of social work education through critical thinking. *The Hong Kong Journal of Social Work*, *49*(3).

Siporin, M. (1985). Current social work perspectives on clinical practice. *Clinical Social Work Journal*, *13*, 198–217.

Suppes, M. A., & Wells, C. C. (2013). *The social work experience: An introduction to social work and social welfare* (6th ed.). Boston: Pearson.

Tinto, V. (2003). Learning better together: The impact of learning communities on student success. *Higher Education Monograph Series*, 2003-1. Higher Education Program, School of Education, Syrcause University.

Titiloye, V. M., & Scott, A. H. (2001). Occupational therapy student's learning styles and application to professional training. *Occupational Therapy in Health Care*, *15*(1), 145–155.

Tsui, M. (2005). *Social work Supervision: Contexts and concepts*. Thousand Oaks, CA: Sage Publication.

Tsang, Annetta (2011). "In-class Reflective Group Discussion as a Strategy for the Development of Students as Evolving Professionals," *International Journal for the Scholarship of Teaching and Learning*, *5*(1), Article 7. Available at: https://doi.org/10.20429/ijsotl.2011.050107

Weiss-Gal, I., & Welbourne, P. (2008). The professionalisation of social work: A cross-national exploration. *International Journal of Social Welfare*, *17*(4), 281–290.

2

ORIENTATION PROGRAMME TO FIELDWORK
Relevance and modalities

Archana Kaushik

Social work is a human service profession that aims to provide help to affected individuals, groups, and communities suffering from social deprivation in order to strengthen and empower them. It is an academic discipline and a practice profession geared towards improving the social functioning and overall wellbeing of the target groups. According to the National Association of Social Workers (1973),

> Social work practice consists of the professional application of social work values, principles, and techniques to one or more of the following ends: helping people obtain tangible services; counseling and psychotherapy with individuals, families, and groups; helping communities or groups provide or improve social and health services; and participating in legislative processes. The practice of social work requires knowledge of human development and behavior; of social and economic, and cultural institutions; and of the interaction of all these factors.
>
> (p. 4–5)

The International Federation of Social Workers and International Association of Schools of Social Work, in 2014, defined social work as:

> It is a practice-based profession and an academic discipline that promotes social change and development, social cohesion, and the empowerment and liberation of people. Principles of social justice, human rights, collective responsibility and respect for diversities are central to social work. Underpinned by theories of social work, social sciences, humanities and indigenous

knowledge, social work engages people and structures to address life challenges and enhance wellbeing.

(p. 1)

As aptly explained in the definition, social work is a practice-based profession, and it makes the attainment and refinement of certain skills, values, and theoretical knowledge crucial for practice. Thus, field training is of vital significance. The globally accepted definition of social work mentioned earlier describes the three pillars on which professional social work rests: knowledge base, value base, and skill base (Figure 2.1).

Knowledge base: In social work practice, trainees or students are required to analyse the social situations that contribute to social deprivations of various kinds. This necessitates the understanding of social structure, social systems and social processes, and cultural norms and values, as well as intra-psychic and inter-personal factors influencing human behaviours, knowledge about vulnerable aspects of disadvantaged population groups, social policies and programmes meant for them, and others. Understanding various methods of working with people (casework, group work, community organization, social action, social welfare administration, and social work research) and different models and theories under each method is also needed to effectively intervene during social work practice. Social work draws on a wide array of theoretical underpinnings from the disciplines of sociology, psychology, anthropology, public health, economics, education, psychiatry, ecology, management, etc., apart from its own set of theories of working with people and service delivery. Theoretical frameworks learned in classrooms provide greater insight to the social work trainees when they interact with clientele groups in the field. Theories help in providing better diagnosis and assessment of social problems, thereby aiding in more efficient design of interventions.

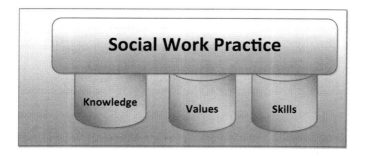

Figure 2.1 Pillars of social work knowledge base
Source: Developed by the author

ORIENTATION PROGRAMME TO FIELDWORK

Value base: Social work is not a neutral (to the extent of being apathetic) profession. It takes the side of the downtrodden and marginalized sections of the society. Its value base includes social justice and empowerment. It works on the rights-based perspective that helps in identifying barriers that are structural in nature. It stands in solidarity with the marginalized and disadvantaged social groups and strives to ameliorate poverty, minimize vulnerability, and promote social inclusion. So Dalits living in abject poverty are not to be blamed for their own condition; rather, the state and society are held responsible for not being able to ensure a rightful share of public goods and services to the poor Dalits. Thus, poverty is seen as a violation of human rights. The social work profession works for to promote social change, social cohesion, and empowerment. A set of social work principles that emerge out of the value base are taught and inculcated among the trainees, and they are expected to abide by these values, ethics, and principles in all situations during their fieldwork practice.

Skill base: Social work practitioners require a range of skills and competencies while working in the field. During their fieldwork training, social workers are expected to learn and refine their skills specific to their settings. Effective intervention is directly related to efficient demonstration of these skills. Some of the prominent ones are assessment and diagnosis, observation and analysis, communication, rapport formation, counselling, persuasion, motivation, creating awareness, mediation, mobilizing, advocating, networking, referring, planning, organizing, implementing, coordinating, monitoring, reporting, documenting, evaluating, etc. Dunlap (2013) has provided ten core skill-groups that are required by professional social workers in most interventions:

1 Assessment skills
2 Communication skills
3 Advocacy and leadership
4 Problem-solving skills
5 Critical thinking skills
6 Respect for diversity
7 Intervention skills
8 Documentation skills
9 Organizational skills
10 Understanding of human relationships

Fieldwork provides a laboratory for social work trainees to learn and become dexterous in these core skill sets. As a general practice, schools of social work have demarcated two days a week where students go to different agencies and communities for each academic year to learn and practice these skills. Students are expected to integrate theories learned in classroom situations into the field practice along with skill enhancement and abiding of values and ethics of the social work profession. The entry points of professional social work training are at graduation and post graduation. In both cases, there is a huge variability among students who join social work for their graduate or post-graduate degree on the bases of their educational levels, socio-cultural milieu, personality, socialization, locale, and such other factors that have direct bearing on their learning and skill development. As social workers, the values and attitudes that we received and imbibed as part of our socialization, our communication and ability to understand social issues and problems, our inclination and dexterity to relate to people of different socio-cultural backgrounds significantly influence our effectiveness in social work practice. Thus, there may be apparent disguised similarity among social work trainees attending classes in a given social work educational institute, when in reality, they all are at different learning levels due to the baggage of socio-cultural values they carry with them. This makes an orientation programme highly significant before social work trainees enter field situations or a live laboratory.

Orientation programme: Dictionary definitions of orientation are "finding direction" (Cambridge Advanced Learners' Dictionary) or "the adjustment or alignment of oneself or one's ideas to surroundings or circumstances" (Oxford English Dictionary). In the context of the social work discipline, an orientation programme aims to acquaint newly enrolled students with the concept and modalities of social work and fieldwork. Most students at the time of joining the course are novices and have various myths and misconceptions regarding social work profession and practice, which need to be addressed before social work trainees enter their respective field settings. Unlike laboratories of natural sciences, where trial and error are allowed and accepted as a mode of learning, discovery, and invention, in human service professions like social work, such liberty is not available. Social work trainees directly interact with individuals, groups, and communities encountering problems, vulnerabilities, and challenges, and their interventions, despite being naïve, affect human lives. Thus, learning through mistakes is not acceptable in fieldwork. Inexperienced and immature trainees may, although unintentionally, harm clientele groups if not provided orientation right at the time of their admission to the course.

Although in India, the social work profession is still considered in a nascent stage, being a social work professional is a highly responsible job, as our interventions have direct implications on human lives. In fieldwork, too, invariably, trainees are not given mock and fabricated situations to learn and practice skills and competencies. This, therefore, becomes imperative for social work educational institutions to design and conduct orientation programmes with much caution, precision, and deliberation. An orientation programme should have the following objectives:

- To acquaint the students about the concept, meaning, and scope of social work practice.
- To develop a basic understanding of the social issues that are addressed by social workers.
- To locate the significance and modalities of fieldwork training as an integral part of social work.
- To inculcate basic skills among students required to initiate rapport with clientele groups and identify and address their needs and problems.
- To develop self-awareness to identify personal strengths and weaknesses that may act as facilitators and inhibitors in effective social work interventions.
- To provide field exposure visits to students for direct observation and experience of certain sites of engagement.
- To inform about the significance and process of documentation and report writing.

Because the scope of the social work profession is quite vast, designing an orientation programme becomes quite challenging. Social work trainees are placed in different organizations requiring different knowledge and skill bases. For instance, the expected roles played by trainees in an urban slum community would be different than those in children's home under the Juvenile Justice Act. Moreover, problems encountered by clients and success or failure in interventions are intangible, and one cannot be sure whether a strategy or intervention would be better than another. This enhances the scope of intuitive learning rather than providing complete reliance on related theories. Thus, in contrast to other social science disciplines, in social work equal emphasis is laid on learning and refining skills involved in interventions and not just information provision in terms of concepts and theories. Nonetheless, an orientation programme is beneficial for students in the following ways:

- It helps in developing a perspective on social problems and issues.
- It instils some confidence to naïve social work trainees, as the orientation programme helps clarify their doubts and apprehensions, misconceptions and dilemmas.
- It provides certain do's and don'ts that need to be kept in mind when in the field. For instance, during the orientation programme, students are asked to respect the cultural diversity and sentiments of the people in the field setting, which may require being careful

in terms of clothing, their demeanour, usage of certain words, and other factors.

- It creates awareness about different components of fieldwork and processes and protocols to be followed.
- It helps students in inculcating theories learned in classroom setting into field practice.

Critical aspects of learning in the orientation programme

The learning of students is the most important aspect of the orientation programme, but merely providing instructions in a formal setup is not enough. One needs to explore the extrinsic and intrinsic factors that facilitate or inhibit learning. Organizers need to understand how people learn, which often determines the quality and usefulness of the knowledge gained and skills imbibed. Some argue that only learning from experience leads to usable knowledge, but this unstructured way of gaining knowledge is a slow as well as 'hit and miss' process. Not all students/ trainees can have same learning from experience, and not all trainees can be exposed to the same experience. Although orientation programmes are poor substitutes for learning by experience (here, students themselves learn from the field setting), they do help in speeding up the learning process when combined with experiential learning through field visits. Therefore, invariably field trips are arranged as a part of the orientation programme. Structured and formal ways of learning, as in the case of orientation programmes, have their own set of benefits and loopholes. In contrast to learning through direct exposure to the field setting, the orientation programme provides guided learning through a controlled and safe environment and by providing immediate feedback to participants.

Single-loop and double-loop learning

The unique requirement of orientation programmes organized for social work trainees is to bring the desired change in their attitude and value system. Not all students who are enrolled in social work courses have the same level of empathy, compassion, acceptance of diversity, and such other values and skills that are required to work in the field. It thus becomes crucial for organizers to provide learning in such a way that basic values and skills are set right among trainee social workers. However, bringing change is thinking, reflected in attitudes and behaviours, can be an uphill task. The prescriptive mode of learning does not work. Argyris and Schon (1974, 1978) have provided the concept of single-loop and double-loop learning. These concepts help participants challenge their limited thinking and behaviour patterns and offer the scope to learn desired behaviours.

Single-loop learning entails changing methods and strategies to achieve set objectives. It means 'doing things right.' Double-loop learning is related to changing the objectives themselves. It involves 'doing the right things.' Single-loop learning is concerned with improving efficiency to obtain established objectives. If is used effectively, errors can be corrected within existing norms, practices, and traditions. Single-loop learning involves a purely intellectual pursuit involving improvements in understanding and performance within current understanding. Respecting diversity can be one example, where any deviation by any member can be handled and rectified by group norms of the class, and the organizers are not required to work on it repeatedly.

On the other hand, double-loop learning stresses challenging one's own habits, assumptions, and ways of thinking. It is also called generative learning. It is dynamic and at times upsetting, as it involves changing the established patterns of thinking and doing things. It means that one must challenge and restructure deeply held assumptions and act in a new and unfamiliar way. It requires a change of deep-rooted habits. Double-loop learning entails emotional and intellectual learning, requiring a change in goals and direction and leading to deep personal change. For instance, a student who is socialized to accept and propagate a feudal mind-set would not be able to work with the poor from a rights-based perspective unless his or her attitudes and beliefs of 'superiority of upper caste and discriminatory practices against Dalits' are not challenged and changed. Double-loop learning depends on awareness. Participants must be open to learning new analytical techniques.

Levels of knowledge

In orientation programmes, organizers face the challenge of having different levels of motivation and retention rates among participants. To what an extent knowledge is expected to be imparted is a contentious issue that needs to be resolved. Krathwohl, Bloom, and Masis (1964) have identified six levels of knowledge in their taxonomy of educational objectives in the cognitive domain:

1 Awareness: to recall, recognize
2 Understanding: to translate from one form to another
3 Application: to apply or use information in a new situation
4 Analysis: to examine a situation and break it down into parts
5 Synthesis: to put together information in a new way
6 Evaluation: to judge based on explicit criteria

Being aware that we have a set of human rights to enjoy is indeed a lower level of knowledge than understanding how we use these rights and let others use them. Translating notions of human rights in our daily life is a higher level of learning and applying than understanding their purpose. Being able to analyse social barriers like poverty and the caste system is yet a higher level of knowledge. Being able to use a rights-based approach in field situations and modalities of ensuring takes even higher and more complex levels of knowledge. And the highest level of knowledge is evaluation: the ability to draw conclusions and make decisions based on established criteria. Continuing with the same example, the ability to identify gaps in systems and make interventions for policy-level changes for ensuring human rights is evaluation. In a human services profession like social work, the best outcome of orientation programmes would be ensuring that participants reach the evaluation level of learning.

Pedagogy vs. andragogy

Andragogy is the term used for 'adult learning,' in juxtaposition to pedagogy, or strategies for teaching children. One of the most common mistakes that resource persons or teachers make while addressing college or university students is making use of pedagogical principles instead of andragogical ones. They tend to treat adult learners as children. Adult learning is self-directed, problem-centred desire to learn and an ability to relate the learning to experiential reality. In contrast, children are relatively like 'tabula rasa,' or a clean slate. They are dependent on teachers, and different strategies are required to maintain and sustain their interest. It is important to treat undergraduate and post-graduate students as responsible and intended learners and not as immature and disinterested ones.

Adult learning principles

Adult learning principles are almost the opposite of traditional teaching practices. These principles support and encourage natural learning that makes use of experiential learning, learning by doing, and by being involved, by trying, by discovering, and by creating. Malcolm Knowles (1980), the father of adult learning theory, coined the term 'andragogy' to differentiate adult learning strategies from child learning strategies, called pedagogy. This differentiation would be clear with the following principles of adult learning, which are today widely practised, while designing content and modalities of workshops and training programmes.

1   Adults bring a lot of experience with them to workshops, and therefore have something to contribute and something to lose.

ORIENTATION PROGRAMME TO FIELDWORK

2 Adults want workshops (or similar platforms) that focus on real-life, here-and-now problems and tasks, rather than on academic situations.

3 Adults are accustomed to being active and self-directing.

While designing orientation programmes for adult learners, it may be noted that adult learning is unique to each individual and everyone learns at his or her own pace and in his or her own way. Adults make active use of their experiential learning to gauge what is being told in the orientation or training programme. Adult participants' personalities are largely crystallized, and it is not easy to bring changes in their perceptions, values, and attitudes. Very few adults are willing to change their self-concept. Any forceful efforts to change their beliefs may have boomerang effects. For learning to occur, it is important to provide a supportive and challenging climate, encourage questioning, and value difference. Adults don't automatically accept answers provided to them; they test the knowledge offered against their experiences. Learning can only be encouraged and not coerced.

The best adult learning experiences are based on the 'felt needs' of the learners, but at times they are not aware of their own learning needs. Learning must have a personal meaning, and it must be of direct and immediate value. Organizers of orientation programmes must keep in mind that adults only learn what they want to learn; to do what they want to do. Therefore, it must be ensured that the orientation programme provides useful information relevant to the participants, and they must be involved in a collaborative and cooperative process that supports participants in sharing their experiences.

Learning styles

Participants in any training or orientation programme are not homogeneous. They differ based on their familial backgrounds, personality types, and intentions to learn due to numerous factors. For effective design and implementation of orientation programmes, organizers should not believe in a 'one size fits all' approach. Individuals make use of a combination of various senses to learn and grasp. Some learn fast when they read the material, whereas others can grasp better if they do things on their own. Usually, attention is not paid to this variability among participants in learning during orientation or training programmes. Organizers need to understand and adapt delivery content and materials based on participants' preferences and learning styles. Roger Smith (1982) has defined learning style as "a person's highly individualized preferences and tendencies that influence his or her learning." Kolb (1984) has four types of learning styles, popularly known as the 'four-box model,' that reflect the critical distinctions of learning styles (Figure 2.2).

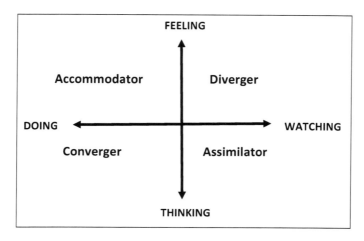

Figure 2.2 Kolb's four-box model of learning styles
Source: Adapted from Kolb (1984)

The accommodator style is based on feeling and doing. Accommodators prefer hands-on work, carrying out plans, role playing, enacting, demonstrating, experimenting, etc. They are skilful in doing things and getting things done and leading and do not hesitate in taking risks. At times, they are impractical and follow their instinct rather than logical arguments. From a social work viewpoint, they have the capacity to work in the grassroots arena effectively.

The diverger style rests on feeling and watching. Their creative visualization is very strong, and they are good at brainstorming problems. They can see many viewpoints. They can gather information and analyse it effectively. In the social work discipline, such trainees are good at problem assessment and finding 'out-of-the-box' solutions.

The assimilator style is based on thinking and watching. They are dexterous in outlining problems and making intervention plans, as well as in creating models and theories. Social work trainees with this style of learning are good at formulating ideas and theorizing problems and models of intervention.

The converger style is based on thinking and doing. They prefer practical use of ideas, finding solutions, making decisions, and checking and assessing ideas. They are focused and task oriented rather than on interpersonal relations. Trainees in social work with this learning style can relate macro-level issues with micro-level ones and emphasize implementing ideas.

Self-scoring inventories and scales are available that can be administered before the orientation programme begins to have an idea of learning styles of the participants, and that would help in making orientation programmes effective.

Types and contents of orientation programmes

Social work educational institutions generally hold orientation programmes for their students at the beginning of each academic year. Based on the level of students, objectives and contents of orientation programmes differ. BA first-year students during their orientation programme may be informed about the basic concepts of social work, its meaning, its values and ethics, and the principles that are followed while practising social work in the field. They are also informed about the various components and modalities of fieldwork. Their exposure visits to agency and community settings are arranged, and information is provided to them on the procedures and rules to be followed in fieldwork, attending individual and group conferences, etc. They are told about the fieldwork reporting format and general guidelines to be adhered to in their respective fieldwork settings.

For BA second-year students, the objectives of the orientation programme are on skill refinement, as students are mostly aware of the nuances of fieldwork. They are informed more about methods of social work, like community organization and social action. Use of programme media and creative arts in their fieldwork form part of their orientation programme.

In the third year of graduation in social work, contents of the orientation programme are more complex and specific. Advocacy issues, counselling micro-skills, research methodology, and models of empowerment of the deprived are some of the topics of which students are made aware.

The first year of post-graduate study is the time when students from various disciplines join social work. Many of them are novices and need to be informed about the basic concepts of social work. At least one session is devoted to theoretical understanding, say, sociology, psychology, political science, casework, group work, etc., so that students get the bird's-eye view of the entire course and its contents. Likewise, the relevance of the fieldwork practicum and its process, procedures, and protocols are delineated. Students visit a few agency and community settings and learn about social needs, social problems, and social work responses.

In the final year of post-graduate work, orientation is usually a week long and covers specific areas like programme planning and execution, counselling micro-skills, psychotherapy, and family therapy. Students are made aware of different settings and areas of specialization, like corporate social responsibilities, social defence, occupational social work, disability, gerontological social work, industrial social work, social work with families and children, etc.

In addition, an orientation is given to one or a few students when they reach their respective fieldwork setting by their agency supervisors or related staff. Trainees are informed about the structural and functional aspects of the organization, programme components, profile of the target groups, and setting up of rules and procedures to be followed by students and outlining of the term plan.

Students' feedback

The orientation programme was an eye opener for me. It has completely changed my perspective on social work profession and practice. Now I can identify several values and perceptions that were inculcated in me during my childhood socialization and that are not democratic in nature. . . . I have inculcated some sense of superiority in myself as I belong to higher caste, which I realized during my orientation sessions.

(Student after attending orientation programme of MA (first year of post graduation) at Department of Social Work, University of Delhi)

He participated in a group activity on understanding marginalization. Students were given chits, and they were supposed to behave according to their perceived identity and role mentioned in the chits. In this activity, students enacted the roles of Dalits, the disabled, children from slums, and landless labourers and were asked to identify social barriers.

Such activities that illicit emotions, critical thinking, and consciousness raising are quite powerful in bringing the desired change in the attitudes and behaviours of the students and trainees.

"I feel empowered as I learned how to develop research proposals and project proposals. It was wonderful and will help me in my fieldwork," expressed one third-year social work student from Aditi College.

Many trainees appreciate learning skills and knowledge on topics that can gain them recognition in fieldwork agencies and help in their job performance. An orientation programme that can stimulate higher-order thinking skills among the participants and provide opportunities for honing the skills that they can use in the field and that is able to ensure active participation from students is considered an effective one.

Orientation programmes can be ranked at different levels based on the effectiveness or success in achieving the objectives (Figure 2.3). The following aspects make an orientation programme less effective:

- Adopting a traditional teaching and grade-school approach where the students are the ignorant and passive receptors of knowledge and the focus is on simply conveying information.

ORIENTATION PROGRAMME TO FIELDWORK

- Resource persons adhere to traditional teaching in a 'jug and mug' fashion where the big jug (the teacher) fills up the little mugs (the students).
- Teachers or resource persons pay little attention to learning readiness and the learning climate. Teachers tell, and students are expected to pay attention. In such situations, students have learning that is fragmented, hard to recall, and even harder to use.
- Scolding, punishment, and other coercive tactics are used to 'discipline' the students, who are taken as lazy, disinterested, and unintended learners. Such sessions can stimulate only the cognitive faculty (mainly memorizing) and only superficially.

The following aspects make orientation programmes more effective:

- Fine blend of sessions with theoretical content and exercises for value and skill inculcation.
- Keeping the socio-cultural background of participants in mind while designing the contents and activities of the orientation programme.
- The speakers and resource persons should have 'delivery skills' such as presenting, facilitating, and leading. They should be technically competent in their respective fields.
- Appraising the differential learning needs and levels of the participants.
- An open and supportive environment where participants can trust that they will not be judged and can openly share their attitudes, perceptions, and feelings even if they are unacceptable on moral grounds.
- Participative approach where all members are encouraged to actively participate in the activities and discussions.
- Offering quality learning materials, providing relevant examples with which all or most students can relate.
- Participants or students are engaged in open and non-judgmental communication with healthy boundaries. They are taken as mature adult learners who are interested in learning.
- Resource persons communicate and interact with students, providing deep learning that involves both intellectual and emotional understanding.
- Participants are given opportunities to learn by doing, and they are facilitated to actively get involved and draw their own conclusions.
- Organizers ensure that sharing of learning and ideas takes place in an atmosphere of common goals, respect, and mutual support.

A moderate level of effectiveness would be achieved when these parameters are in the mid-range in an orientation programme.

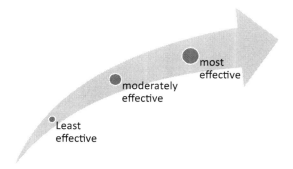

Figure 2.3 Levels of effectiveness of orientation programmes
Source: Developed by the author

Conclusions

The social work profession has carved an important niche in Indian society due to its response to social problems. Orienting students to this human service profession is crucial. Learning is a mental process that leads to know knowledge and skills, which students start gaining in their orientation programme. When students are treated as adult learners and a conducive atmosphere is created for learning that is characterized by trust, support, and congeniality, the highest levels of learning take place. When an orientation programme is properly designed, trainees look forward to becoming dexterous and competent social work professionals.

References

Argyris, C., & Schon, D. A. (1974). *Theory in practice: Increasing professional effectiveness*. San Francisco, CA: Jossey-Bass.
Argyris, C., & Schon, D. A. (1978). *Organizational learning: A theory of action perspective*. Reading, MA: Addison-Wesley.
Dunlap, A. (2013). *Ten skills every social worker needs*. Retrieved October 30, 2017, from www.socialworkhelper.com/2013/08/06/10-skills-every-social-worker-needs/
International Federation of Social Workers. *Global definition of social work*. Retrieved October 30, 2017, from http://ifsw.org/get-involved/global-definition-of-social-work/
Kolb, D. A. (2014). *Experiential learning: Experience as the source of learning and development*. Eaglewood Cliffs, NJ: Prentice-Hall.
Knowles, M. S. (1980). *Andragogy in action*. San Francisco, CA: Jossey-Bass.
Krathwohl, D. R., Bloom, B. S., & Masis, B. B. (1964). *A taxonomy of educational objectives*. New York, NY: David McKay Co.

National Association of Social Workers. (1973). *Definition of social work*. Retrieved October 30, 2017, from https://quizlet.com/99482734/nasw-definition-for-social-work-flash-cards/

Smith, K. K. (1982). Rabbits, lynxes, and organizational traditions. In J. Kimberly & R. Quinn (Eds.), *New futures: The challenges of managing corporate traditions*. Homewood, IL: Dow Jones-Irwin.

3

FIELDWORK REPORT
A pragmatic exercise

Sheeba Joseph

Introduction

Fieldwork in social work education refers to a praxis-oriented approach. The training mainly focuses on skill development, and deliberation of thought comes from a broader perspective. It is a systematic process of observing, amassing, and implementing creative, innovative ideas. It fosters the development of intellectual and emotional processes and attitudes. The belief underpinning fieldwork is that mere classroom teaching cannot comprehend the practical situation in social work education. Thus, fieldwork provides the student with the opportunity to integrate classroom knowledge with experiential learning in a relevant social work setting. It is an inevitable segment of fieldwork. One must put forth colossal effort to make the practice stupendous. The voyage of fieldwork helps students explore new avenues for developing a just approach in their career.

The field practicum is an active course that encourages students to apply knowledge, skills, and values within an organization and community. The field practicum is a vital dimension in undergraduate and graduate social work education. The hours of field practice groom the trainees to enter the work arena as professional social work practitioners. Theoretical knowledge acquired with the help of the self-preparation method will create a curiosity among the students to know the practical aspects. Then the fieldwork experience will be more interesting, and the trainees will be ready to take up challenges. That leads to an engaged mind.

In other words, it is a practice-based professional discipline anchored on a unified curriculum consisting of both theory and fieldwork components (Twikirize and Tusasiirwe, 2015). Hall (1990) asserts a generally accepted view that field instruction and education are of equal importance as theoretical academic instruction. The key features in common shows the concept of linking theory to practice. Field practice education is a natural necessity in a social work programme.

> In social work, field education is the signature pedagogy, the central form of instruction and learning in which a profession socialises its students.
>
> (CSWE, 2008, p. 8)

The general purpose of fieldwork is therefore to acquaint students with actual social work situations in preparation for professional social work practice. Hepworth, Rooney, and Larsen (2002) observe that fieldwork engages the student in supervised social work practice and provides opportunities to marry theory and practice. Especially in agency settings, students will be able to carve out a clear space for their work in a multi-disciplinary team and gain experience.

The chapter describes possible mandatory requirements of the fieldwork report and its advantages. The fieldwork report begins with the plan for the current day and ends with the plan of action/future plan for the next visit. The report is the voyage of a trainee in the process of experiential learning. Report writing provides an opportunity for the social worker trainee to organize and present information, observations, reflections, and actions in a methodical way and to reflect upon their role in interaction with people, administration, and research. The report should be precise, expressive, and comprehensible (PEC). The report should not be too elaborate – it should be the exact reflection of the fieldwork experience, not an exaggeration. At the same time, it should express the feelings of the trainee towards every pragmatic learning insight. The report should not contain bogus information. In addition, it should be understandable for the reader. It is better to avoid complicated words, or if you don't want to use a word frequently, use the synonym, which will enhance your report writing skill. Because it is recorded by the trainee during fieldwork, the report should be written in past tense. The format of the report varies according to the institution, but the major thrust remains the same. Dash and Roy (2015) developed a model (RD Model) of report writing in social work, which was used as a model for the sections discussed in this chapter.

Prelude to the report writing format

The first four points are the initial slices of the report. For instance, he or she must include the visit number, the day and date of the visit, the duration, and the place of visit.

Preamble

1 **Visit Number:** The trainee is required to specify the visit number here.
2 **Day and Date:** The day and date should be mentioned as per the day allocated for the fieldwork by the organization.
3 **Duration:** Hours spent in the field.
4 **Place of Visit:** The trainee is supposed to mention the place/locality/community where he or she visited during the day.

Introduction

In the introduction, the trainee can give a brief outline of the fieldwork or can introduce the reader to fieldwork practice. For example, start with a quotation on fieldwork, and later a brief write-up on fieldwork can be mentioned. You can speak about the importance of fieldwork, the advantage of experiential learning, and define/explain the fieldwork practicum in your own words or theoretical interpretations by researchers.

Example: Fieldwork is the heart of social work education. Learning becomes meaningful if it is coupled with hands-on training. The trainees in social work education get the opportunity to turn every mistake into learning experiences. This experiential learning helps the students to encounter deprived individuals, their hitches, their reactions to the problems, and their attitude towards social workers and their intervention strategies and this enables the trainee to realize his or her ability to help.

Objectives

In concurrent fieldwork practice, every week the trainee must submit a report to both supervisors. In the first visit report, one can always mention the broader objectives of fieldwork. The Social Work Review Committee (1978) on Social Work Education in India has evolved specific objectives for fieldwork training. They are as follows

To develop professional skills through practical learning, apply acquired knowledge for the study of relevant facts, analysis of the problem, and selection of appropriate means of solution towards the problems.

To develop the skills for solving the problems in work at the micro and macro level.

To provide concurrent opportunity for the integration of classroom learning in the field practice and vice versa (feedback mechanism for both field and class).

To develop skills required for professional practice at a particular level of training.

To objectively develop professional attitudes involving impartiality and non-judgemental attitudes.

To develop professional values and commitments such as human dignity and worth.

To develop an awareness of self and one's professional ideas.

These are the theoretical objectives that came out of the deliberation of the Social Work Review Committee meeting. Apart from the general objectives, a fieldwork trainee should have specific objectives on the type of work allotted to them. It is important to understand that without objectives, the trainee will be like a sailor in the middle of the sea without a compass. Thus, specific objectives show the direction towards the destination. Always remember your objectives should be SMART (Table 3.1).

Formulate the objectives in simple and understandable language, being specific. The objectives that you formulate should be measurable as well as attainable. The trainee should mention objectives that are realistic and can be achieved in the stipulated time frame.

For example, in the initial reports, the trainee can mention the objectives in the following way. The examples quoted in this chapter are in the context of a non-governmental organization working for the promotion of rural health and education.

To get acquainted with the agency setting (description and background of the organization, its focus of interventions, target population, geographic coverage, vision, mission and goal, the structure)

To meet the director/agency supervisor for preliminary interaction.

To build a professional rapport with the personnel in the social welfare organization.

To organize/coordinate a blood donation camp.

To conduct a baseline survey of the locality.

Plan of the day

Planning every activity meticulously with the guidance of faculty and the agency supervisor is an integral part of fieldwork. There are four

Table 3.1 SMART objectives

S	Specific
M	Measurable
A	Attainable
R	Realistic
T	Time bound

Source: Doran (1981)

components in fieldwork training: the social welfare agency, the trainee student, the faculty supervisor, and the agency supervisor. A novice in fieldwork should always go to the field with proper planning. A fieldwork conference helps the trainee discuss the concerns and share ideas with the faculty supervisor for better performance. The trainee should also consult the agency supervisor and discuss the plan of action for the subsequent week. In a developing country like India, where dearth of real social worker is clearly visible, as a beginner, the trainee should grab as many as learning opportunities from the field as possible so that the learning experience will be an added advantage for them in the future. During the initial visits, trainees may not have any planned activity, but the agency supervisor may entrust them with some responsibilities to perform. Very often, I have come across a monotonous style of writing in the planned activity segment (i.e., to visit the agency, to meet the agency people, to visit the field, etc.). Here are few examples in the Indian context:

- *To visit the organization to discuss the upcoming medical camp*
- *To visit the community for casework follow-up*
- *To coordinate the SHG meeting with the group members*
- *To participate in the participatory rural appraisal (PRA) exercise.*

Activities performed by trainee or the work done

Many times, students complain that they didn't do any work – we did the data entry, filing, and wrote the address on the envelops. It is the responsibility of the faculty to orient the trainees to the functioning of an organization. Pursuing a BSW/MSW will not make you eligible to receive a red-carpet welcome in the organization. You may have to sit for hours on the first day to meet the director/fieldwork supervisor. You should go with an attitude to learn, re-learn, and un-learn many things. Adaptability is one of the good qualities one should possess to be an effective social worker. As mentioned, every bit of work that you do is a learning experience and an asset for your future. A social worker should be a jack of all trades, although this is an era of specialization. It is very important for the trainee to consider the experiences as valuable. The actual work done by the trainee should be mentioned in this area, preferably in bulleted format with a brief description of the role performed by the trainee.

A few examples of work done by the fieldwork trainees in the course of fieldwork are as follows: documentation, filing of certain documents, visited various departments, interacted (professionally) with the supervisor, visited the field, participated in a meeting/activity of the organization, casework session with client, group work meeting group therapy/group counselling, took sessions on various topics decided in consultation with the agency supervisor.

FIELDWORK REPORT

Theory(ies) applied

Theory is neither something that can be indifferently passed over as an unimportant matter nor overstressed. Theories form the supportive structure, providing a sense of intellectual and emotional security to the professional practitioners besides giving them direction and an ability to predict outcomes (Mathew, 1992). Existential casework (Krill, 1969) helps in the process of disillusionment, that is, a person who has distorted perceptions of himself or herself has to go through a process of disillusionment about self and others. Wrong assumptions are replaced, and correct ideas are established. For example, a trainee social worker who is doing a casework intervention with a child who has developed a pessimistic approach in life needs an existential casework approach.

For instance, when a case of poor social functioning has become your area of intervention, reality therapy can be applied to make the client aware of the present situation.

Tools, techniques, and methods applied

In this section of the fieldwork report, the trainee will mention the tools and techniques applied during fieldwork. This is an opportunity for the trainee to enhance practice, knowledge, attitude, and skills. When a trainee is working in the grassroots level in the initial phase of social work education, they should be cognizant of how to interact with people during the house visits as well as community visits. Many tools can be used in fieldwork. A few are listed here to provide a thumbnail sketch of various applications:

- *Rapport building*
  Society is a web of social relationship said by Maciver (1937), and human beings are involved in a network of relationships and emotional bonds. Perlman (1957) opined that rapport building is a condition in which two persons with some common interest between them, whether long term or temporary, interact with feeling. The main purpose is to create an atmosphere for the development of personality, to help the client find a better solution for his or her problem and emotional problems, and to help the client make a more acceptable adjustment to their personal problems.
- *Active listening*
  The concept of active listening was developed by Carl Rogers (1966) in his client-centred therapy. We listen to what the person is saying, both content and feelings expressed, and we verbally acknowledge that we are hearing them. The primary purpose is not to check out to see if we have received the intended message, but rather to let him

or her know that we are listening to and understanding what he or she is expressing. We only rephrase the statements of the sender – we do not evaluate, give an opinion, provide advice, or interpret. This is often practised when the trainee is involved in any method of social work, for example casework, group work, and community organization

- *Observation*
  Observation is a technique used by the trainee if they practice generalist social work, social casework, social group work, community organization, and in all other arenas of social work. It helps the trainee to understand the real nature of the situation. In social casework, the worker ought to pay attention to the personal appearance of the client; in group work practice, the worker needs to observe the interaction pattern between the group members and their participation of each in the activities; in community organization, the organizer keenly observes the community members' interest in mobilizing community resources, the acceptance level of each coming from different backgrounds. The trainee can be a participant observer or a non-participant observer, depending upon the context.

- *Home visits*
  The trainee should be aware of the purpose of home visits. Home visits help the trainee/worker to see the environment in which the patient lives and observe the family and relevant social interactions. It is also an opportunity to persuade the clients to optimize utilization of resources. Another aim is to reduce anxiety and tension, especially in the case of mentally ill patients. It helps strengthen the bond between the client in the institution and the family, and it also facilitates the rehabilitation of discharged clients from the institutions. Finally, home visits can provide follow-up services to the client.

- *Interview*
  Interviewing is communicating with a conscious purpose. Kahn and Cannell (1957) define interviewing as a specialized pattern of verbal interaction initiated for a specific purpose, focused on a specific content area, with consequent elimination of extraneous variables. One should apply the following four aspects to have a successful interview: honesty, empathy, non-possessive warmth, and unconditional acceptance. The trainee must record the interview techniques used during the fieldwork practicum. Specific mention of the techniques will help the trainee practise those techniques in similar situation. Some of them include exploration, ventilation, topical shift, logical reasoning, partialization, explaining, encouragement, informing, generalization (universalization), reassurance, externalization of interest, individualization, resource utilization, limit setting, confrontation, clarification, and interpretation.

Observation

Here, the trainee is not simply repeating skills used. Rather, this refers to what the trainee observed in the field. Seeing and observing are two different areas. Observation is the practice of noticing features about people, things, or situations in the context of social work. The trainee must mention whether he or she used observation as a technique while dealing with the clients/groups/community.

The purpose is to use the observed data to understand the situation, client, group members, community members, and the way the agency functions. For example, in casework practice, the worker has to be cognizant of the following with reference to the client: the general outward appearance; facial expression, posture, and gestures; and the characteristics, particularly the emotional nuances of interactions that take place between the clients and others. As a trainee, once we reach the organization, your learning has already started. You may see information displayed on the notice board, like the vision and the mission, the code of conduct, organizational structure, various information, education and communication (IEC) materials pertaining to the areas of intervention, and so on. The report should reflect the approach of the agency towards imparting a learning experience to the trainee. The initial reports will portray this type of information. Once the involvement becomes intense, the trainee will develop a professional approach while applying the techniques. He or she will come to know how to bifurcate the relevant and irrelevant data.

The trainee should follow a reflective and reflexive approach. The observation section should include one's own experiences, thoughts, and feelings. Consider and report how your observations may have affected the observed, as well as how you may have been affected by what and how you've participated and observed. Ponder and report on the origins and implications of your own perspective.

Pragmatic learning experience(s)

Pragmatic learning experience refers to the practical knowledge the trainee gained from the field. It tries to gauge the quantum of theoretical knowledge one could integrate into the practical situation/field. Being a praxis-oriented learning approach, social work education always emphasizes the ability of oneself to apply theory to practice. Pragmatic learning could be considered as the way the trainee conceives a concept, understands it, feels it, internalizes it, and applies it according to the context or situation and the outcome of application. As academicians, we have come across a lot of responses from students stating the difference textbooks and the real world. Through various components of social work education, we try to equip trainees with various skills, a positive attitude, enough knowledge, and practical thinking. Every day should be a pragmatic learning experience for the trainee, and the report should certainly reflect that.

For example: The trainee learned various social work skills in the process of classroom learning and how far he or she is able to practise that in the real situation, how effectively it was used, the outcome of the skill used, and how he or she could apply that in another situation with another client or group/community. So rather than students complaining that they didn't do anything and nothing was learned, a trained fieldwork supervisor can help the trainee develop insight to understand every situation as a learning experience that adds a drop of knowledge to the existing knowledge one already possesses.

Ethical dilemmas faced

Despite a century of social work education, in India we still don't have our own code of ethics. Thomas (2015) tried to contribute a code of ethics for social workers in India implemented through the IGNOU social work curriculum. Ethics are a set of standards one needs to uphold while practising professional social work. Thomas (2015) has presented 12 core values in social work, which helps an individual to learn, practise, and ponder our behaviour towards clients/colleagues. Integrity, competence, reliability, respect for others, loyalty to the profession, cultural sensitivity, commitment, and responsibility are among them. In a country like India where diverse culture and religion exist, it is quite predictable to face ethical issues while practising professional social work. The trainee must write down such information and the techniques or strategies applied to overcome it in the report. It is important to internalize all the principles that we study in social work. Preaching is not important; instead, how far you are able to apply that daily life is important.

For example, in certain communities men having sex with men is considered an unnatural thing, as a trainee who learned this teaching as part of his or her belief system has already developed a mind-set and thought process aligned with that. When they practise in the field and are confronted with such situations, they face ethical trauma: the belief says it is wrong, but the teachings in social work speak about the right of the client to self-determination. Similar situations can happen in the field. You should be able to set apart your principles, ideas, and thoughts and not impose them on the clientele.

Evaluation

Evaluation serves as an important exercise for purposeful teaching and learning in social work education. It helps one understand the strength and weakness of the trainee in terms of professional competence. Evaluation acts as a stepping stone to overcome all the hiccups or bottlenecks that the trainee faced while working in the field. It appraises the work done by the trainee during the day. The trainee needs to evaluate the experiences of the fieldwork day objectively. One should not be influenced by personal biases and prejudiced thoughts while writing the evaluation. The approach towards the evaluation segment should be constructive. It helps in improving professional practice as we learn what strategy works and the shortcomings. The trainee should take this part seriously, as it serves a yardstick to measure the effectiveness of the day's learnings. Always try to find out whether the planned activities were accomplished or if the objectives were achieved. That helps the trainee better evaluate that day's performance and its efficacy.

Future plan

The trainee needs to mention the plan for the next visit (if applicable) in the report. Those points should be shared with the faculty supervisor as well as the agency supervisor through the weekly report. The trainee should consult the agency supervisor on the last day of the visit to update the activities conducted and to discuss the future plan. This helps the trainee to decide and deliberate with other team members on what strategy could be adopted to implement the programmes chalked out in advance. It will help the trainee foresee the challenges that may arrive and can take precautionary measures to overcome these hurdles.

This chapter will now turn to a few guidelines to improve the quality of writing.

Guidelines to improve the quality of reports

The rule of thumb in report writing says that reports should be precise, expressive, and comprehensible (PEC). Reports that are inaccurate, incomplete, or unclear can lead to confusion, resentment, and inflated errors. So it is very important to have a thoughtful tactic while conscripting the report.

1 The trainee should analyse the reader(s) and determine what information they really need. For example, the trainee must submit the report to both the faculty supervisor and the agency supervisor. As academicians, we have come across reports that contained absolute criticism about the functioning of the organization. Imagine if the same report was shared with the agency supervisor. Things that are negative could be stated in a better way to the agency to prevent damaging the professional relationship.

2 Avoid using acronyms, first names, and jargon. For example, if the trainee has to mention human immunodeficiency virus in the report, spell it out initially along with the acronym in brackets so that you can use the acronym for the remainder of the report.

3 Before beginning to write, organize the information to be presented in a logical structure. Construct the outline of the report, present your ideas in an orderly way, and the reader will be more likely to understand.

4 Two to three drafts may be needed before the final version is produced.

5 Use language that is simple and clear. Select words carefully (i.e., only those words which the reader can understand). Avoid words that have different meanings in different contexts. Avoid using slang or phrases that might offend or hurt the feelings of others. For example, portly, stout, obese, and fat, or firm, obstinate, stubborn, and pig-headed all have the same basic meanings, but each strikes the reader in a different way. The emotion or attitude the word implies should be well thought out.

6 Avoid the usage of words or phrases that remove the trainee from being accountable for what he or she has mentioned in the report. Such ambiguous language gives the reader the impression that the report writer is unsure of what is stated. Follow a very objective approach in formulating the report.

7 Sentences should not be lengthy or too complex, as this lessens the force of expression and distracts the reader. Most often, the straightforward subject–verb–object sentence is the best because it can be read quickly and is seldom misunderstood.

8 Use active voice wherever possible. The passive voice adds unnecessary words, weakens the sentences, and makes it unclear.

9 Give specific attention to all the segments while drafting the report.

10 Use a dictionary to find the exact meaning of the words used, the correct spelling, whether a word should be capitalized, and correct punctuation marks. A thesaurus, which has synonyms and antonyms, will add freshness and variety to the words selected.

Conclusion

Fieldwork gives a reality check to the trainees in terms of the reports that need to be written. It is important to read about theories, but it is equally (if not more) important to use their understanding of theories in the reality of the field. Because fieldwork is contextual and contingent, it does not always go the way a student expects it to. So while recording the fieldwork activities, it is desirable to follow a methodical approach. Fieldwork involves learning by doing; it exposes the students to different social situations and makes them absorb the diverse needs of the target populations/beneficiaries. Reports will help the trainee to substantiate what he or she did in the field. It acts as a reference for the trainee, for the organization, and for the institution.

References

Alpert, H. (1954). 1964 Robert M. Maclver's contributions to sociological theory. In M. Berger, T. Abel, & C. H. Page (Eds.), *Freedom and control in modern society* (pp. 286–292). New York, NY: Octagon Books.

Beers, W. C. (2014). *The mental hygiene movement*. Whitefish, MT: Literary Licensing LLC.

Council on Social Work Education. (2008). *Purpose: Social work practice, education, and educational policy and accreditation standards*. Retrieved May 3, 2017, from www.cswe.org/File.aspx?id=41861

Dash, B., & Roy, S. (2015). *Field work in social work education: Contemporary practices and perspectives*. Atlantic Publishers.

Davies, M. (2008). *The essential social worker*. Farnham: Ashgate.

Doran, G. T. (1981). There's a S. M.A.R.T. Way to write management's goals and objectives. *Management Review, 70*, 35–36.

Dubois, B., & Karla, M. K. (1992). Social work- an empowering profession. Boston, MA: Allyn and Bacon.

Hall, N. (1990). Social work training in Africa: A fieldwork manual. *Harare Journal of Social Development in Africa*. Kopje, Zimbabwe. Retrieved May 5, 2019, from https://books.google.co.in/books/about/Social_Work_Education_in_Africa.html?id=WZ-5AAAAIAAJ&redir_esc=y.

Hepworth, D. H., Rooney, R., & Larsen, J. A. (2002). *Direct social work practice: Theory and skills*. USA: Brooks/Cole-Thomas Learning.

Kahn, R. L., & Cannell, C. F. (1957). *The dynamics of interviewing: Theory, technique and cases*. New York, NY: Wiley.

Krill, D. (1969, April). Existential psychotherapy and problems of the Anomie. *Social Work, 14*(2), 33–49.

Maciver, R. M. (1937). *Society – A textbook of sociology*. London: MacMillan and Co., Ltd.

Mathew, G. (1992). *An introduction to social case work*. Mumbai: TISS.

Perlman, H. H. (1957). *Social casework*. Chicago, IL: University of Chicago Press.

Review of Social Work Education in India: Retrospect and Prospect. Report of Second Review Committee, appointed by the UGC, New Delhi, 1978 (p. 52–57).

Retrieved May 2, 2019, from https://www.academia.edu/11701453/S_R_E_in_Field_Work_Practicum_Some_Learning_Reflections

Rogers, C. R. (1966). To facilitate learning. In M. Provus (Ed.), *Innovations for time to teach*. Washington, DC: National Education Association.

Sheafor, W., & Bradford, A. G. (1988). *Techniques and guidelines for social work practice*. Boston, MA: Allyn and Bacon.

Subhedar, I. S. (2001). *Field work training in social work*. Rawat Publications.

Thomas, G. (2015). *Social work: a value based profession*. Rawat Publications.

Twikirize, J. M., & Tusasiirwe, S. (2015). *Social work fieldwork: Guidelines for students and supervisors*. Kampala, Uganda: Fountain Publishers.

Upadhyay, R. K. (2012). *Social case work*. Rawat Publications. Retrieved May 3, 2017, from www.sjsu.edu/people/fred.prochaska/courses/ScWk242Spring 2013/s1/Session-5-Slides-Observation-and-Qualitative-Fieldwork.pdf; http://sho dhganga.inflibnet.ac.in/bitstream/10603/16128/10/10_chapter%203.pdf

4

TRANSFORMATIVE LEARNING IN SOCIAL WORK EDUCATION IN INDIA
Role of social work camps

Ramesh B

Introduction

Fieldwork practice in social work has a pivotal role in transforming social work trainees from a personal self to professional self. The evolution of social work can be traced to several practitioners in the West. However, it was Marry Richmond who pioneered professionalism in the practice of social work. Hence, social work is considered a practice-based profession wherein learning by doing is instrumental for the transformative development of social work trainees. On the other hand, the term fieldwork may be described as gaining experience by utilizing practical knowledge and developing the skills to deal with the problems of fellow human beings living at all strata of the society. Rural camp is a part of the fieldwork practicum where the integrated practice of social work is deployed (Subhedar, 2009).

Fieldwork training makes the students employable and confident to face the interviews and challenges in professional practice. The main objectives of community camp are to test all social work method tools and techniques in the field, to facilitate social work trainees to obtain skills out of the fieldwork experience, to possess a social work attitude, to practise the theories in the field, and to understand how to confront professional problems while practising. Community social work camp as a part of fieldwork practice in India is unique in nature and scope and is organized by the trainees under the guidance of social work faculty. It enables students to understand social structure, community problems, system and subsystem inter-relations, tangible and intangible culture, level of government and non-government intervention and its effect, social institutions, and community-based organization, inculcating a sense of social responsibility among trainees so as to sensitize them to the dynamics of the community. Also, it will give community, group, and individual experience in teams (*ibid*).

This chapter explores the field practicum models in India. That the social work camp is one of the special programmes meant to indigenize social work education, with a specific focus on training macro-practice in India, a community-based, living-learning field practicum model has been explored in the context of transformative learning theory. Although the chapter explores social work camp features and challenges, it also narrates the model of social work living-learning field practicum model for social work education. The chapter also observes that the rural camp is a source of transformative learning among social work trainees. Ultimately, it develops their overall personality in a professional manner by teaching them to adopt the innovative scientific techniques and skills of social work methods.

Social work camp

Social work camp, conducted for seven to ten days' duration in a rural/tribal setting, is expected to provide opportunities to experience rural/tribal life, analyse its dynamics, and observe the functioning of government machinery (local self-government) and voluntary organizations. The primary objective of the camp is to provide the student with an opportunity to acquire skills in planning, organizing, handling regulations, decision making, and collectively contributing to the chosen cause in the area where the camp is held. Generally, the camps are held in rural/tribal areas. However, if the departmental council desires, the camps can also be organized in relief areas (disaster areas) and tribal areas as innovative learning projects.

Micro-planning exercises and participatory rural appraisal (PRA) activities are also part of social work camp. This will be an opportunity to practise the community organization method. This experience aids peer participation in planning activities for one's own group and for local people. It also helps develop skills to carry out, evaluate, and report on the experience. The camp shall be conducted under the guidance of two faculty members.

Before conducting the community camp, pilot committees shall be formulated. The committees consist of Master of Social Work (MSW) students. Through the committees they make plans for screening communities with the help of their fieldwork agency experience and faculty supervisor guidance. Later, they should finalize a few communities to conduct a pilot visit. During this visit a socio-demographical module shall be used to assess the needs of the communities. After collecting data social work trainees will present their need assessment in different communities. Based upon the intensity of need and problems found, they shall finalize a camp site. Then social work trainees are required to visit the camp site to build rapport with the community people. In this process the trainees shall trace out key persons and assess some felt needs based on focus group discussion (FGD). The needs of the community shall be addressed priority-wise through the camp. Thus, the programmes of the ten-day camp shall be structured based on the felt needs of the community.

To meet the expenses of these programmes, existing resource utilization and resource mobilization from outside the community shall be planned with the same FGD. In addition to that, all community-based organizations (CBOs), non-governmental organizations (NGOs) and local self-governments shall be used to mobilize existing funds through the student. Once the camp date is finalized pre-camp committees are formulated. These committees are (1) invitation committee, (2) resource mobilization committee, (3) finance committee, (4) logistic committee, (5) purchasing committee, and (6) transportation committee. All first-year MSW students shall be assigned to a committee so that they can get group experience, get a sense of responsibility, and can enhance their skills. However, these pre-camp committees exist up to the commencement of camp, and they do all the planning and preparation activities during this time. Once the community camp commences, different tasks shall be deployed, such as (1) programme committee, (2) stage committee, (3) *shramadhan* committee, (4) cultural committee, and (5) food committee. Through intra- and inter-group experiences the camp supervisor observes the group dynamics and how the group builds intimacy and bonds during individual and group evaluations at night and tries to mould the social work trainee's personality according to the social work profession.

Typically, each day in the rural camp starts with physical exercises and includes home visits, a socio-economic survey, community participatory activities, and community participatory cultural events and finally ends with students' daily reflection on the learning experience called evaluation. These activities are designed to ensure a high level of community interaction for students. It needs to be noted that the rural camp practicum is intended to emancipate dialectical and dialogical learning for the students, as they are both the subjects and the centre of the learning process. Finally, before withdrawing from the community, whatever programmes, activities, and interventions have been conducted there shall be continued by the community members thereafter. Hence, the withdrawal strategies can be used to bring sustainable changes in the community.

Next this chapter explores some social work camp case studies. It describes the model living-learning field practicum model adopted in rural/tribal camp containing the innovative practices which trace the transformative learning among the social work trainees.

Case Study I: Mysore University's Department of Social Work has conducted a rural/tribal camp for 7 to 10 days to provide opportunities to experience rural life, analyse rural dynamics, and observe the functioning of local self-government and voluntary organizations. This experience aids peer participation in planning for activities for their own group and for local people. It also helped develop skills to carry out, evaluate, and report on the experience. In 2006 the department conducted a community camp at Hanagalli village, Mysore district. The social work trainees identified the felt needs of the community and conducted awareness regarding watershed and rain water harvesting. The social work trainees opined that after undergoing the camp they had developed leadership qualities, learned to practise social work skills, and their attitude towards the community has been changed significantly.

Case study II: Kuvempu University's Social Work Department conducted a social work camp at Maleshankara village, Shimoga district in 2007. The village people had been displaced due to the Sharavathi Power Project. As a result, they were vulnerable and were dwelling in a new village called Maleshankara. After ten days of the camp, social work trainees transformed from personal self to professional self through the experience they got working in various committees and adhering to stringent individual and group evaluation practice. Especially during that camp a social action method was practised to bring about radical change in the community. The social work faculty supervisor and social work trainees recognized that the youths were experiencing deteriorating health and loss in economic stability due to arrack (alcohol) shops. Hence, the social work faculty supervisor and trainees devised strategies to combat this menace. As a result, the faculty supervisor delivered a motivational speech against liquor and its effect on health to all self-help groups women for around one and half hours. The women were inspired by the speech and eventually ensured that the arrack shop was closed. Indirectly the social work faculty supervisor and trainees created strong dislike for arrack. Practising social work methods in the village changed the village and the social work trainees. After completing the MSW course, the trainees became practitioners, and some became educators due to the experience, learning, and transformation that took place during the course of rural camp at Maleshankara village. In fact, they all are still practicing the exposure they have got in their respective fields.

Case study III: Tumkur University's Social Work Department and Tumkur University and the Post-Graduation Departments of Social Work of the affiliated colleges in collaboration with the Navyadisha non-governmental organization conducted a social work rural camp at Oordigere village, Tumkur district in 2014. The core intention of the camp was to expose social work trainees to rural life, along with bringing awareness about the importance of sanitation. The prime activities of the camp were to motivate people to construct toilets and use existing toilets in households. For this reason, the social work trainees planned various awareness programmes like street plays, cultural programmes, home visits, etc. By becoming involved in these activities the trainees' professional capacity is enhanced. By the end of the camp, the social work trainees felt happy with the outcome. Their perceptions and perspectives were transformed by the camp experience, and they learned how to practise social work even more effectively in the field.

Case study IV: A rural camp was organized by the Department of Social Work at Christ College, Bangalore, with an intention to assess the impact of the Chetana Project, which the Centre for Social Action (CSA) was planning to implement. It provided an opportunity for students to gain practical skills and be exposed to rural areas. The students of Christ University (MSW 2013–2015) were required to go for a cross-cultural field study in the village of Hoskote. The objective of the study was to conduct an impact assessment of a former CSA project which is now handled by CMRC. The rural camp was held from 16 February to 22 February. The students were divided into several committees. The class was divided into ten different committees to look after different aspects of the rural camp. At the camp site, the students were divided into five groups to visit the different villages in Hoskote. The CFCD-Chetana Project between KNH-CCCYC and CSA worked for seven years and spread across Kolar and Bangalore Rural districts, as well as Hoskote and Malur Taluks. It was a project meant to enrich the performance of CSA in promoting child-focused community development programmes in a participatory manner, with the goal of improving the quality of life of marginalized communities and their children. Over the seven years of the project, CSA, with the guidance of KNH-CCCYC, has tried several strategies and innovations in order to draw the best results out of the project.

Out of several committees framed during camp, the social work trainees have learned the following:

- Values such as cooperation and coordination were learned while conducting FGDs.
- The students discussed the loopholes in the government plans for the implementation of effective measures pertaining to community problems.
- The community at times would deviate from the main objective of socio-economic development and enter into politics (Work, 2014).

Case study V: A rural camp was conducted by the Department of Social Work, Government First Grade College, Narsimharajapura, Chikkamagaluru district in 2016 at Honnekoodige village. The social work trainees identified the felt needs of the village, such as a lack of connected roads, with associated problems like a lack of markets, unauthorized liquor sales, and the threat of wild animals. During camp, social work trainees dealt with these felt needs by conducting social action activities and by networking and advocating for concerned departments. These endeavours helped to community to fulfil these needs, and in turn the social work trainees learned how to utilize existing resources and mobilize external resources. Ultimately, the trainees learned how to conduct social action activities, networking, and advocacy.

Case study VI: The social work post-graduation students of Hemadri College, Tumkur, conducted a social work rural camp at Melehalli village of Kora Gram Panchayath, Tumkur, Karnataka, in 2016. The social work trainees conducted a socio-economic survey and used both qualitative and quantitative methods to collect data, such as home visits, surveys, participatory rural appraisal (PRA), and FGDs. Udai Pareek's Rural Socio-Economic Assessment Scale was used to assess the socio-economic status. It was discovered that a majority (56.27 per cent) of the respondents fell in the middle class and 21.25 per cent of them fell in the upper middle class. There were 825 people dwelling in 120 households. From wealth mapping as a part of the PRA conducted in the village, the campers found that the cumulative income of all households per year (120 households) was 425,000,000 INR. But when it came to expenditures it was 305,000,000 INR. Their income sources were agriculture-related crops like ragi (millet), coconut, tamarind, mango, and allied agricultural products. Regarding expenditure of food grains, soap, toothpaste, shampoos, clothes, and so in terms of their festival expenses, the average was 4,000 INR for *Ugadi,* 2,000 INR for *Deepavali*, and 1,000 INR for *Sankranthi* festivals in each household. For local Gramadevathe (village god) fairs and the Anjaneya fair the households preferred to organize collectively, and they were found to spend approximately 200,000 INR (this was a pooled amount). From this study it was found that the people of Melehalli village spend more on corporate company products, and their expenditure would be especially high during festival seasons. This research-based experience created inspiration among many trainees, and they came to know how to conduct scientific research at the grassroots level (Ramesh, 2017).

Rural camps and transformative learning theory

Paulo Freire (1970) in "Pedagogy of oppressed" articulated the theory of transformative learning, which he referred to as conscientization, or conscious rising (Welton, 1995). Jack Mezirow was influenced by Freire and contributed to transformative learning theory. He said that thinking is the process of making meaning from our experience through critical self-reflection. He eventually named this process perspective transformation to reflective change (Mizirow, 1991). However, social work trainees will have a different perspective towards communities and people when they encounter them in real life, and through the social work camp their entire perception and perspective will change.

The rural camp provided a platform for students to think critically about their core assumptions and inferences that they make about different cultures and realize how their worldview about other cultures is influenced by their perceptions and biased assumptions. This awareness was achieved while social work students critically examined their worldview when negotiating and acting on their individualized purposes, values, feelings, and meanings when contrasted with those learned in an uncritically assimilated form (Mezirow, 2000). During the camp, decisions were examined from a more critical perspective, resulting in students' constructing revised and new interpretations of the meaning of social realities (Taylor, 2008).

Community-based, living-learning model

The University of San Diego developed the model of living-learning communities (LLC). LLC is an academic strategy to create an environment in which more intellectual interaction will occur among students, faculty by linking the core curriculum to on-campus living. Although LLCs can be traced back to the British model of the residential college, the structural and pedagogical roots of today's LLC are found in the debates over the aims of a strong liberal education in the 1920s. LLC experiments conducted throughout the 20th century established that an integrated college experience promotes intellectual communication between faculty and students, improves students' grade point averages, enhances civic engagement, increases retention, eases both the academic and social transition to college, and decreases negative student behaviours (Diego, 2015).

Perception change

Building a rapport between the community and the students was found to enrich the learning environment. It was found that student perceptions about people were transformed by the end of the rural/tribal camp. In the initial days of the camp, students were preoccupied with a biased mind-set about rural/tribal communities, and such perceptions were found to have undergone significant change as they approached the community members.

Indigenizing social work practice

The social work profession has undergone significant changes in the West. In India it was Clifford Manshardt who started social work education in

1936 at Dorabji Tata Institute of Social Work, which is now known as the Tata Institution of Social Sciences (Gore, 1977). It may thus be understood that it was through the efforts of such pioneers that social work education in India was borrowed from the West. Hence, it is obvious that some implication problems were encountered in the initial stages of social work professional development in India. Nevertheless, regarding the practice fieldwork, and especially community-based practice, some practitioners have developed indigenous models to practise in the Indian scenario. In addition, some indigenous social work literature was developed by practitioners and educators where both have developed complementarily to each other.

The process of developing and implementing indigenized social work theories and models for practice is a solid requirement in developing countries. Several efforts were made after the post-colonial period to develop indigenized social work education and practice (Boroujerdi, 2002). Developing countries are experiencing a dichotomy in terms of the influence of colonialism, modernization, and industrialization, on one side, and traditional customs, values, and traditional beliefs on the other (Gray, 2008). These contrasting ideologies result in a cultural conflict when Western theoretical models are applied to social work practice in developing countries (Ejaz, 1991). Social work education has been taking place in India for 80 years, but there is still an absence of indigenous orientation to the knowledge component and lack of linkages between classroom learning and field realities.

Implications

Implications are drawn based upon case studies in various social work camps held in different places. The next section discusses this in light of a proposed learning transformation model.

Proposed social work learning transformation model

Social work trainees accomplish more in terms of learning by being involved in different committees. Both inter- and intra-group experiences occur during the ten-day camp. The purpose of pre-camp committees is to plan and prepare trainees and the community for the camp experience. The committees' responsibilities and learnings are depicted in Figure 4.1 and Figure 4.2.

Pre-camp committees

Without detailed plans for a camp, it is doomed to failure. Social work trainees should form several pre-camp committees to divide the work and

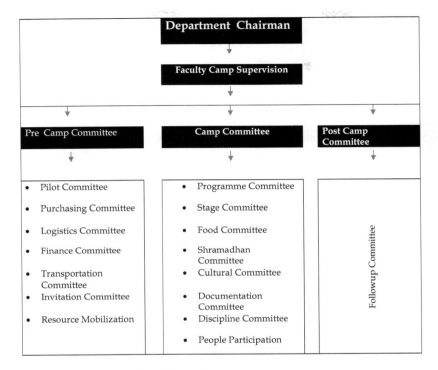

Figure 4.1 Camp committee formation
Source: Developed by author

have intra- and inter-group experiences. These pre-camp committees as follows:

- *Pilot Committee:* A pilot committee should be formulated to discover the needs of the community for conducting the camp in coordination with agencies and trainees. The major responsibility lies with the pilot committee to deploy a tool (questionnaire) to assess the socio-economic status of the community, to employ FGD with key persons and stakeholders of the community, to assess community support for the camp, to finalize the camp site based on intensity of needs (problems), to plan programmes for ten days, and other responsibilities. Learning and transformation that occur through involvement with this committee include assessment skills, communication skills, and skills in establishing rapport, depending upon trainees' level of involvement.
- *Finance Committee:* The resources required for conducting the camp in terms of staffing, materials, machinery, and money (both cash and

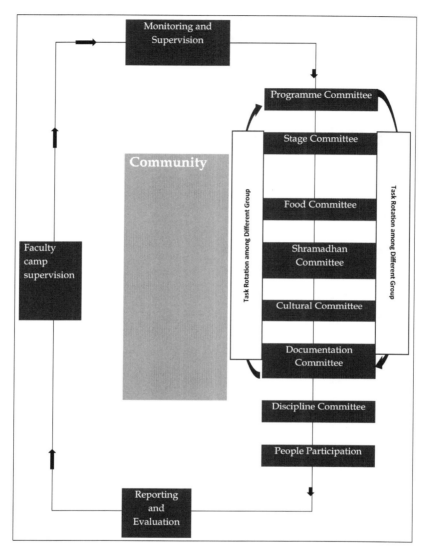

Figure 4.2 Proposed social work learning transformation model through committees
Source: Developed by author

in kind) will be devised and mobilized by the finance committee. The committee will be responsible for all resources which are needed for camp from both the institution and communities. In addition, the committee monitors the finances and accounting for disbursements.

TRANSFORMATIVE LEARNING

Each committee should submit an estimated budget to the finance committee for review and incorporation in the overall document. The other responsibilities that lie with the finance committee are maintaining in-resources and out-resources records, making a budget for camp, keeping all receipts and vouchers (accounts) of all committee expenses, maintaining camp expenses in terms of cost-effectiveness, and other responsibilities. Learning and transformation through participation on the finance committee include improved skills in terms of recording and documenting, budgeting and resource utilization skills.

- *Purchasing Committee:* This committee should purchase all materials required for ten days of camp, in accordance with the demand of various committees and the consent of the finance committee. The purchasing committee is also responsible for collecting all materials needed from other committees, procuring existing resources in the community and among trainees, making a separate list of requirements based on the nature of materials (grocery, stationary, etc.), collecting quotations from different shops and finalizing lowest bidder, and so on. Learning and transformation that occur through participation on the purchase committee include improved skills in bargaining and communication, among other things.

- *Resource Mobilization Committee:* Resources are the backbone for organizing a camp. Hence, all kinds of resources in terms of cash and kind (man, machine, material, and money) should be mobilized both within the community and outside it, which is the responsibility of the resource mobilization committee. Other responsibilities include consulting CBOs and NGOs working in that community, identifying material and non-material resources, linking needs and resources, effectively utilizing existing resources, and so on. Learning and transformation that will occur through participation on the resource mobilization committee include improved skills in communication, rapport building, liaising, and others.

- *Transportation Committee:* Transportation must be made available from the college to the camp site, and travel arrangements for all resource persons should be arranged by the transportation committee. Other responsibilities that lie with this committee include arranging vehicles to transport all materials required for the camp. Learning and transformation that occur through participation on the transportation committee include improved skills in escorting guests, time management skill, coordination skills, and more.

- *Logistics Committee:* The logistics committee is responsible for the smooth operation of the camp. By working with every other committee, they will create a master schedule that outlines all activities of the camp at any given time. Other responsibilities that lie with this committee are arranging accommodations for all trainees: separate washroom and toilet facilities must be provided for men and women, bedding and cooking areas need to be arranged, and first aid supplements must be procured. Learning and transformation that occur through participation on the resource mobilization committee include improved skills in assessment, communication, and observation, among other things.

- *Invitation Committee:* Making the invitation protocol wise (arranging hierarchy wise guest list) and arranging stage programmes and planning them for all ten days are the responsibilities of the invitation committee. Other responsibilities of this committee include inviting the delegates for all ten days, inviting the community, and inviting all CBOs and NGOs who are working for that community. Learning and transformation that occur through participating on the logistics mobilization committee include improved skills in delineating guests according to designation, communication, and networking, among other things.

Camp committees

During the camp it is crucial to formulate group committees based upon requirements. In all groups each committee's responsibilities should be rotated so that social work trainees can gain a wide variety of experience and learning.

Programme Committee: The programme committee is responsible for organizing and scheduling programmes for each day. Other responsibilities include reminding the guests and resource persons the day before and planning for the dais; the master of ceremony, invocation, welcome, and thanks shall be prepared, as shall the programme. Learning and transformation that occur through participation on the programme committee include improved strategizing, performance and, stage decorum, among others.

Stage Committee: The stage committee is responsible for preparing the stage, procuring materials for decorating it, maintaining electronic devices which are used for the programme, and so on. Learning and transformation that occur through participation on the stage committee include improved skills in creativity, resource utilization, and division of labour, among other things.

Food Committee: Providing food and beverages for social work trainees is the primary responsibility for this committee. Other responsibilities include planning menus, mobilizing foodstuffs from the community if required, preparing food and beverages for social work trainees, serving food, and rendering hospitality to guests. Learning and transformation that occur through participation on the food committee include improved skills in coordinating, resource mobilization, life skills, and other areas.

TRANSFORMATIVE LEARNING

Shramadhan Committee: Social work trainees conduct *shramadhan,* a voluntary contribution involving physical effort. In India it is a way of helping community and contributing to help and change the environment around for the betterment of community. With the participation of community members because it is important to ensure that the community people maintain hygiene after the camp is done. The major responsibilities are to procure instruments for doing shramadhan, mobilizing the community to carry out this activity, motivate people to work for hygiene, unite community youth when it comes to cleanliness, and so on. Besides learning and transformation through the *shramadhan* committee, motivating, resource utilization, and other skills will be improved.

Cultural Committee: The cultural committee is primarily responsible for ensuring that community members participate in the camp. Innovative cultural programmes can be used to create awareness among people in the form of street plays, songs, dances, and skits. Trainees can use information communication technologies to disseminate awareness even more effectively. The responsibilities of the committee are to ensure complete participation of the students in all activities, to ensure maximum participation from the people in the village, to build rapport with the village community, to spread awareness among the communities, and to create a pleasant atmosphere in the village. Through the cultural activities Social Work trainees can manifest their latent talent to bring awareness among people. Communication and rapport establishment skills will be improved through participation in the committee. Also, participating in the cultural activities significantly improves their personality in terms of appearance, verbal mannerism, gesticulation, mental alertness, stability of thoughts, leadership skills, and positive attitude among Social Work trainees.

Discipline Committee: The discipline committee plays a vital role in bringing about changes in the social work trainees and the camp site. This committee is responsible for maintaining order during the field study and avoiding trouble-causing behaviours, ensuring standardized and regulated behaviour for all during working hours, maintaining a conducive atmosphere during group meetings, holding meetings and discussions, maintaining a hygienic and clean environment at the campsite as well as in the community, ensuring cleanliness of places of common usage like toilets and eating areas, encouraging punctuality and adhering to schedules, and maintaining safety of students during their stay and during travel.

People Participation Committee: Recently, the people participation committee has been diminishing. Therefore, social work trainees can create innovative strategies, with create and updated tactics to ensure more people participate. Without people participation, the entire camp will be useless.

Methodology used for conducting the camps

Baseline surveys, observation, FGDs, meetings, PRA, home visits, in-basket household budgeting, micro-research, cultural activities (i.e., street plays, songs, dances, etc.), analysis and interpretation of the data collected, and preparing of the report can all be practised effectively where these are required.

In-basket household budgeting

The use of budgets for specific types of households has a long tradition. In the literature, they have mainly been used for the measurement of poverty, and the budgets therein are typically known as standard budgets, although other terms such as 'example budgets' and 'budget standards' have also been used. It is our view, however, that the term 'standard budgets' carries too prescriptive a meaning, with the implication being that an individual household has to comply with 'the standard.' Yet we also believe that these budgets should be used as a tool with which to help consumers and their advisors 'benchmark' individual spending patterns.

Fisher distinguishes three types of reference budgets. The first is the detailed budget approach. All the items in these reference budgets are described in detail, and it is obvious that their development requires a great deal of investigation and, therefore, manpower. In the categorical approach, expenditure is only specified for certain consumption categories. This produces the outcome of the detailed budget approach, but without the need for comprehensive investigations. These budgets are based on the experience of, for example, budget counsellors. The third type of reference budget is based on average consumer expenditure, and the results of household expenditure surveys may be used therein (Marcel Warnaar, 2009). This method can be used during home visits. Trainees can conduct innovative in-basket exercises to assess household earnings and spending in different baskets; further spending will be bifurcated into mandatory and not mandatory expenses, and finally trainees can create a household budget for the entire year and avoid unnecessary spending; in addition, they shall develop financial literacy.

Do's in social work camps

- Trainees shall have a professional relationship with the community people.
- Social work trainees shall have professional relationships among themselves.
- Trainees shall conduct all activities with the guidance of the faculty supervisor.
- Trainees should be sensitive to the dynamics of the community.

- Trainees shall test all social work knowledge and methods in the community with the guidance of the supervisor.
- Trainees shall get inter-group and intra-group experience by participating in all work.
- Trainees shall plan, organize, withdraw from, and evaluate the community camp.
- Trainees' skills shall be enhanced through increasing utilization of all committee responsibilities and supervisor-assigned activities.

Don'ts in social work camps

- Unethical personal conduct with community people.
- Unethical personal conduct with trainee counterparts.
- Sympathetic approach towards community rather empathetic.
- Using derogatory language with trainee counterparts and community people.
- Giving false assurance to community people.
- Discrimination on the basis of caste, creed, religion, gender, and region.

Conclusion

Social work camps play a pivotal role in learning and transformation among trainees and help to inculcate skills and a professional attitude and promote indigenous practice with new strategies and tactics with unique communities. In the case studies described in this chapter not only transformative learning but also certain professional interactions occurred among the social work trainees and faculty camp supervisors, professional knowledge was applied and tested, and trial-and-error processes took place during camp. Communities are the laboratories for a social work–tested body of knowledge and for transforming social work trainees from personal selves to professional selves. Rural camp provides an opportunity for the students to get practical exposure to dealing with individual problems, group development, and organizing communities; if the situation demands it, the trainees can use social action methods, conduct social work research to assess facts and social welfare administration and implement their resources based on the needs of the community. The rural camp motivates the trainees to think about innovative strategies. Hence, alongside transformative learning, professional development will also take place. Therefore, even a community-based, living-learning model can be practised during social work camp.

Especially in India, private practice has not emerged yet. Instead, integrated social work practice at the community level takes place. Although there may be any number of macro-level theories with implications for direct practice, it is my belief that the theory of community development is perhaps the most practical framework for social workers seeking lasting change for individuals and the communities and societies in which they live. It focuses on the centrality of oppressed people in the process of overcoming externally imposed social problems. Social work, at its foundation, shares much in common with the tenets of community development (Tan, 2009).

References

Boroujerdi, M. (2002). Subduing globalization: The challenge of the indigenization movement. In *Gobalzation and the Margins* (pp. 39–49). New York, NY: Palgrave Macmillan.

Diego, U. O. (2015). *Proposed living learning communities*. Retrieved October 3, 2017, from sandiego.edu: www.sandiego.edu/wscuc/documents/effectiveness/attachments/LLC.pdf

Ejaz, F. K. (1991). Social workeducation in India: Perceptions of social workers in Bombay. *International Social Work, 34*.

Freire, P. (1970). *Pedagogy of Oppressed*. New York: Herder and Herder.

Gore, P. A. (1977). Social work education in India. In B. N. Ganguli (Ed.), *Social development* (pp. 260–290). New Delhi: Sterling Publication Pvt Ltd.

Gray, M., & Coates, J. (2008). *Indigenous social workaround the world: Towards culturally relevant education and practice*. Aldershot: Ashgate.

Marcel Warnaar, A. L. (2009). *Handbook of reference*. European Community Programme for Employment and Social Solidarity.

Mezirow, J. (2000). Learning to think like an adult: Gore concepts of transformation theory. In *Learning as transformation: Critical perspectives on a theory in progress* (pp. 3–33). San Francisco: Jossey-Bass.

Mizirow, J. (1991). *Transfermative dimentions of adult learning*. San Fransisco: Jossey-Bass.

Ramesh, B. S. (2017). Globalization impact on festival economy of India. In R. Raghuramapatruni (Ed.), *Selected readings on international business* (pp. 225–233). New Delhi: Abhijeet Publications.

Subhedar, I. (2009). *Field work training in social work*. Jaipur: Rawat Publication.

Tan, A. (2009). Community development theory and practice bridging the devide between micro and macro levels of social work. *North American Association of Chri, 15*.

Taylor, E. W. (2008). Transformative learning theory. In *New directions for adult and continuing education* (pp. 5–15). Hoboken, NJ: Wiley Periodicals, Inc.

Welton, M. R. (1995). *In defence of the life world: Critical perspective on Adult learning*. Albany, NY: SUNY Press.

Work, D. O. (2014, February). *Rural camp report-2014*. Retrieved October 3, 2017, from christuniversity. https://christuniversity.in/uploads/userfiles/rural_camp.pdf

5

ESSENTIAL GUIDELINES FOR SUCCESSFUL FIELDWORK SUPERVISION

Akileswari S

Introduction

In social work, the signature pedagogy is field education. The intent of field education is to connect the theoretical and conceptual contributions of the classroom with the practical world of the practice setting. It is a basic precept of social work education that the two interrelated components of the curriculum – classroom and field – are of equal importance within the curriculum, and each contributes to the development of the requisite competencies of professional practice. Field education is systematically designed, supervised, coordinated, and evaluated based on criteria by which students demonstrate the achievement of programme competencies (Council on Social Work Education [CSWE], 2008).

The development of students in terms of knowledge, skills, attitude and competencies, inculcation of values and ethics, integration of theory and practice, and creation of a learning environment in the fieldwork practicum largely depends on supervision. The concept of fieldwork supervision in social work education is dual: (1) supervision by the faculty members and (2) supervision by the agency supervisors. Subhedhar (2001) states that the supervisory process aims at the development of the field practicum, integration of theory and practice, and creation of an environment through which the students should be able to learn practical aspects of social work theories and philosophies. It rests upon democratic values and ideals, which are not the denial of responsibilities.

Supervision holds the key to the professional development of a student. It is a dynamic educational process involving the faculty supervisor, student, peers, and agency supervisor to develop knowledge, skills, and attitudes in accordance with the professional standards of social work practice. It is mainly the supervised nature of fieldwork training that facilitates professional development (Sajid, 2000).

Concept of fieldwork supervision

Fieldwork supervision consists of three key components, namely, the faculty supervisor, the agency supervisor, and the student, which are interconnected for the purpose of knowledge transfer. The faculty supervisor is attached to the department, and the agency supervisor is attached to the agency, with the student moving between the two in the pursuit of competency acquisition. This process is pinned down to a framework called the school–agency interface. This interface was presented by Bogo and Vayda (1987) as shown in Figure 5.1.

Definition of fieldwork supervision

> Supervision is a traditional method of transmitting knowledge of social work skills in practice from the trained to the untrained, from the experienced to the inexperienced student and worker.
> (*Encyclopedia of Social Work*, 1965 cited in Kadushin & Harkness, 2002)

Fieldwork supervision: a brief history

The history of supervision goes back to the very beginnings of the social work profession; indeed, it is inextricably bound up with the

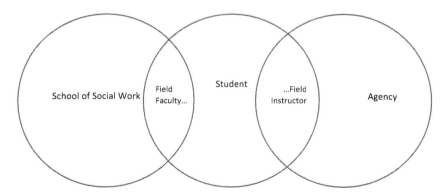

Figure 5.1 School–agency interface for fieldwork supervision

Source: Bogo and Vayda (1987), The Practice of Field Instruction in Social Work: Theory and Process

ESSENTIAL GUIDELINES

development of the profession (Pettes, 1967). There is evidence to suggest that the teaching function of supervision was recognized as early as 1869 when the Charity Organization Society was formed in England. The pedagogical function of the supervisor received further impetus with the opening of schools of social work during the 1920s in the United States. The students who were placed for fieldwork in social welfare agencies were supervised by the agency staff. Supervision was influenced by the increasing emphasis on casework. The major experimentation was the use of group supervision, peer group supervision, etc. (Pathak, 1975).

Since its beginnings, fieldwork supervision has always been a subject of discussion in all the social work curriculum framing and reframing exercises that have taken place across the globe. The emphasis on strengthening fieldwork supervision continues; accordingly, this chapter presents a set of essential guidelines for successful supervision.

Framework of guidelines for fieldwork supervision

In order to make the process of supervision in practice and learning professional, meaningful, and successful, it must be organized within a framework of guidelines, which are discussed in the next sections.

Objectives of fieldwork supervision

Fieldwork supervision should be carried out based on certain objectives. Subhedhar (2001) lists the general objectives of fieldwork supervision as:

1 To provide an opportunity for students to learn social work techniques in practical situations in different fields and to meet the needs of professional education.
2 To organize and accelerate the process of learning the practical aspects of social work theories and philosophies in the different fields of social work.
3 To facilitate achievement of learning goals, especially the practical use of principles and philosophies, skill, and techniques, in social work practice.
4 To help students acquire professional skills and develop their social attitudes.
5 To help students assess their strengths and weaknesses in the proper perspective.
6 To assist students in developing their social perspectives and social outlook for effective social work practice.

Administration/organization of fieldwork supervision

Fieldwork supervision, be it at the school/department or at the agency, involves certain administrative responsibilities. The objectives of supervision can be realized only if these two partners take up the following responsibilities:

1   The school/department should consider the following parameters for the selection of 'practicum-worthy' agencies for fieldwork training:

- The students should be placed only in agencies which have professionally qualified supervisors (i.e., under the supervision of a professional social worker). The NAAC (2005) dictates that agency supervisors should be professional social workers.
- The agency supervisors should have the required experience to engage in student supervision. The University Grants Commission (1980) in its report of the Second Review Committee on Social Work Education insisted that field instructors must be persons of tested knowledge and experience with the ability to teach in practice situation. Field instructors should be persons with practice experience of at least three years and a high academic rating parallel to the expectation of teaching faculty.

2   The role of the school/department in the school–agency interface:

- The agency supervisors should be provided with a printed fieldwork manual with clear guidelines on supervision. The manual should specifically carry instructions pertaining to the role of the agency supervisor in maintenance of students' attendance.
- Payment should be made to the agency supervisors for their services. Payment to the agencies/agency supervisors would make them have a moral responsibility and work towards ensuring quality in the fieldwork training provided by them. Also, payment for services denotes that the work of the agency/agency supervisors is recognized. However, there could be the danger of causing a financial burden to the students.
- Agency supervisors' meetings should be held every year to enhance the administration/organization of fieldwork and the learning experience of the students. These meetings should be also utilized to guide the agency supervisors on the fieldwork supervisory requirements. These meetings help mutually inform the expectations and requirements of each other and to discuss the issues and problems that arise during fieldwork practicum and supervision.

3   The role of the school/department in enhancing the fieldwork supervision at the department level:

- The weekly timetable of the department should include an exclusive period for individual and group conferences.
- Private spaces for the faculty supervisors in the form of rooms, cubicles, or cabins should be provided in order to enable the supervisors and students to engage in confidential supervisory sessions.
- The number of students allotted to the faculty supervisors should be a number that would permit quality supervision.
- Guidelines for supervision should be provided to the faculty supervisors. The guidelines should include the stipulation of the frequency of minimum contact with the agency.
- Fieldwork should be included as part of the workload for the faculty.
- Faculty supervisors should be given allowances for commuting to fieldwork agencies.

Preparation of supervisors

The NAAC (2005) insists on preparing supervisors in order to ensure quality standards in supervision. However, the fact that faculty supervisors and agency supervisors have undergone fieldwork training does not ensure that they can become competent supervisors. The skills required to become a good supervisor need to be built through a continuous process of training. The field instructors, be they school based or agency based, should be trained (Devi Prasad & Vijayalakshmi, 1997). The agency supervisors are considered equal partners in the development of professional social workers, but they seem to be totally neglected in terms of capacity building. Unless their skills and competencies are built, the quality of their supervisory inputs given to the students will be substandard. Hence, there is a dire need for the departments of social work to pay attention to such supervisory skill building programmes for agency supervisors. Opportunities for agency supervisors to periodically provide inputs from the field during classes would enable them to hone their teaching and training skills.

The supervisory skill development to prepare the faculty and the agency supervisors should be undertaken by the school/department encompassing a plethora of training activities such as:

- Periodic orientation on fieldwork supervision for the faculty and agency supervisors.
- Making reading materials available for faculty and agency supervisors on fieldwork supervision.
- Organizing supervisory skills training programmes through seminars, conferences, symposia, and workshops for the faculty and the agency supervisors.

- Arranging for periodic refresher courses in fieldwork supervision and encouraging the faculty members to take the course.
- Inviting the agency supervisors/practitioners to give feedback on developments in the field to the faculty so they can be kept up-to-date and so that supervision can be provided based on these developments.
- Arranging for social work staff meetings which reflect fieldwork supervision and involving the faculty members in the discussions.
- Carrying out annual self-appraisal for the faculty supervisors with regard to fieldwork supervision and using it for planning the next year, in consultation with the head of the school/department.
- Encouraging faculty supervisors to practise social work so that they can be aware of and knowledgeable about the dynamics of the field and provide guidance based on this experience, which will make a significant difference in their supervision. Providing faculty with sabbatical leave will enable them to gain field experience. This would enhance the quality of supervision provided to the students. Only through practice can faculty supervisors can become good educators.
- Inviting the agency supervisors to take part in academic meetings which focus on the designing/redesigning of the fieldwork practicum and the inter-linked dimension of supervision.
- Providing adequate preparation for the beginning supervisors (both faculty and agency supervisors) for the tasks and problems that are to be faced.

Other support for faculty and agency supervisors in the process of preparation include:

- Providing emotional support to help to carry out the role as faculty and agency supervisors.
- Recognizing faculty and agency supervisors for outstanding performance in fieldwork supervision; an important source of support in working with the field of agencies is a system of reward and recognition for their instructional and supervisory contributions (Schneck & Glassman 1991). Lacerte and Ray (1991) identified that the agency supervisors valued recognition offered in the form of free workshops, orientations, adjunct professor status, networking with other supervisors, and guest lecturing in the classroom.

Competencies for supervision

Supervision is not only a responsibility; it also requires specific competencies to effectively meet its objectives. The possession of the following

ESSENTIAL GUIDELINES

competencies would make the faculty and agency supervisors efficient during the process of supervising students.

- **Professional Practice Competencies** – These competencies denote that a fieldwork supervisor has the knowledge, skill, attitude, ethics, and values necessary. The fieldwork supervisor with professional practice competencies possesses:

  1 A sound knowledge of social work theory and practice.
  2 The professional skills and attitude and demonstrates them in terms of ethics and values.
  3 The professional attributes such as humility, integrity, optimism, and commitment to work.
  4 Ability to give a holistic approach to practice-based research and researched fieldwork.
  5 A professional self which is consciously maintained to meet the requirements of the profession.

- **Education Competencies** – These competencies denote that a fieldwork supervisor can develop professional practice and competence in fieldwork. The fieldwork supervisor with education competencies enables:

  1 The imparting of the required knowledge and skills to the students and shapes their attitudes.
  2 The students to apply the theoretical knowledge to practice during fieldwork.
  3 The development of critical self-awareness among the students.
  4 The professional attributes and ethical behaviour among students.
  5 The students to understand the types of recordings and to develop their ability to write reports or to create the necessary documentation.

- **Supervision Competencies** – These competencies denote that a fieldwork supervisor provides adequate guidance to the students to enable them to make certain achievements in fieldwork. The fieldwork supervisor with supervision competencies helps:

  1 To create a non-intimidating and non-authoritarian environment of learning for the students.
  2 The students develop maturity in dealing with difficult situations in the field.
  3 The students to discuss their views in a democratic way during individual and group conferences.
  4 The older, frustrated, and emotionally disturbed students create strategies due to the raw realities in the field.

5   The students to be gender sensitive and nurture a spirit of optimism among them.

- **Evaluation Competencies** – These competencies denote that a fieldwork supervisor effectively evaluates the fieldwork performance of the students. The fieldwork supervisor with evaluation competencies evaluates:

1   By providing the students with prompt and constructive feedback throughout the fieldwork.
2   By reading the reports of the students and understanding the activities carried out by them.
3   By correcting the records/documents in advance and only discussing them during the individual and group conferences.
4   Objectively and shows no discrepancy or disparity among students.
5   Each student in consultation with the respective agency or faculty supervisors.

- **Administration Competencies** – These competencies denote that a fieldwork supervisor develops and implements a set of rules and regulations for the students in terms of fieldwork. The fieldwork supervisor with administration competencies ensures:

1   That the qualities of regularity and punctuality required for fieldwork are inculcated in students.
2   The accountability of the students to their placement agencies.
3   That frequent visits are made to the fieldwork agencies and/or the field to assess the performance of the students.
4   That a realistic report is given to the department about the students' fieldwork.
5   That discipline is maintained among the students during fieldwork and other related activities.

- **Relationship Competencies** – These competencies denote that a fieldwork supervisor maintains a professional relationship with the students. The fieldwork supervisor with relationship competencies maintains:

1   A professional relationship with the students and has a disciplined control of personal needs and reactions.
2   A relationship without any personal biases or any expectation in terms of personal gain.
3   A meaningful relationship with respect for the students and faith in their potentialities.
4   Positive qualities and acts as a role model with whom the students can identify.
5   Regular contact with all the fieldwork agencies or institutions and maintains a cordial relationship with them.

ESSENTIAL GUIDELINES

Process of supervision

The preparation for supervision and acquisition of related competencies would enable the supervisors to successfully accompany the students through the process of supervision. The process of supervision both at the school and in the agency takes place through the methods of (1) individual conferences, (2) group conferences, (3) spot instructions, and (3) fieldwork seminars (Singh, 1985). During this process, Singh (1985) delineated the roles of the supervisor in different phases, such as (1) orientation phase, which involves explaining the fieldwork programme to the students; (2) induction phase, which involves introducing the student to the agency/field, the client system, the supervisor–supervisee relationship, and report writing; (3) implementation phase, which involves helping the students to carry out their fieldwork assignments, clarifying their doubts and analysing their experiences and feelings; and d) evaluation phase, which involves formulating a pattern of evaluation, all directed towards fostering growth and awareness in the students. The 'areas of supervision' that were pointed out were skills such as observation, interviewing, relationship, recording, administrative procedures, training, fact-finding, planning, implementation, analysis, and organization.

As pointed out by Singh (1985), the process of fieldwork supervision, which consists of various phases, requires the faculty and the agency supervisors to adopt certain supervisory practices to make the teaching-learning process successful.

1   Supervisory practices for faculty supervisors:

- Planning an agenda/structure in advance for fieldwork supervisory sessions.
- Holding individual conferences of at least 30 minutes' duration per student per week.
- Checking students' records every week, reading them carefully, making written comments, and discussing them in the conferences.
- Holding one group conference in a month with at least one presentation by each student in a year.
- Guiding the students based on the requirements of the fieldwork manual.
- Enabling the students to outline their fieldwork plans and programmes and guiding them in their implementation.
- Enabling the students to relate theories taught in class with practice.
- Encouraging the students to practise all the methods of social work during their fieldwork.

- Making visits to the fieldwork agencies for discussion of the students' plan, possible assignments that could be taken up, and the progress made by the students with agency supervisors.
- Relating well with the agency supervisors.
- Participating in the community programmes organized by the students and observing them.
- Making available model fieldwork records and recording formats for casework, group work and community organization and enabling the students to prepare sound reports.
- Teaching the students to respect the agency and the agency supervisor and value the learning opportunity provided by them.
- Insisting on the code of conduct among the students.
- Inculcating ethical behaviour among students.
- Acting as a mentor to identify issues that block the learning of the students.
- Providing feedback to the students periodically and helping them progress in the right direction.
- Effectively redressing any student grievances related to fieldwork.
- Taking up written or oral review of fieldwork at the end of each year that the students share.
- Maintaining greater transparency and fairness and a regular and candid appraisal of the evaluation process.

2 Supervisory practices for agency supervisors:

- Engaging only the number of students to whom quality supervision could be ensured.
- Ensuring adequate infrastructure/conducive and comfortable space to create an ambience for the students to learn.
- Maintenance of attendance of the fieldwork students.
- Understanding and following the fieldwork manual provided by the schools/departments and assimilating the fieldwork requirements of the students.
- Arranging suitable fieldwork experiences for the students that would shape their knowledge, skills, and attitudes and inculcate professionalism.
- Allocating time to supervise the fieldwork students along with the regular agency work.
- Adequately planning and preparing an agenda/structure in advance for the supervisory sessions with the students and readily answering their queries related to the realities of fieldwork.
- Enabling the students to relate theories taught in class with practice.
- Encouraging the students to practise all the methods of social work during their fieldwork.

- Periodically consulting the faculty supervisor regarding the assignments planned and discussing the ways and means of providing a quality fieldwork experience for the students.
- Providing periodic feedback to the faculty supervisor about the progress made by the students.
- Providing periodic feedback to the students and enabling them to progress in the right direction.
- Encouraging peer group supervision to facilitate learning.
- Being concerned about the physical and emotional health of the students when they are in the field.
- Ensuring the safety of the students when they are in the field.
- Effectively redressing the student grievances related to fieldwork.
- Objectively evaluating the student and transparently communicating the same.
- Taking up written or oral review of fieldwork at the end of each year that the students share.

Functions of supervision

During the various phases of the supervisory process, the faculty and agency supervisors need to perform certain vital functions. Middleman and Rhodes (1985) identified nine functions of supervision which are applicable to the context of fieldwork supervision. They are:

- Integrative Functions:

  (1) **Humanizing:** The humanizing function includes commending supervisees on specific actions, expressing publicly and valuing the work of students, adjusting the work environment, openly pointing to or admitting their own mistakes, and deliberately allowing the supervisees to save face.

  (2) **Managing Tension:** The tension managing function includes encouraging diverse points of view; helping others see something from a different perspective; assuming a mediating position; allowing time for ventilation or expression of anger; bending, modifying, or adjusting a procedure; and using humour in tense situations.

  (3) **Catalyzing Function:** The catalyzing function includes encouraging supervisees to take on special assignments or participate in training opportunities, encouraging supervisees to work together on a common problem, discouraging 'yes, but' responses to new situations or to change, encouraging new ideas, conveying optimism about ideas actions, and offering new ideas/plans.

- Service Delivery Functions:

    (4) **Teaching:** The teaching function includes presenting, discussing, or describing concepts, theory, or data; inviting a speaker to present information on a topic or to teach skills; planning for students to present some content; coaching supervisees in new activities, skills, and behaviours; and sharing or circulating articles, books, reports, and studies.

    (5) **Career Socializing:** The career socializing functions include encouraging supervises to grow both during the work and outside of it; making choices or decisions based on a value issue; taking ethical stands, even if unpopular; acting in relation to student behaviour out of regard for professional standards and norms; challenging agency policy that conflicts with professional imperatives; asserting or distinguishing a social work belief from the orientation of another profession; and encouraging self and supervisees to interpret a social work perspective on social issues, the profession's image, or client concern for others in the community.

    (6) **Evaluating:** The evaluating function includes offering verbal assessment of supervisees' work; helping develop performance goals in the areas of self, supervisees, programme, and service; providing written feedback on performance to supervisees; reviewing performance expectations with new supervisees; soliciting feedback on and reviewing own performance; and conducting or analysing studies of programme performance, such as work conditions, programme impact, client needs, client satisfaction, and so forth.

- Linkage Functions:

    (7) **Administering:** The administering function includes delegating tasks related to service goals; interpreting and translating agency goals, policies, and procedures into assignments, activities, and tasks; monitoring the timely completion of essential paperwork (case notes, recording, reports, statistics, eligibility certification forms); taking the initiative to affect or enhance communication networks, written and verbal; accessing and reviewing information (agency reports, computer printouts); and disseminating relevant information to the supervisees.

    (8) **Advocating:** The advocating function includes taking a stand on behalf of the supervisee(s); taking a stand on behalf of self and other supervisors; developing a position statement and expressing or disseminating it; initiating contacts with public media; participating in community events to enlighten or influence

about the commitments to proposed changes in policies, regulations, and procedures; and joining action groups (internal and external).

(9) **Changing:** The changing function of the supervisors includes encouraging review of standard operating procedures; implementing useful suggestion of others (supervisee or supervisor); disagreeing with and confronting a superior; collecting and providing information about other approaches, thinking programmes, and data related to closing gaps in service delivery; and implementing an innovative plan or idea.

Supervisor–supervisee relationship

Another important aspect of fieldwork supervision is the supervisor–supervisee relationship. This relationship determines the course of supervision and influences the learning needs of the students. Lager (2010) is of the opinion that the establishment of a positive relationship begins with an open discussion by the supervisor regarding his or her style of supervision. Supervisory style can be best defined as the way the fieldwork supervisor shares his or her theoretical orientation, practice, and supervisory philosophies. Supervisory style consists of a series of behaviour patterns used by the supervisor to establish a working relationship with the student. It can generally be categorized as (1) active, which is problem oriented, directive, and interpretive, or (2) reactive, which is process oriented, indirect, and non-interpretive (Munson, 2002).

Shulman (2009) termed the relationship established during supervision as a helping relationship which requires interactional skills. The interactional skills refer to the development of core communication, relationship, and problem-solving skills, which would facilitate the supervisory process towards the objective for which the relationship was established. Shulman (1993), in his examination of interactional supervision, articulates a staged approach wherein supervision includes a cluster of skill sets that supervisors employ to facilitate growth and development in supervisees. These include but are not limited to (1) sessional tuning in skills; (2) sessional contracting skills, or identification of agenda items with attention to staff concerns; (3) elaborating skills, to facilitate deeper and richer conversations; (4) empathic skills, which offer support and validation of supervisee experiences and feelings; (5) reaching for feelings, or reflection on affective messages; (6) acknowledging feelings and communicating this understanding of feelings; (7) sharing feelings, which assist the supervisor's presentation of self as human beings, with vulnerability, anger, warmth, etc.; (8) making a demand for work necessary to facilitate continued work in the face of ambivalence and resistance; (9) understanding the change process and the importance of acknowledging safety needs during change; (10) partializing worker concerns and breaking down complex challenges; and (11) assisting staff who are distracted or avoiding activities to maintain focus.

An ideal supervisor should display leadership, a willingness to help, friendliness, and understanding. They should show moderate behaviour in providing freedom and responsibility to students and in being strict. They should not show much uncertainty, dissatisfaction, and admonishing behaviour. Equal levels of proximity and influence make an ideal supervisor. (Wubbels, Maihard, van der Rijst, & van Tartwijk, 2009)

The faculty and the agency supervisors need to exhibit certain supervisory behaviours as identified by Shulman (1981) in order to build a positive and a healthy supervisor–supervisee relationship.

Supervisory Behaviours:

- Effective stress management to focus on fieldwork supervision.
- Availability when fieldwork supervisees need the supervisors.
- Explaining how work can be done together and describing the kind of help that will be provided.
- Helping the students talk about subjects they are not comfortable discussing.
- Sharing thoughts and feelings.
- Understanding students' feelings.
- Encouraging the students to talk about things the supervisors say or do that might be upsetting to them.
- Sensing the students' feelings without the need to verbalize them.
- Helping the students sort out their concerns in a situation and look at them one at a time.
- Sharing suggestions about the subjects that are discussed for their consideration.
- Creating an atmosphere in which the students feel free to discuss their mistakes/failures and successes.
- Helping the students to talk openly about fieldwork-related concerns.
- Permitting students to make their own mistakes.
- Allowing students to talk openly to their fellow students concerning placements.
- Having a detailed and accurate grasp of policy and procedures in the institution/agency.
- Communicating the students' views to the administration about policy and procedures.
- Being helpful to the fieldwork students.
- Building a satisfactory working relationship with the fieldwork students.

Outcome of fieldwork supervision

The fieldwork supervisory framework aims at developing the knowledge, skills, and attitude and maintaining the professional ethics and values. Thus, the outcome of this system is the expectation that students would acquire the following core competencies of social work (CSWE, 2008):

- Identify with the social work profession and behave professionally.
- Apply social work ethical principles to guide professional practice.
- Apply critical thinking to inform and communicate professional judgments.
- Engage diversity and flexibility in practice.
- Apply human rights and social and economic justice.
- Engage in research-informed practice and practice-informed research.
- Apply knowledge of human behaviour and the social environment.
- Engage in policy practice to advance social and economic wellbeing and to deliver effective social work services.
- Respond to realities that shape practice.
- Engage, assess, intervene, and evaluate with individuals, families, groups, organizations, and communities.

Supervised fieldwork helps in the attainment of these competencies and thereby ensures that the students have grown to become social work professionals who are ready for practice.

Conclusion

It is obvious that a system of fieldwork supervision has grown over the years; old practices have been replaced by new practices, and innovations are continually developed. It is the moral obligation of social work educators and practitioners to incorporate the essential guidelines to keep fieldwork supervision alive without letting it get diluted and dissuaded by the rigours of time. Otherwise, there is the danger of the strengths of the profession turning into its weaknesses.

References

Bogo, M., & Vayda, E. (1987). *The practice of field instruction in social work: Theory and process.* New York, NY: Columbia University Press.

Council on Social Work Education. (2008). *Educational policy and accreditation standards.* Retrieved September 18, 2012, from www.cswe.org/File.aspx?id=13780

Kadushin, A., & Harkness, D. (2002). *Supervision in social work.* New York: Columbia University Press.

Lacerte, J., & Ray, J. (1991). Recognizing the educational contributions of field instructors. In D. Schneck, B. Grossman, & U. Glassman (Eds.), *Field instruction in social work: Contemporary issues and trends* (pp. 217–225). Dubuque, IA: Kendall/ Hunt.

Lager, P. (2010). Administrative and environmental aspects in social work supervision. In G. Thomas (Ed.), *Social work practicum and supervision* (pp. 206–219). New Delhi: Indira Gandhi National Open University (IGNOU).

Middleman, R. R., & Rhodes, G. B. (1985). *Competent supervision: Making imaginative judgements*. Upper Saddle River, NJ: Prentice-Hall.

Munson, C. E. (2002). *Clinical social work supervision* (3rd ed.). New York: Haworth Press.

National Assessment and Accreditation Council. (2005). *Manual for self-study of social work institutions*. New Delhi: National Assessment and Accreditation Council.

Pathak, S. H. (1975). Supervision in social work: Historical development. *The Indian Journal of Social Work*, *35*(4), 317–323.

Pettes, D. E. (1967). *Supervision in social work*. London: George Allen & Unwin Ltd.

Prasad, D. B., & Vijayalakshmi, B. (1997). Field instruction in social work education in India. *The Indian Journal of Social Work*, *58*(1), 11–77.

Sajid, S. M. (2000). Field work in social work education: Issues and problems in curriculum designing. In A. S. Navale (Ed.), *Social Work Review*, Special Issue on Social Work Profession, 121–130.

Schneck, G. B., & Glassman, U. (1991). *Field education in social work: Contemporary issues and trends*. Dubuque, IA: Kendell Hunt Publishing Company.

Shulman, L. (1993). *Interactional supervision*. Washington, DC: NACW Press.

Shulman, L. (2009). *The skills of helping individuals, families, groups, and communities*. Boston: Cengage Learning.

Shulman, L., Robinson, E., & Luckyj, A. (1981). *A study of content, context and skills of supervision*. Vancouver: University of British Columbia Press.

Singh, R. R. (Ed.). (1985). *Field work in social work education- a perspective for human service professions*. New Delhi: Concept Publishing Company.

Subhedhar, I. S. (2001). *Field work training in social work*. Jaipur: Rawat Publications.

University Grants Commission. (1980). *Review of social work education in India: Retrospect and prospect*. New Delhi: University Grants Commission.

Wubbels, T., Maihard, T., van der Rijst, R., & van Tartwijk, J. (2009). A model for the supervisor-doctoral student relationship. *Higher Education*, *58*, 359–373. Retrieved February 9, 2012, from http://link.springer.com/article/10.1007/s10734-009-9199-8/fulltext.html

6

ESSENTIAL GUIDELINES AND TECHNIQUES FOR ASSESSMENT AND EVALUATION IN FIELDWORK

Nita Kumari

Introduction

Social work, both as an academic discipline and as a profession, is primarily a practice-oriented profession that strives towards promoting human and community wellbeing; respect for human diversity; social and economic justice and human rights; and enhancing the quality of life of all individuals, regardless of their caste, colour, creed, sex, and religion. The uniqueness of the profession is that it imparts learning by giving practical experiences to students. This profession makes itself distinct from other professions by giving the utmost importance to positive change in society and continuously driving individuals to do something constructive in nature.

In 2000 the IFSW and IASSW gave an international definition of social work:

> The social work profession promotes social change, problem solving in human relationships, and the empowerment and liberation of people to enhance wellbeing. Utilizing theory of human behaviours and social systems, social work intervenes at the point where people interact with their environments. Principles of human rights and social justice are fundamental to social work.
>
> (IFSW & IASSW, 2000)

In July 2014 another global definition of social work was approved at the general meeting of IFSW and General Assembly of IASSW which is as follows:

> Social work is a practice-based profession and an academic discipline that promotes social change and development, social

cohesion, and the empowerment and liberation of people. Principles of social justice, human rights, collective responsibility and respect for diversities are central to social work. Underpinned by theories of social work, social sciences, humanities and indigenous knowledge, social work engages people and structures to address life challenges and enhance wellbeing.

(IFSW & IASSW, 2014)

According to Dash and Roy, "Social work is [a] value based, ethical and spiritual practice based profession that aims at addressing the overall problems and sufferings of individuals, families, groups and communities to attend a peaceful life" (Dash & Roy, 2015, p. 4).

From these definitions, it is quite clear that social workers always follow a formal procedure to help their clients achieve positive change in their lives using social work skills and methods. They develop the capacity of clients to deal with their problems more effectively and efficiently and connect them with needed resources. Moreover, through social work intervention, social workers induce changes in the existing structure, if required, for overall growth and development.

The curriculum of social work therefore has developed both a theoretical course structure and a planned and supervised fieldwork practicum. Through supervised fieldwork practicum, a student can develop the requisite skills for working with people. According to Singla, supervised fieldwork training helps build the student's capacities and enables them to apply social work theory to real-life situations in social service agencies or in communities (Singla, 2015, p. 90). The practicum is considered necessary to prepare the students to perform practice roles. A number of scholars have suggested that classroom-based cognitive education needs to be integrated with practical field experience in order to teach professional practice (Caspi & William, 2002). Hence, the schools of social work not only have a theoretical base but also train students by giving them practical exposure through fieldwork training. The fieldwork has various components on which the student is assessed and evaluated throughout their course.

Fieldwork in social work and its importance

The field practicum is central to the education of social work students (Canadian Association of Schools of Social Work, 2000; Council on Social Work Education, 1994), providing the primary opportunity for students to integrate knowledge, values, and skills into their professional self-concepts (Bogo & Vayda, 1998; Rogers & McDonald, 1995). The pivotal role of facilitating and directing the learning process in these practicums is left to practitioners in their roles as field instructors. These practitioners are charged with the complex responsibility of teaching

ESSENTIAL GUIDELINES AND TECHNIQUES

adults, which includes the responsibility of empowering students to become autonomous, self-directed, self-regulating professionals (Livingston, Davidson, & Marshack, 1989)

Conceptualized early as apprenticeship training, fieldwork has matured to take its place as one of the core components in professional social work education at both the undergraduate and graduate levels that gives experiential learning to students. During fieldwork students not only develop themselves personally and professionally but also integrate classroom knowledge and skills. In the words of Agnimitra, in fieldwork students acquire a desirable attitude and create a value frame under the supervision of expert academicians and practitioners (Agnimitra, 2015, p. 28). The Council on Social Work Education (CSWE)[1] has described fieldwork (also called field education, field practicum, field instruction, field education, or internship) as the "signature pedagogy" that represents the central form of instruction and learning in which a profession socializes its students to perform the role of practitioner. Like any other profession, social workers also require pedagogical norms with which they connect and integrate theory and practice (CSWE, 2008, p. 8). The term signature pedagogy was created by Shulman, who characterizes it as a form of teaching and learning used in a particular profession, through which the 'novices are instructed in critical aspects of three fundamental dimensions of professional work-to think, to perform, and to act with integrity' (Shulman, 2005, p. 52).

The Delhi School of Social Work published a document in 1957 titled "Fieldwork Supervision: In an Indian School of Social Work," highlighting the importance of practice in social work. Essentially social work skills are concerned with problem solving, and as such they rest upon knowledge contained in the social and biological sciences pertaining to man and society. This knowledge is gained partly in the didactic sessions of the curriculum, but it becomes meaningful only when the student tests it in situation after situation in the field. Thus, it can be seen that practical experience must be closely integrated at every step with what the student learns in the classroom (Gore, 1957, p. 3).

Various authors have defined fieldwork in their own ways. According to I. S. Subhedar (2001, p. 22):

> Fieldwork in social work education refers to training and education. . . . It consists of accumulating knowledge in different situations. It is a dynamic process of observing, amassing and implementing creative and innovative ideas. Moreover, it fosters the development of intellectual and emotional processes and attitudes [. . . .] Fieldwork programme provides an opportunity to the students to apply their theoretical knowledge taught in the classroom appropriately in different practical situations.

105

In their fieldwork manual Twikirize and Tusasiirwe (2015, p. 6) stated that "Fieldwork placements represent a laboratory where theories taught at the university are tested and practiced under the supervision of a qualified practitioner, for the student to acquire skills." The latest definition of fieldwork has been given by Dash and Roy (2015), which says that

> Field work is an ethical and value based professional and scientific application of social work methods, principles, techniques, and theories of social sciences for the alleviation of human sufferings and developing their capacities and skills to solve their psychological and social problems.
>
> (Dash & Roy, 2015, p. 5)

In a nutshell, in social work education, any kind of practical experience deliberately arranged for the enhancement and testing of knowledge and for the development of skills may be termed fieldwork. Fieldwork is like a laboratory for learning and serves an educational purpose (i.e., to reinforce, concretize, and extend theoretical learning).

Nature and purpose of fieldwork

In the field of social work, professional training is provided to students wherein they learn by doing the work they are being trained for. During fieldwork, the student is expected to concretize knowledge of social work theory by working face to face with individuals, groups, and communities. In the classroom, the student is taught different concepts, theories, descriptions of relationships, and theoretical knowledge useful for practice. However, students test the validity themselves by directly working in the field with the real-life situations, needs, and problems of people. An array of opportunities are provided to students during fieldwork to develop intervention strategies using their knowledge, skills, and techniques. While engaging in the field, the students can capture the field dynamics and can have a healthy and fruitful discussion in the classroom interactions, individual conferences, and group conferences so that the knowledge and different experiences can be exchanged with fellow students and faculty. Hipp and Munson, among others, very rightly believe that the engagement of the student in a mutual teaching and learning process sets the stage for responsible and participatory learning throughout the educational experience and, by extension, throughout one's career (Hipp & Munson, 1995; Livingston et al., 1989; Taylor, 1993).

Fieldwork is aimed at preparing students for practice as professionals, and so it involves not mere knowledge but also skill in the use of knowledge. The CSWE, in its curriculum policy statement (1969), formulated the objectives of fieldwork/practicum as to:

ESSENTIAL GUIDELINES AND TECHNIQUES

Enhance and improve student's learning within all areas of the curriculum; Endow students with opportunities for development, integration and reinforcement of competence through performance in actual service situations; Permit students to acquire and test skill relevant to emerging conditions of social work practice; Foster the integration and reinforcement of knowledge, value and skill learning acquired in the field and through particular courses and concentration; and Provide students with opportunity to delineate and comprehend questions for research which arise in the course of practice.

(cited in Dsouza, 2014, p. 3)

However, according to Agnimitra, fieldwork comprises the following objectives:

1   Help students understand the socio-economic, cultural, and political milieu and develop capacity for critical examination of factors instrumental in causing and perpetuating social problems and their consequences.
2   Provide students with an opportunity to apply theory in practical situations for problem solving with individuals, groups, and communities.
3   Help students identify, plan, and implement social work intervention strategies and assess their impact on different client systems in various settings.
4   Enable students to appreciate the role of the social work profession in empowering individuals, groups, and communities and in facilitating social change.
5   Facilitate students to develop skills and appropriate personality traits required for professional social work practice.
6   Provide opportunities for working with and responding to varied situations and challenging circumstances (Agnimitra, 2015, p. 31).

Educators often justify the inclusion of fieldwork because it covers a wide range of educational objectives. These include helping students to consolidate and apply classroom learning, to acquire various skills, and to contribute to affective goals such as personal and social development (Kent, Gilbertson, & Hunt, 1997; Job, 1999; Kent & Foskett, 2000). Lonergan and Andresen (1988) summarize the educational goals of fieldwork as follows:

1   To provide opportunities for practising techniques that cannot be carried out elsewhere (acquisition of practical/intellectual/methodological skills).

107

2 To demonstrate/illustrate objects or phenomena not accessible in other settings, enabling direct contact with, perception of, or interaction with them (acquisition of knowledge).
3 To promote group interaction (social growth).
4 To reinforce things previously presented in the classroom (application and consolidation of learning).
5 To stimulate higher-level understanding of matters already encountered elsewhere (deepening conceptual development).
6 To stimulate, in cases where the field is a natural environment, an attitude of appreciation, concern, and valuing of that environment (appraisal and adoption of attitudes and values) (1988, pp. 64–65).

Research on students' experiences in fieldwork has revealed that fieldwork has both an intellectual and affective focus (Job, 1996; Lai, 2000). Fieldwork takes place in a multi-sensory learning environment, which is different from the classroom, and engages students' emotions and feelings (Cook, 2011; Lai, 1999, 2000, 2006). The experience often provides students with meaningful personal experiences, which in turn lead to an exploration and increased understanding of places, ideas, and concepts, as well as to develop a feeling of personal concern and responsibility (see Kent & Foskett, 2000; Lai, 1999; Stimpson, 1995). The opportunity to collaborate with classmates in group work often allows students to develop valuable inter-personal relationships outside the school routine (Lai, 2000). In addition, outdoor work is an experiential activity in which students' experiences prior to, during, and after fieldwork are inter-connected. Student interest before and learning experiences after fieldwork are often much richer than their teachers have intended (Lai, 1999). Munowenyu (2002) also argues that teaching in the classroom and fieldwork are intertwined because both help promote students' understanding of the subject. Social work is a systematically planned and rigorous programme that evaluates and assesses students based on various components, which have evolved over time. These components are discussed next.

Components of fieldwork

The essential set of components within the ambit of a fieldwork programme in most schools of social work includes (1) orientation programme and observation visits/exposure visit, (2) concurrent fieldwork, (3) individual conference, (4) group conference; (5) rural camp or educational camp; (6) skill development workshop, and (7) block placement or block fieldwork training (Agnimitra, 2015; Singla, 2015; University of Delhi, 2015; Jamia Millia Islamia University, 2015; UGC, 2001).

Orientation programme and observation visit/exposure visit

A well-planned and well-organized orientation not only provides information useful for student performance but also benefits the fieldwork site by enhancing the potential for greater student productivity. The orientation programme is organized at the beginning of the academic session, which occurs before the fieldwork starts. During the orientation, newly admitted students are informed about the social work profession, its philosophy, methods, and practice sites, and are provided an understanding about the educational programme, that is, course structure (papers offered) and their content. In addition students develop basic knowledge, skills, ethics, values, and attitudes in order to facilitate the beginning of fieldwork; students are familiarized with various dimensions of the fieldwork programme, such as its learning requirements, different components, processes, and procedures. Students are also acquainted with the types of organizations they may be placed with and the range and scope of possible assignments, as well as do's and don'ts in the field.

For the rest of the semester the orientation programme is aimed at enhancing the learning experience of students already initiated into the social work programme. This orientation programme provides an opportunity to build upon the core knowledge and skill base that they have acquired over the previous semesters. The major objectives of such orientation are to facilitate in-depth understanding of contemporary issues, perspectives, and challenges in the field of social work practice; develop an understanding of the new and emerging social work domains and how students can engage themselves in such practice sites; strengthen perspectives on empowerment, social justice, and rights- based issues for social change; enhance knowledge of human behaviour, skills, and techniques to effectively work with the clientele group in the field; and increase understanding of the professional roles and relationships and the ethics of the profession to be followed in the field.

The orientation programme is combined with the exposure visits to the different agencies, which expose students to a wide range of social work practice. The students develop an understanding of the organization and identify different concerns that the organizations are focusing on and their response to the same. During these visits, students record their observations, analyse them, and reflect on their experiences. These visits improve observation skills, develop a spirit of enquiry; enable the students to make social work interventions, and prepare them for their concurrent field placements.

Concurrent fieldwork

This is one of the core components of fieldwork in social work education and lasts the entire academic year. Each student is assigned to an agency/

organization with set objectives for his or her learning experiences where he or she can acquire essential skills, tackle ethical dilemmas, practise various methods and test professional values, and learn to apply knowledge gathered through academic coursework. The student is supposed to go for fieldwork twice in a week (specific days decided by the institute/ university) and the other four days are for theory classes. Students must spend a minimum of six to seven hours per visit in the field setting under the guidance of a faculty supervisor and an agency supervisor. At the beginning of the fieldwork session, the supervisor, along with the student, makes a learning plan/action plan based on the fieldwork situation. The fieldwork supervisor is responsible for assigning the students a learning experience, guiding the learning through regular fieldwork conferences (individual and group conferences), and providing occasional feedback about their fieldwork performance. Students' records are the main basis for providing this instruction.

Some of the factors that influence the placement decisions include the distance to be commuted by the learner and any interest or preferences of the students (in case of second- or third-year students). Ideally, a maximum of three students are preferred for placement in one agency, and the student is expected to work within the limitations of the organization. While placing the students in a group, it is believed that students learn how to adjust, cooperate, coordinate with each other, and acquire teamwork skills. During their fieldwork, students gain knowledge of the needs and problems of client groups and critically review the programmes, services, and service delivery systems meant for the people in need of professional intervention.

Students can be placed in any of the government or non-government organizations, open communities, or communities through agency placement. Some of the fieldwork settings where students are placed include organizations working for the welfare of the scheduled caste, scheduled tribes and other backward classes: child welfare; youth welfare; welfare of the disabled; environmental conservation and development; providing legal aid; correctional institutions; schools; hospitals; centres for the disabled and elderly; organizations working with people living with HIV/ AIDS or leprosy; mental health institutions; industrial/corporate settings; and organizations working with homeless populations and the urban poor, etc.

Individual conference

The individual conference, which is held at least once a week, consists of face-to-face contact between the faculty supervisor and the student during which the student apprises the supervisor about every aspect of his or her involvement with the client and shares their experiences or problems confronted in the field. During the conference, the supervisee gets guidance and needed help to integrate theory and practice and develop concept clarity pertaining to social work practice. The supervisor monitors and evaluates the student's development of responsibility, knowledge, skills, techniques, attitude towards people, and ethical standards followed in the practice of social work and provides consistent feedback.

Some of the objectives of the individual conference are to assist the student in understanding and adapting to the agency/community where the field placement takes place; assess the student's ability to understand the fieldwork process; provide relevant feedback and encouragement; assist students in identifying their weakness and strengths during practicals; clarify and interpret various behaviours exhibited by the student; listen carefully to the students and share experiences that enhance the students' development; develop an understanding of integrating theory into practice; and generate confidence and inculcate a scientific approach in students.

Group conference

The group conference is an essential component in the training of students that helps in linking education and practice in social work. Group conferences are aimed at enhancing the knowledge base of the students through sharing of each other's field experiences. The students increase their understanding of connections between different phenomena that are observed and experienced by them in different field situations. As it is not possible to provide students with adequate exposure to all type of settings through direct field placement, group conferences familiarize students with the diverse social work practice settings through the experiences of other students placed in different fieldwork settings. The group conference facilitates the development and expansion of professional skills (such as project management, sensitizing people on various issues, campaigning, advocacy, responding to emergencies and conflicts, and so on) and competencies in students through the medium of presentations and focused discussions in a formal group setting provided by the college/department. The students are expected to prepare their group conference paper in consultation with their faculty supervisor, and the performance of students as presenters, recorders, chairpersons, and participants is minutely observed and evaluated by the faculty supervisors as part of their evaluation. Some of the objectives of the group conference are to provide an opportunity for students to prepare a formal, academic, and practice-oriented paper. Through such experience they learn how to write in a structured manner, communicate and express clearly through written as well as oral formats, and learn to integrate theory and practice; develop and enhance understanding of various social work settings;

provide a platform for students to share, discuss, and clarify conceptual issues, use of theoretical application, and real-life situations/actual field experiences encountered by students; encourage students to offer suggestions regarding a case/event/situation which the presenter is expecting from the group; and learn to perform the roles of presenter, chairperson, and recorder in a formal discussion within the time limit.

Rural camp or educational camp

Rural camp is another important component of fieldwork training, usually organized for a week for final-year students. The students are taken to a village setting where they are exposed to rural life and the needs, problems, challenges, limitations, and other issues related to the setting. The organization working at these sites is approached for help in coordinating the rural camp. Some of the objectives of rural camp include enabling the students to understand the rural life, including the culture, traditions, beliefs, livelihood pattern, economic structures, and ways of finding solutions to their own needs and problems; getting insight into the reasons behind rural problems, the possible intervention strategies for solving them, and the role of the social worker in the intervention process; facilitating good bonding among the students, developing team spirit, group living, and undertaking leadership roles; and developing sensitivity towards the needs and problems of the peer group as well as of the rural population.

During the camp, students are instructed on the objectives, how to meaningfully utilize the opportunity, and their expected conduct and behaviour during the programme. Students are also instructed on the organization's objective, functioning, and various schemes and programmes. Then the students are divided into subgroups and sent to different parts of the village to get an in-depth understanding about the socio-economic, cultural, political aspects of the village and make use of different techniques (participatory rural appraisal and participatory learning and action can be used for social, resource mapping, and transact walk) and use various resources to conduct meetings with different stakeholders (pradhan,[2] school teachers, anganwadi workers,[3] self-help groups,[4] elders and other influencing leaders of the village, etc.) and plan intervention strategies. They can conduct activities such as role-play, rallies, and use of slogans and songs to sensitize the villagers on the issues of health, education, sanitation, drinking water, women's health, nutrition (child health), and various schemes and programmes of the government.

Such rural camps are truly beneficial for the students in terms of conceptual clarity; practical knowledge of techniques such as PRA and rural life from a social work perspective; use of social work methods, skills, techniques, and attitudes; and managing and administrating the camp under the guidance of faculty. Students not only get exposed to the village setting but can also draw a connection between the problems at the village level and those in the urban areas.

Skill development workshops

The skill development workshop is a platform in which the values, principles, methods, techniques, tools, etc., are translated into practice skills, that is, 'learning by doing.' Through the experimental learning in the workshop, insights are acquired to develop the personal self and the professional self. The main aim of the skill workshop is to build the confidence and strengthen knowledge, skills, aptitude, and attitudinal base of students. The activities that may be included in a skill workshop are (1) role-plays; (2) use of motivational songs and other interactive visual media; (3) preparation of street plays, including script writing/street theatre; (4) simulation exercises; (5) screening of films; (6) practising counselling techniques; (7) practising participative techniques; (8) workshops on communication; (9) mock interviews; and (10) strategic planning for advocacy (University of Delhi, 2015, p. 13). Such skill development workshops may help students become more independent learners and encourage better interaction in the classrooms. The sessions in the worships may explore the latest concepts and new and occasionally radical approaches to learning and teaching. The students develop attributes such as creativity, better decision making, and are better equipped to perform in a demanding teaching environment. They can better respond to today's fast-changing learning needs and develop skills and emergency response actions through these workshops.

Block placement/block fieldwork training

Block fieldwork is carried out towards the end of the course. Students are required to undergo four- to six-week block fieldwork training in a social welfare agency or project in India. It is treated more as a pre-employment experience, and the student must work in the chosen agency on a full-time basis. The objectives of block placement are to provide an opportunity to handle professional responsibilities independently and familiarize students with the realities of the field; expand the opportunities for students to have an in-depth learning experience in diverse settings, both nationally and internationally; increase motivation, confidence, and awareness of self in the role of professional social worker; enable students to understand their weaknesses and strengths and ability to manage tasks; develop an understanding of working within the limitations and how to overcome the challenges and problems inherent in implementing a programme; and develop skills that help students further their own learning by using their ideas to form opinions, solve problems, and use a range of strategies in their learning.

A student then is expected to submit reports either weekly or at the end of block placement (depending upon the rules of the institution/department/university) to their respective college/department.

Supervision in fieldwork

As discussed, there are plenty of opportunities for practical learning by the way of fieldwork in social work education. However, effective and helpful supervision is a very vital factor in the success of fieldwork programmes. The guided practice learning through fieldwork makes the educational programme holistic and complete. Fieldwork training is a supervised practice under the guidance of a faculty supervisor in the college/department and a field supervisor in the agency, with the primary aim to facilitate, ensure, and increase humanistic, competent, and independent social work practice, which ultimately benefits the social work clientele. In the words of Singh (1985):

> Supervision is a two-way process between supervisor and supervisee in which the supervisor instructs, enables, guides, supports and communicates with the student in his quest for developing social work skills, knowledge and attitudes. According to Sajid, objectives of supervision are to: facilitate an educational and learning environment which encourages the student to participate freely in discussing issues arising out of applying theory in a practice setting; encourage students for self-knowledge, awareness and development; assist students to acquire a capacity for critical analysis of the issues involved in any practice setting; inculcate among students values and attitudes appropriate to the practice of professional social work; and help students evolve a framework of social work practice appropriate to the requirements of field setting as well as assist students to assume an independent professional status.
>
> (Sajid, 1999 cited in Nasreen, 2015, p. 78)

Faculty supervisors have several responsibilities. Some of them are to assess the student's understanding and ability to adjust to the field setting; facilitate in identifying learning needs, formulating learning objectives, and preparing an action plan; assess the student's ability to make use of theory in practice; help students develop maturity in dealing with different circumstances and learn to appreciate and respect the multiplicity and diversity of society, cultures, and communities; help them grow as

ESSENTIAL GUIDELINES AND TECHNIQUES

professional social workers, conscious of the demands of the profession and develop the capability to handle situations independently; monitor continuously the progress of students and provide feedback to them about the performance; arrange periodic visits and meetings with the agency supervisor/instructor wherein the proposed course of action by the student is discussed and an affirmative response is obtained from the agency; read and check the fieldwork reports and provide necessary guidelines to the students regarding report writing; develop insight into the process of social work intervention using social work philosophy, principles, methods, and skills; provide regular, timely, and systematic inputs; and assess the performance of students (University of Delhi, 2015, p. 11).

Assessment and evaluation in fieldwork

Fieldwork is subjected to a continuous process of evaluation, which is a particularly important responsibility and frequently a difficult one. It enables the supervisor and student to focus on directions that are most beneficial and valuable to the student's professional development.

Fieldwork evaluation has numerous purposes, serving the needs of the college, the agency, and the student themselves. The school must determine whether the student is functioning satisfactorily for his or her level of education, the clinic must know whether the needs of the clients seen by the student are being met, and the student must know how he or she doing in order to make both short- and long-term decisions regarding his or her professional future. It is in this last area that the procedures used by the supervisor can substantially increase the value of evaluation to the student (Billig, 1971, p. 66).

Generally, at the end of the programme, a fieldwork assessment is done both internally and externally. Students prepare a fieldwork self-assessment report as per the guidelines in a prescribed form and submit it to the respective college supervisors/instructors. The college supervisors also prepare an assessment report regarding the performance of the students. In most of the schools of social work, assessment of fieldwork is done by the internal supervisor and viva-voce taken by the external examiner. In terms of internal assessment, the student is assessed on parameters such as honesty, sincerity, ability to establish and maintain professional relationships with clients, agency staff, co-workers etc.; attendance (attentiveness in fieldwork, individual and group conferences, workshops, submitting reports along with log sheets, maintaining a certain percentage of attendance in overall fieldwork activities etc.); theoretical knowledge of the fundamental concepts, philosophy, ethics and values, methods, principles, and skills and techniques of social work; knowledge about the agency/community, including its structure, functioning, policies, programmes and activities, services, clients, networking with other organizations, etc; performance in the field, for example, identification and assessment of needs/problems, ability to integrate theoretical knowledge with field practice (i.e., methods, principles, skills, techniques) in accordance with the learning plan and ability to utilize administrative skills, etc.); development of a professional attitude in terms of assigned tasks, programme planning and management, decision making, ability to work within agency limitations, willingness to accept mistakes and remedy them through practice learning instructions, sense of responsibility, and professional commitment, ability to adjust with co-workers, agency staff, clients, and/or community people, ability to work cooperatively; quality of reports that include clarity of learning plan, agency/community profile; narration of incidences, presentation of facts, mode of presentation of facts, ability to observe and analyse given situations, language and style of report writing etc.; and quality of content of the group conference paper, language, presentation style, clarity of the theme, tackling clarifications, and level of participation, etc. (University of Delhi, 2015, p. 17).

During the evaluation process, a student is assessed as to what extent he or she has meaningfully made use of classroom theory into practice in the field. It must reflect specific tasks and skill expectations, and definitive statements about the extent to which these expectations have been realized are provided. The student is expected to make use of various skills and techniques in the helping process, such as observation (client's demeanour, speech pattern), interest and concern (appropriate questions, attentive listening), warmth, support, and acceptance (use of humour, non-verbal expressions, appropriate reassurance), professional function and agency service (clear and concise interpretive statement, provide operational conception), inviting the client to identify and elaborate on concerns, needs, and expectations (use of appropriate 'what,' 'who,' and 'how' questions, focusing and partializing relating to manifest and latent content and to subtle nuances), and the establishment of mutually acceptable conditions for work and role responsibilities (inviting doubt, hesitation, clarifying role confusion and expectations, defining respective responsibilities) (Gitterman & Gitterman, 1979).

Assessment and evaluation in fieldwork: some essential guidelines

There are some gaps when assessing and evaluating the performance of the students. This section suggests some points to be incorporated in fieldwork evaluation and in general.

1   In order to evaluate the professional development of students, evaluation is done on various parameters, such as progress on the work, regularity, and punctuality maintained in the field; individual conferences,

ESSENTIAL GUIDELINES AND TECHNIQUES

group conferences, and related assignments; quality of reports submitted; use of theoretical application in the field; and self-evaluations written by the students. Strong emphasis should also be given on detailed descriptions of changes in a student's perception and beliefs over time in view of the code of conduct of the social work profession. Kaudshin and Harkness suggested that such descriptions could include the student's awareness of his or her emotional response to various situations, conflicts experienced during various situations in the field, and application of social work principles to resolve the conflicts. A student needs to constantly observe and carefully examine his or her thoughts and feelings during fieldwork. This would be a step towards self-awareness. Self-awareness will enhance a person's adherence to the values and principles of the social work profession. Self-awareness is of prime importance to the supervisee and practitioner, as client problems can affect the emotional wellbeing of a worker, and this in turn can adversely affect the helping relationship (Kaudshin & Harkness, 2002, p. 41). In order to achieve self-awareness, Bist Swati has recommended that a few classes on yoga and meditation techniques could be introduced and encouraged for social work students. This would enable the students to pay attention and check their thought processes during interactions in the field and personal life situations (Bist, 2015, p. 107). Such sessions could be included in skills development workshops.

2 Though the schools of social work have their own fieldwork expectations from the students, there is no clearly written fieldwork curriculum that would benefit students by proving an understanding of the required learning goals in the beginning of the field placement. Later during the evaluation, it would help the supervisor to assess to what extent the student is able to achieve these learning goals. Shardlow and Doel (1996) have also recommended some of the advantages of having a fieldwork curriculum: The requirement of social work practice can shape the content of what is learned by students through a practice curriculum; students are empowered through the existence of an explicit written practice curriculum by having an understanding of the required learning at the start of the placement; and practice teachers are empowered through the development of the curriculum as a common currency so there is an opportunity for and a reason to become connected with each other. In addition, it is possible to organize practice learning so that simple or core skills, basic knowledge, or fundamental values are learned before the more complex elements are attempted. It is possible with a practice curriculum to know when learning has been achieved in given areas, and then to move on to other components of the curriculum or to find ways to compensate for deficiencies in the learning environment. The curriculum allows

for a range of different learning opportunities and learning methods to be used – this can be well organized and planned before the start of the placement, and the examination of practice competence can be structured and harmonized to fit with the pace of learning (Shardlow & Doel, 1996, p. 80).

3 When the student is placed in an agency under the direct supervision of an agency supervisor, he or she directly observes and assesses how the student is demonstrating competencies while dealing with the client/agency, whether he or she is sensitive towards the culture, customs, feeling, beliefs, and other issues and concerns of the client. However, during the final evaluation of the student, no role of importance has been delegated to the agency supervisor. Apart from eliciting feedback from the agency supervisor, if they could be involved in assigning marks (some percentage should be decided by the institution) to the students or given the opportunity to write their remarks in the evaluation form, this would be more meaningful when evaluating the students. Another important aspect is that the college and the agency should develop clearer and more mutually understandable concepts of generic social work practice through reciprocal and collaborative testing of experiences in the college as well as in allotted placement agencies. There should be an exchange of ideas on social work education between both the supervisors. Professor Agnimitra has also suggested that agency supervisors supervising students for the first time should be assisted to attend seminars on field instruction. These sessions could facilitate the integration of field and classroom experiences, as field supervisors are given access to syllabi, course outlines, bibliographies, curriculum statements, field manuals, and other relevant documents. Agency supervisors can also be integrated within consultative committees and advisory boards to provide input and feedback on the overall educational curriculum and field practicum component (Agnimitra, 2015, p. 46).

4 During the orientation programme and observation visit, it has been observed that many students miss orientation programmes and then compensate with assignments (given by the faculty supervisor) in order to complete fieldwork hours. Similarly, during group conferences, the students who are more vocal are repeatedly given more opportunities to perform the role of chairperson and recorder. In such a situation, the students who are sincere but not very vocal are ignored. It is therefore necessary to encourage and motivate each student to actively participate in such conferences and to be regular in attending orientation programmes. Another way of ensuring complete participation is that they could be evaluated by allotting marks.

5 Preparation for evaluation should begin early in the placement, once the student has been allotted a faculty supervisor. The student should

ESSENTIAL GUIDELINES AND TECHNIQUES

have a fair idea of his or her strengths and weaknesses as he or she goes along. The final evaluation should bring into focus the various components already discussed and a review of growth since the beginning of the placement. The supervisor's feedback about the student's functioning should never come as a surprise to the student at the evaluation session; rather, it should be participatory. At least one week before, the supervisor should discuss the upcoming evaluation with the student, give an explanation about the standards and expectations for the level of education, deal with any anxiety, and explain the outline that will be used. When meeting for the evaluation, both the supervisor and learner need to objectively assess the learner's learning outcomes. Professor Agnimitra is also of the view that during evaluation, students need to be guided to realistically and objectively reflect on their performance and learning. The supervisor should counsel the supervisee to help them improve on aspects found unsatisfactory, to strive towards optimization of learning, and to accept criticism positively. She also suggested that an upgrading of supervisory skills and competence through refresher and capacity building modules for the supervisors are therefore mandated (Agnimitra, 2015, p. 47).

6   One more aspect which has been raised by Williamson and generally overlooked while evaluating a student's effectiveness in his or her fieldwork placement is the role played by the agency and the supervisor. To what extent and in what ways have the agency's procedures and arrangements, and the supervisor's activity or busyness with other responsibilities, contributed to a student's poor showing? Were the assignments made by the agency appropriate to the student's level at the time he or she entered the placement? Was he or she given adequate support? Were the orientation and preparation given by the agency sufficient and appropriate? What has the agency done to help with the difficulties? "Evaluation should not proceed apart from some consideration of these factors" (Williamson, 1961).

7   Some schools of social work have collaborations with overseas universities and have a student exchange programme in fieldwork. Such programmes enhance the understanding of students of how social workers in other countries are assisting clients to understand and accept various problems and situations. How they are assisting a client in clarifying a problem or resolving a conflict, and how they are empowering the client to make their own decisions and actively solve the problem? It is a unique opportunity to gain insights into new culture, observe social work in a different milieu, and learn to be sensitive and work with another country's social workers with different values and attitudes. When coming back to their own country, students can share their knowledge with other students and faculty

and can address differences and similarities in ethical issues in the two cultures. If such exchange programmes are given space, it would make the programme holistic in all aspects.

Conclusion

There is no doubt that fieldwork prepares students for professional practice in social work and the supervisor plays a vital role in the professional development of a new practitioner. A supervisor generally assesses and evaluates the student's level of learning and capacity to adapt to the complexities of the various problems confronted in the field and various parameters, components, and guidelines provided by the institution. Evaluation can be a positive and productive learning experience for both student and supervisor if approached with adequate preparation on both sides. In the process of evaluation, students should also become accountable at all levels, that is, of the clients' needs and the satisfaction of those needs, of the effectiveness of the agency, and of the effects of intervention on the community/clientele group. This chapter has attempted to address the evaluation criteria followed by schools of social work and identify some gaps in assessing and evaluating students in their fieldwork.

Notes

1 CSWE is the accrediting agency for social work education in the United States.
2 The pradhan is head of the village.
3 Anganwadi workers are the basic functionaries of the Integrated Child Development Services (ICDS is an Indian government welfare programme).
4 The self-help group is a village-based financial intermediary committee usually composed of 10 to 20 local residents.

References

Agnimitra, N. (2015). Field work in the contemporary context: Vision and engagement. *Journal of Social Work Education, Research and Action, 1*(1), 28–49.
Billig, S. (1971). Some elements in supervisor evaluation of field work students. *The Journal of Education, 153*(3), 66–72. Retrieved February 8, 2016, from www.jstor.org/stable/42772998
Bist, S. (2015). Social work education for undergraduate students: Issues and challenges in field work. *Social Work Journal, 6*(1), 103–113.
Bogo, M., & Vayda, E. (1998). *The practice of field education in social work* (2nd ed.). Toronto: University of Toronto Press.
Canadian Association of Schools of Social Work. (2000). *Board of accreditation manual.* Retrieved February 2, 2016, from http:// www.cassw-acess.ca/ xACCR/aclx2.html
Caspi, J., & William, J. R. (2002). *Educational supervision in social work.* New York, NY: Columbia University Press.

Cook, V. (2011). The origins and development of geography fieldwork in British schools. *Geography, 96*(2), 69–74.

Council on Social Work Education. (1994). *Hand book of accreditation standards and procedures* (4th ed.). Alexandria, VA: Author.

Council on Social Work Education. (2008). *Purpose: Social work practice, education, and educational policy and accreditation standards.* Retrieved December 1, 2016, from www.cswe.org/File.aspx?id=13780

Dash, B. M., & Roy, S. (2015). Field work practice in social work education: Major components, issues and challenges. In B. M. Das and S. Roy (Eds.), *Field work in social work education: Contemporary practices and perspectives.* New Delhi: Atlantic Publishers.

Dsouza, H. (2014). Field instruction in social work education (Unpublished PhD Theses), Submitted at Tata Institute of Social Sciences in School of Social Sciences, pp. 3–21. Retrieved February 8, 2016, from http://hdl.handle.net/10603/21385

Gore, M. S. (1957). *Fieldwork supervision in an Indian school of social work.* New Delhi: Delhi School of Social Work.

Gitterman, A., & Gitterman, N. P. (1979). Social work student evaluation: Format and method. *Journal of Education for Social Work, 15*(3), 103–108. Retrieved February 8, 2016, from www.jstor.org/stable/23038937

Global Definition of Social Work, IFSW & IASSW. (2014). Retrieved November 30, 2016, from http://ifsw.org/get-involved/global-definition-of-social-work/

Hipp, J., & Munson, C. (1995). The partnership model: A feminist supervision/consultation perspective. *The Clinical Supervisor, 13*(1), 23–38.

International Definition of Social Work, IFSW & IASSW. (2000). Retrieved November 30, 2016, from http://ifsw.org/policies/statement-of-ethical-principles/

Jamia Millia Islamia University. (2015). *Field work manual for masters of social work.* New Delhi. Retrieved April 5, 2017, from http://jmi.ac.in/upload/menu upload/field_work_manual_msw_2015.pdf

Job, D. (1996). Geography and environmental education: An exploration of perspectives and strategies. In A. Kent, D. Lambert, M. Naish, & F. Slater (Eds.), *Geography in education: Viewpoints on teaching and learning* (pp. 22–49). Cambridge: Cambridge University Press.

Job, D. (1999). *Beyond the Bikesheds: Fresh approaches to fieldwork in the school locality.* Sheffield: Geographical Association.

Kaudshin, A., & Harkness, D. (2002). *Supervision in social work.* New York: Columbia University Press.

Kent, A., & Foskett, N. (2000). Fieldwork in the school geography curriculum: Pedagogical issues and development. In R. Gerber & K. C. Goh (Eds.), *Fieldwork in geography: Reflections, perspectives and actions* (pp. 171–193). Dordrecht: Kluwer Academic Publisher.

Kent, M., Gilbertson, D. D., & Hunt, C. O. (1997). Fieldwork in geography teaching: A critical review of the literature and approaches. *Journal of Geography in Higher Education, 21*(3), 313–332.

Lai, K. C. (1999). Freedom to learn: A study of the experiences of secondary school teachers and students in a geography field trip. *International Research on Geographical and Environmental Education, 8*(3), 239–255.

Lai, K. C. (2000). Affective-focused geographical fieldwork: What do adventurous experiences during field trips mean to pupils? In R. Gerber & K. C. Goh (Eds.), *Fieldwork in geography: Reflections, perspectives and actions* (pp. 145–169). Dordrecht: Kluwer Academic Publisher.

Lai, K. C. (2006). Fieldwork and outdoor education for environmental and geographical education for sustainability. In C. K. J. Lee & M. Williams (Eds.), *Environmental and geographical education for sustainability: Cultural contexts* (pp. 155–171). New York, NY: NOVA Science Publishers, Inc.

Livingston, D., Davidson, K., & Marshack, E. (1989). Education for autonomous practice: A challenge for field educators. *Journal of Independent Social Work, 4*(1), 69–82.

Lonergan, N., & Andresen, L. W. (1988). Field-based education: Some theoretical considerations. *Higher Education Research and Development, 7*(1), 63–77.

Munowenyu, E. (2002). Fieldwork in geography: A review and critique of the relevant literature on the use of objectives. *The Journal of Doctoral Research in Education, 2*(2), 16–31.

Nasreen, A. (2015). Challenges in supervision of differently-abled student: A case study from social work field practicum. *Journal of Social Work and Development Issues, 4*, 76–84.

Rogers, G., & McDonald, L. (1995). Expedience over education: Teaching methods used by field instructors. *The Clinical Supervisor, 13*(2), 41–65.

Shardlow, S., & Doel, M. (1996). *Practice learning and teaching.* London: Macmillan Press Ltd.

Shulman, L. (2005). Signature pedagogies in the profession. *Daedalus, 134*(3), 52–59.

Singh, R. R. (1985). *Field work training in social work education.* New Delhi: Concept Publishing House.

Singla, P. R. (2015). Fieldwork as signature pedagogy of social work education: As I see it! *Social Work Journal, 6*(1), 90–102.

Stimpson, P. (1995). Fieldwork in geography: A review of purpose and practice. *New Horizons in Education, 36*, 85–93.

Subhedar, I. S. (2001). *Fieldwork training in social work.* Jaipur: Rawat Publications.

Taylor, I. (1993). Self-directed learning and social work education: A critical analysis. *Issues in Social Work Education, 23*(1), 3–24.

Twikirize, J. M., & Tusasiirwe, S. (2015). *Social work fieldwork: Guidelines for students and supervision.* Kampala: Fountain Publishers.

UGC. (2001). *Social work education model curriculum report.* New Delhi: University Grants Commission.

University of Delhi. (2015). *Syllabus for undergraduate programme, department of social work.* New Delhi: University of Delhi. Retrieved February 5, 2016, from www.du.ac.in/uploads/Administration/AC/10072015/.../10072015_Annexure-59.pdf

Williamson, M. (1961). *Supervision – new patterns and processes.* New York, NY: Association Press.

7

CONTEMPORARY FIELD-LEVEL NEEDS AND ESSENTIAL STRATEGIES IN SOCIAL WORK PRACTICUM

Asok Kumar Sarkar and Indranil Sarkar

Introduction

Professional social work education has an 80-year history in India, though it has started long before in the UK and United States. Social work education cannot be realistic without field-level learning. Fieldwork in social work is all about the concept of 'learning by doing.' According to Garrett (1959), fieldwork in social work is vital as the new social worker learns to deal with the dynamics of human personality in the context of individual needs. Mallick (2007) states that the fieldwork curriculum exposes students to a variety of problems and helps them develop as a professional person. Agnimitra (2015) feels that fieldwork is the signature pedagogy of students to validate and corroborate classroom teaching and to be engaged with the social-political realities. In fact, field-level learning enables the new social worker to develop skills and helps them to become professionally competent (Sarkar, 2011). In the early days, the social work education system in India followed the US model, which was clinical, micro-based and curative in nature (Mandal, 1989; Devi Prasad and Vijayalakshmi, 1997). But in a country like India with vibrant cultures and a multi-layered social strata the Western perspectives did not fit properly. The University Grants Commission (UGC) undertook an initiative to give a better shape to the social work education system and hence formed review committees in 1960,[1] 1975,[2] and 1990.[3] It also published a Model Curriculum Report[4] in 2001. Despite this, as of today, any uniform curriculum for field-level learning is neither observed nor suggested in the Indian schools of social work. It is vital to have a uniform fieldwork curriculum, but of course with a focus on zone-specific or culture-specific problems and contemporary professional requirements (i.e., markets of professional social workers).

Contemporary field-level needs

A quick survey of *The New Social Worker*, a social work careers magazine,[5] details the expectations, difficulties, and perceptions of many social work students, new graduates, and field placement issues. Again, our experiences in the Indian context, which we get very frequently from our graduated students, add many field-level realities.

When the new social workers of Indian schools of social work get new jobs, they face multiple problems as they deal with the social issues using the tools and strategies they have learned during their education, which were mostly orthodox and were not relevant to the contemporary field-level needs. Most of the time the organizations need to train the new social workers after their appointment to make them capable, to groom them, and to orient them on the approach the organization follows. Thus, social work education should include space for practising several essential strategies, which are highly relevant for new social workers to survive in the development sector. This chapter discusses eight strategies in detail to clarify why the Indian social work field needs them. All these strategies are modern, are systematic, and will give the new social workers a lens for looking into the current social issues and will help them to work effectively.

Essential strategies

Rights-based approach

In India, social work education initially followed the American model. With time, several new approaches in terms of action and style of thinking emerged. In the late 1990s, a very relevant approach to social work (i.e., rights-based approach) originated. According to UNFPA,[6] a rights-based approach to development is a framework that integrates the norms, principles, standards, and goals of the international human rights system into the plans and processes of development. A rights-based approach seeks to identify the disadvantaged individuals, groups, and communities and tends to investigate why their rights are violated. According to Boesen and Martin (2007), a rights-based approach identifies rights-holders and their entitlements and corresponding duty bearers and their obligations, and works to strengthen the capacity of duty bearers to comply with their obligations and rights-holders to claim and exercise their rights.

Before 1997, most UN development agencies pursued a 'basic needs' approach, and now they work to fulfil the rights of people. As a strategy, it can be very useful for the ground-level workers, as it orients them to understand the basic rights of any human being and trains them to protect those rights. The human rights are designed in such a manner that they directly promote the wellbeing of people, which coincides with the philosophy of social work education. For the new social workers and the professional social workers, a rights-based approach can be a perfect framework to understand and take in the social policies at the national and international level, as those are also framed to fulfil only basic human needs.

Social work education talks about dealing with any sort of problem which creates a hindrance in the proper functioning of an individual, group, or community. Social workers are meant to deal with problems related to women, children, youth, elders, etc. Thus, the student social workers must be trained in such a way that they should be able to deal with any of these issues. It will be better if a framework is provided during the training period in the field so that they can easily understand and deal with the problems in the future. A rights-based approach can provide such a framework. If students are trained to use the lens of a rights-based approach, they will be able to understand what rights are getting violated and how an individual, group, or community can be empowered by protecting and demanding their rights. For instance, a child who is working in the shops or staying in the streets actually has multiple rights violated: right to education, right to care, and right to protection; in case of genital feticide, the right to life is getting violated; in case of students dropping out, the right to education is getting violated. In a similar manner, in every aspect of social work, some sort of right is being violated. To deal with these social issues, if the student social workers practise using the framework of a rights-based approach, they will be able to prepare a plan. They will be able to locate the stakeholders and the steps which need to be taken.

Evidence-based practice

The core concept of evidence-based practice has always been in social work education from the beginning, as it was noticed in the process of casework (study, diagnosis, intervention, evaluation, and termination). It was always been appreciated in social work to collate theories and field experiences before planning and implementing any action. Gibbs and Gambrill (2002) stated that basing social work practice on research evidence is an important ethical mandate. In a real sense in the late 1990s it took the form of an inter-disciplinary approach with the core components (best available research evidence, clinical expertise, and client's preferences).

According to Sackett et al. (1997), evidence=based practice is the conscientious, explicit, and judicious use of current best evidence in making decisions about the care of individuals. The approach deals with social issues based on ground-level facts and data in a very collaborative manner with the client throughout the process. It gives the priority to the clients and their own values and expectations while involving them actively in the decision-making process (Gambrill, 1999).

Davies and Nutley (2002) noted that two major strategies to dissemination and implementation of best practices have been used, namely macro- (top-down) and micro- (bottom-up) strategies. Macro-strategies are not based on the felt need of the target group and are not formulated from the ground-level reality, but rather are based on the upper level, which keeps the effectiveness of the policies low. To increase the effectiveness of the policies, a micro-level strategy is needed. The social work practitioners need to be engaged with the micro-level strategy development using evidence-based practice for critical decision making with clients.

The practitioners and student social workers need to engage in evidence-based practice for information gathering, analysis, and decision making with clients and for using critical thinking skills (Gambrill, 1999). Evidence-based practice can be used as a framework for dealing with contemporary social issues. Social workers must be trained with evidence-based practice for developing practice guidelines, manuals, toolkits, and other forms currently used to translate evidence into practice prescriptions; information retrieval and critical assessment skills; systematic review methods, data syntheses, and meta-analytic procedures; methods of social intervention research as a process for developing, testing, refining, and disseminating scientifically validated social work practices; foundations of scientific thinking; research and evaluation methods, as well as quantitative and qualitative modes of inquiry and analysis; and skills for adapting general research findings and guidelines to individualized client circumstances, preferences, and values (Mullen, 1978; Mullen & Bacon, 2003). The social workers who use evidence-based practice need to have the habit of practising EBP reflexively, learn how to phrase empirically answerable questions, learn how to search the empirical literature, learn how to evaluate cutting-edge evidence found in the empirical literature, and learn how to apply evidence in conjunction with professional judgment and client factors (Drake, Jonson-Reid, Hovmand, & Zayas, 2007).

One major obstacle to the use of evidenced-based treatments is their near absence in many training programmes for psychologists, social workers, and residency training programmes for psychiatrists, though some training is provided in the countries like Canada, Great Britain, Holland, Iceland, Germany, and Spain (Weissman & Sanderson, 2001). Training is generally absent in current social work educational programmes. In the immediate future evidence-based practice training must be provided for both new social workers and professional social workers already in practice. For the students, training needs to be organized by the educational institutes, and for the latter group, training opportunities need to be made available by the employing organizations without maintaining any ideological barriers.

Social network analysis

The social network is an integral part of the society which provides social support to individuals. Human beings, being social animals, prefer to avoid isolation. When we talk about social work, it mainly deals with the situations which create a hindrance in the proper functioning of the individuals or groups or communities in dealing with such situations – social networking seems to be a vital part of social work education. The idea of a social network is not new. It was introduced to the social sciences by John Barnes in 1954 as an alternative means of understanding the structure and organization of a rural Norwegian community, yielding greater insights into the behaviour of village people than the examination of social institutions or social roles (Barnes, 1954).

In order to understand the pattern of a relationship or interaction, there is a need to analyse the social network of an individual, group, or community. The social network tends to interpret the social behaviour of any particular individual or the behaviour of other people with whom one is not directly in contact (Mitchell, 1969). Social network analysis investigates the access between members, the level of membership interconnectedness and how far network connections extend, their reciprocations, the durability of the network, the intensity of obligation and reliance felt by members, and frequency of contact between members.

Social work practice teaches us to understand the people and communities and to recognize their needs, problems, and dynamics at both the macro and micro level. Social network analysis can be used as a tool for in-depth understanding about the community and people's day-to-day lives, which include their lifestyle, overlapping networks, complexity of community, social influences, etc. New and established social workers alike must be trained in using social network analysis as a tool. It will be beneficial for research, as well as project designing and implementing plans in a much more effective manner with fewer errors. Social workers must deal with multiple target groups and various social issues affecting their lives, and hence social network analysis can occur at many conceptual levels (i.e., individuals, families, communities, and organizations). It can be used to develop the social network, to identify causes of disfunction, and to promote cohesion or to understand the pattern of a relationship or interaction.

Innovation

In layman's language, innovation is all about creating or developing a new concept or idea. In science, we often see the use of the term innovation, and it has become the ultimate key for satisfying needs of present-day humans. In the race for survival, multi-national companies are fully dependent on the innovation, research, and development team. When it comes to social work education, innovation is not considered a useful tool. The continuing gap between research and practice has long been a problem in social work (Herie & Martin, 2002) and has been well documented (Chavkin, 1993; Epstein, 1996; Hess & Mullen, 1995).

There is a critical need to bridge the practice and research gap. In social work education, research has a vital role to play for identifying the issues, the reasons, and the consequences of particular social issues, and it can be done only with the support of fieldwork practice. This amalgamation will generate the concept of innovation in social work education. There are compelling reasons for the social work profession to take steps collectively to bridge the research–practice gap (Herie & Martin, 2002). Innovation is viewed as the application of better solutions that meet new requirements, unarticulated needs, or existing market needs (Maryville, 1992).

Innovation can be a very important strategy for social work students and for professionals as well. The new social workers must be trained to practice innovation during their under graduation or post-graduate studies so that they can practise while working in various organizations with various social problems in all levels. It is important for social workers to continue the process of innovation during challenging situations, as it can help them deal with situations in a very systematic, simple, and scientific manner. Innovation can improve or replace theoretical or traditional methods of social work to increase efficiency and productivity with different and changing communities and individuals. It can extend the quality of the service, adding new values to social work education. Innovation is a creative and continuous process. The new social workers must be trained to get ideas from communities, individuals, research and development workers, universities, and other sources of new technologies. The new social workers need to filter those ideas and identify those that the profession will focus on. By utilizing innovation as a strategy, new social workers and professional social workers alike can improve productivity, achieve optimal resource utilization, build the value of the service, and establish new partnerships and relationships.

Advocacy

Social work advocacy is the exclusive and mutual representation of a client(s) or a cause in a forum, attempting to systematically influence decision making in an unjust or unresponsive system(s). Advocacy was identified as a professional role as far back as 1887 (Schneider, Lester, & Ochieng, 2008). Social work education promotes the culture of advocacy and carries forward the intuition among its followers to uphold the voice of the unheard or the underprivileged section of society. Social work uses advocacy while dealing with individuals, families, groups, and communities as target beneficiaries. As stated by Freddolino, Moxley, and Hyduk (2004),

> the purpose of advocacy within the profession is to improve the social status of individuals who may be considered vulnerable or oppressed, thereby enhancing their standing within a specific social system whether it is a community, organization, service system, societal institution, or society itself.
>
> (p. 119)

While doing so, if the person is not aware of the process, it can malfunction. Thus, there is a need for the new social workers and professional social workers alike to adopt and understand the approach of advocacy and develop a certain set of skills before engaging in advocacy in actual practice. Advocates must possess an appropriate level of skill and expertise in order to perform their role effectively (Carlisle, 2000).

The educational institute is responsible for developing the skill required by new social workers during BSW and MSW study using a fieldwork curriculum. Regarding professional social workers, the organizations should train them to use the advocacy model. According to Schneider et al. (2008), as client and societal needs evolve, universities should emphasize advocacy in their curricula, and the National Association of Social Workers should promote electoral and legislative initiatives that reflect an emphasis on social and economic injustices. It should be noted that many new social workers opt to become social activists and directly work to change the social setting, and in such situations advocacy becomes very important. Inexpert application of advocacy may cause social tension at the macro level for social activists.

Advocacy in social work practice develops a range of macro knowledge, skills, and values needed to analyse and assess organizations, communities, social policies, and political systems as they relate to the welfare of the individuals, groups, and communities. Social work education must include advocacy to teach students how to formulate macro interventions, advocate for, and work collaboratively in change and capacity building processes within organizations and communities and to influence social policies and political processes that affect the everyday lives and opportunities of clients. In addition, the course seeks to deepen students' understanding of distributive justice, human and civil rights, and the dynamics of oppression, as well as the saliency of advocacy and social change action in the pursuit of social and economic justice through responsible organizational, community, policy, and political practice. This will expand the knowledge base regarding the dynamics of privilege, systemic evaluation, and monitoring of the impact of their own practice within and across system levels; power and oppression; and the ways in which the interests, traditions, and expectations of culturally diverse clients coincide and collide with the interests, traditions, and expectations of relevant organizational actors, community leaders, and social policy makers.

Multi-cultural approach

There is a plurality of cultures and traditions in India. People's culture, ritual, tradition, lifestyle, and even the languages change almost in every district. As per the provisions of Article 14 to 18 of the Constitution of India, everyone holds equal rights and position as a citizen, and thus the concept of multi-culturalism is incorporated in the constitution of the country (Basu, 2007). Multi-culturalism refers to a society that is characterized by ethnic or cultural heterogeneity and by an ideal of equality and mutual respect among a population's ethnic or cultural groups (Burnet, 1988). The value base of social work coincides with an ideology of multi-culturalism which emphasizes the right of all individuals to live according to their own cultural values and beliefs as long as they do not infringe on the rights of others (Seebaran & McNiven, 1979).

Every discipline of education has its own paradigm, and the paradigms are developed for every discipline and are transferred from one generation to another. In the case of social work, a multi-cultural approach can be a useful and effective paradigm or strategy. The target of the social work practitioners can be anyone from any kind of background, and thus the new social workers need to be trained to use the multi-cultural approach as a tool to think critically. At the same time the new social workers who are in the process of becoming professionals also come from different cultures; often they unconsciously hold preconceived notions which hinder their future work as professionals. Inclusion of multi-cultural approach in the training also helps them overcome their own personal biases. Social work practice in India cannot ignore the multi-cultural aspect of its communities. We need to consider on what assumptions education for practice in a multi-cultural society should be built. The new social workers must be trained to work in the rural and urban areas of the country, which are actually going a through a transition period and are having difficulty adapting to the latest technologies and other different developmental issues. At present, the country is full of violence because of political, religious, and ideological differences. Social

CONTEMPORARY FIELD-LEVEL NEEDS

workers need to understand those differences in detail in order to deal with them effectively to identify the core problems and resolve them. Multi-culturalism needs to be included for developing a strong and well-integrated practice-oriented research component using the multi-ethnic/multi-cultural community as a field laboratory. According to Good-enough (1963), communities can be understood by five dimensions of individual and public cultures: language, principles of action, concepts, beliefs, and values. By using a multi-cultural approach, social workers will be able to understand the communities of different backgrounds effectively, which will help to group similar communities and understand their strengths and weakness in a scientific manner. Social work with a multi-cultural approach in a nation like India will promote equality – equality of opportunity (Seebaran & McNiven, 1979).

Risk and resilience perspective

Social work professionals are trained to deal with individual, group, and community-level problems, which mainly include decreasing the risk factors and increasing the resilience capacity of an individual or group or community to cope with difficult situations. The risk and resilience framework is useful for understanding ways in which individuals face adversity. It emerged in the mid-1980s to prevent childhood and youth problems such as school failure, delinquency, and substance abuse (Hawkins, Jenson, Catalano, & Lishner, 1988). Social workers are supposed to identify both the risk and resilience and decrease the risk by promoting the resilience capacity.

Promoting resilience means to develop self-esteem, self-efficacy, and capacity to cope with life challenges. The risk and the resilience both are developed within a person because of multiple factors like socialization (child abuse, chronic family conflict, unskilled parenting, academic failure; peer rejection), environmental conditions, and socio-economic background (poverty, race, gender, health, culture, religion, education, accessibility of resources), as well as personal experiences (racism, sexism, other types of discrimination) (Coie et al., 1993; Kirby & Fraser, 1997). While dealing with a person in depression, a social work professional first must identify the source of the depression, which can be hidden in some past life experiences. Once the issue is identified, the person's resilience needs to be discovered, especially in terms of potential. This potential may be a source of resilience for the individual to cope effectively with depression. As the whole process is very dynamic, a risk and resilience perspective will give a framework for an effective and systematic outcome.

Werner (1990) reviewed several studies and described gender differences in child-rearing practices that differentially affected males and

131

females. Werner noted that resilience in girls was promoted by a few parenting styles that placed emphasis on risk taking, independence, and stable emotional support. For boys, resilience was also promoted by several parenting styles that provided higher degrees of supervision and structure, the presence of a male role model, and support for expressing emotions.

Resilience is closely tied to development. The skills and competences that characterize resilient functioning at one point in time may be obsolete in the face of new developmental challenges or new contingencies in the environment. The main aspects of resilience are being successful despite exposure to high risk, successfully adjusting to high-risk situations, and adjusting successfully to negative life events (Fraser, Richman, & Galinsky, 1999).

Social work departments and universities need to focus on the development of positive experiences during the training and the practice of social work, such as the capacity to be resilient. During the graduation and post-graduation period the new social workers should be trained with this perspective using role -lay in the class and fieldwork. The most important part of the exercise should be the process of promoting resilience within an individual with a problem. They must know that this perspective is one of the vital strategies of social work practice, and knowledge of risk, protection, and resilience has been used to inform curriculum content and intervention strategies aimed at preventing and treating a range of childhood and adolescent problem behaviours (Hawkins, 2006; Jenson, 2006).

Social policy perspective

In a democratic country like India, social policy acts as an integrated part of the administration to maintain the status of the welfare state of the nation. In India the citizens belong to different cultures, traditions, religions, languages, races, etc., and their needs are structured by these factors. In order to fulfil the needs and to improve the situation of deprived people, multiple social policies have been developed. Most of them are concerned with weaker and vulnerable sections of society such as the poor, women, children, disabled, backward classes, etc., so as to bring them on par with the rest of society. A social policy aims to bring such a society where inequalities are reduced to a minimum level.

Policies are the general guidelines or principles which give direction to a course of action by the government for the welfare of the citizens. Marshall (1965) states that social policies have a direct impact on the welfare of citizens by providing them with services or an income source. On the other hand, David Gill (1973) has pointed out the areas which are influenced by social policies in a positive manner, which are quality of life; living circumstances of individuals and groups; and the nature of intra-societal relationships among individuals, groups, and society as a whole. Pinker (1979) has argued that the objective of social policy is minimization of sufferings and maximization of welfare. Analysing all the statements, it's understood that the focus of the social policy is social justice.

Similar to social policy, social justice is a central goal of the social work profession (Weiss, Gal, & Katan, 2006). Social work education promotes social wellbeing, and there is always a need for a specific and effective tool for dealing with the social issues in the field. In such a situation, using a social policy perspective can be a very useful strategy for social workers. While working in the field, social policy can give professionals a basis to talk about the rights of the people, especially what is legally right and wrong. If the social worker is to recognize legal problems as 'legal,' it is obvious that he or she must possess some elementary legal knowledge; and if he or she is to refer his or her client to a solicitor, the social worker should have some knowledge of the legal aid system and perhaps of the competences of local solicitors (Phillips, 1979).

However, policy practice is still neglected in social work practice and in the professional socialization process (Weiss et al., 2006). It must be included in the training module of the social work education, which will provide a legal perspective for dealing with any situation and to develop a broad framework among the new social workers to work with the human rights issues and to maintain a welfare state. If the new social workers are oriented from a social policy perspective, they can educate people in the community who are unaware of the legal framework or provisions and they can help them access the services available for them. Policies like the national policy for women, the national policy for persons with disabilities, the national policy for mental health, and the national policy for older persons, etc., are few social policies which provide the new social workers with a base in their fight to promote justice for all.

A social policy perspective will enable new social workers to understand the frameworks, concepts, and language of social policy; develop an understanding of the links between social policy theory, ideology, policy, and practice; explore different perspectives on social policy and their implications for understanding and addressing major social problems in society; enhance critical thinking and a commitment to social justice; and enable them to understand the need of any social policy which should be developed and to work for its formulation. The new social workers should not be trained only to work with the existing social policies but also to critically examine them and the social situations for the modifications and formulation of the social policies.

They should also have practical knowledge about the strength of mass media; creation of public opinion; public interest litigation; discussions, meetings, and seminars; social planning; building pressure on government; signature campaigns, etc. In order to develop this understanding they can be placed in the courts, police stations, block development offices, panchayats, etc., for their fieldwork.

Conclusion

All eight strategies that have been discussed in this chapter have great potential for professional social work, but social work education will have the critical task of teaching the application of these strategies. Social work educators must become familiar with these and with the micro- to macro-level aspects of the social work practice where they can be applied to strengthen the discipline as a profession. Inclusion of these strategies in the social work education curriculum will make new social workers go through the process of need-based, scientific- and systematic professional socialization, which is an urgent need at present.

New social workers must be well equipped with new knowledge and innovations. They must have the urge to learn newest and best techniques to improve their skills in developing the quality of life of the individuals in a society. It will be beneficial for the social work professionals as well as social work educators to adopt these contemporary strategies. These strategies will provide support to the teaching methods of interventions in the classroom, as well as in the field. It will provide direction for social workers to deal with social problems in different contexts and situations.

Notes

1 The committee was appointed by the Ministry of Education and the University Grants Commission on 2 March 2, which was chaired by Dr. Radhakamal Mukerjee, and the report was published in 1965. The major points the review committee focused on were the importance of social work training, requirements of trained welfare personnel, recognition of training, teaching staff fieldwork, library facilities, coordination of training programme, and organization of social work education (Bhatt & Phukon, 2015).

2 The committee was appointed by the Ministry of Education and the University Grants Commission in 1975, and the report was published in 1980. The prime focus of the committee was to review critically the existing programmes of social work education, including courses, fieldwork, and research in relation to education at all levels and suggest changes with a view to making these programmes more meaningful and relevant and ways of effecting these changes. Other areas of focus were to study and suggest changes or modifications in such administrative matters as procedural problems, funding patterns, and relationship to the various academic structures in their respective universities; examine the present role of institutions for social work education in relation to the National Service Scheme and suggest ways in which they could help effectively in accomplishing the objectives of this scheme (Bhatt & Phukon, 2015).

3 The third committee on curriculum development was appointed in 1990.

4 The UGC Model Curriculum on Social Work Education was developed in 2001. The main purpose of the committee was to examine theoretical approaches of drafting/building a curriculum and to select a design to provide a frame to the curriculum. The committee was formed with the initiative of UGC and TISS, and the meeting was held in Mumbai (Bhatt & Pathare, 2015).
5 *The New Social Worker* magazine publishes articles on social work careers, social work education, social work ethics, technology, books, and more. It has been published quarterly since 1994. It was started by and is published and edited by Linda May Grobman, ACSW, LSW, a social worker with an interest in social work career development. It was published in print format until spring 2007. The magazine's primary focus is on career development for social workers and social work students at all levels. Retrieved 1 March 2019 from www.socialworker.com
6 UNFPA, The human rights-based approach. Retrieved 1 March 2019 from www.unfpa.org/human-rights-based-approach#sthash.9XUL64k4.dpuf

References

Agnimitra, N. (2015). Field work in the contemporary context: Vision and engagement. *Journal of Social Work Education, Research and Action*, 1(1), 28–49.

Barnes, J. (1954). Class and committees in a Norwegian Island Parish. *Human Relations*, 7, 39–58.

Basu, D. D. (2007). *Introduction to the constitution of India*. Agra: Adhwa and Company Law Publishers.

Bhatt, S., & Pathare, S. (2015). *Social work education and practice engagement*. New Delhi: Shipra Publications.

Bhatt, S., & Phukon, D. (2015). *Social work education in India: A resource book*. New Delhi: Alter Notes Press.

Boesen, J. K., & Martin, T. (2007). *Applying a rights-based approach: An inspirational guide for civil society*. Copenhagen: Danish Institute for Human Rights.

Burnet, J. (1988). *Multiculturalism. The Canadian Encyclopedia* (Vol. 3, p. 1401). Edmonton: Hurtig.

Carlisle, S. (2000). Health promotion, advocacy and health inequalities: A conceptual framework. *Health Promotion International*, 15(4), 369–376.

Chavkin, N. F. (1993). *The use of research in social work practice: A case example from school social work*. Westport, CT: Praeger.

Coie, J. D., Watt, N. F., West, S. G., Hawkins, J. D., Asarnow, J. R., Markman, H. J., . . . Long, B. (1993). The science of prevention: A conceptual framework and some directions for a national research program. *American Psychologist*, 48, 1013–1022.

Davies, H., & Nutley, S. (2002). *Evidence-based policy and practice: Moving from rhetoric to reality, Discussion Paper 2*, Scotland: St Andrews University, Research Unit for Research Utilization.

Drake, B., Reid, M. J., Hovmand, P., & Zayas, L. H. (2007). Adopting and teaching evidence-based practice in master's-level social work programs. *Journal of Social Work Education*, 43(3), 431–446.

Epstein, I. (1996). In quest of a research-based model for clinical practice: Or, why can't a social worker be more like a researcher? *Social Work Research*, 20, 97–100.

Fraser, M. W., Richman, J. M., & Galinsky, M. J. (1999). Risk, protection, and resilience: Toward a conceptual framework for social work practice. *Social Work Research*, 23, 131–143.

Freddolino, P. P., Moxley, D. P., & Hyduk, C. A. (2004). A different model of advocacy in social work practice. *Families in Society: The Journal of Contemporary Social Services*, 85(1), 119–128.

Gambrill, E. (1999). Evidence-based practice: An alternative to authority-based practice. *Families in Society: The Journal of Contemporary Human Services*, 80(4), 341.

Garrett, A. (1959). Learning through supervision. *Smith College Studies in Social Work*, 24(2).

Gibbs, L., & Gambrill, E. (2002). Evidence-based practice: Counterarguments to objections. *Research on Social Work Practice*, 12, 452.

Gill, D. (1973). *Unravelling social policy*. Cambridge, MA: Schenkman Publishing Co.

Goodenough, W. H. (1963). *Cooperation in change: An anthropological approach to community development*. New York, NY: Russell Sage Foundation.

Hawkins, J. D. (2006). Science, social work, prevention: Finding the intersections. *Social Work Research*, 30, 137–152.

Hawkins, J. D., Jenson, J. M., Catalano, R. F., & Lishner, D. L. (1988). Delinquency and drug abuse: Implications for social services. *Social Service Review*, 62, 258–284.

Herie, M., & Martin, G. W. (2002). Knowledge diffusion in social work: A new approach to bridging the gap. *Social Work*, 47(1), 85–95.

Hess, P. M., & Mullen, E. J. (Eds.). (1995). *Practitioner-researcher partnerships: Building knowledge from, in, and for practice*. Washington, DC: NASW Press.

Jenson, J. M. (2006). Advances and challenges in preventing childhood and adolescent problem behavior [Editorial]. *Social Work Research*, 30, 131.

Kirby, L. D., & Fraser, M. W. (1997). Risk and resilience in childhood. In M. W. Fraser (Ed.), *Risk and resilience in childhood: An ecological perspective*. Washington, DC: NASW Press.

Mallick, A. (2007). Field work training in social work curriculum: Reflections on learning and teaching. *The Indian Journal of Social Work*, 68(4), 573–580.

Mandal, K. S. (1989). American influence on social work education in India and its impact. *International Social Work*, 32(4), 303–309.

Mark, W. F., Richman, J. M., & Galinsky, M. J. (1999). Introduction: Risk, protection, and resilience: Toward a conceptual framework for social work practice. *Social Work Research*, 23(3), 131–143.

Marshall, T. H. (1965). *Social policy*. London: Hutchinson.

Maryville, S. (1992). Entrepreneurship in the business curriculum. *Journal of Education for Business*, 68(1), 27–31.

Mitchell, J. C. (1969). The concept and use of social network. In J. C. Mitchell (Ed.), *Social networks in Urban situations: Analyses of personal relationships in central African Towns*. Manchester: Manchester University Press.

Mullen, E. J. (1978). Construction of personal models for effective practice: A method for utilizing research findings to guide social interventions. *Journal of Social Service Research*, 2(1), 45–63.

Mullen, E. J., & Bacon, W. F. (2003). Practitioner adoption and implementation of evidence-based effective treatments and issues of quality control. In A. Rosen & E. K. Proctor (Eds.), *Developing practice guidelines for social work intervention: Issues, methods, and a research agenda*. New York, NY: Columbia University Press.

Phillips, A. (1979). Social work and the delivery of legal services. *The Modern Law Review, 42*(1), 29–41.

Pinker, R. (1979). *The idea welfare*. London: Heinemann.

Prasad, D. B., & Vijayalakshmi, B. (1997). Field instruction in social work education in India: Some issues. *The Indian Journal of Social Work, 58*(1), 65–77.

Sackett, D. L. et al. (1997). *Evidence-based medicine: How to practice and teach EBM* (2nd ed.). Edinburgh: Churchill-Livingstone.

Sarkar, A. (2011). Methods and techniques oriented field work training in social work. *Learning Community: An International Journal of Education and Social Development, 2*(3), 375–383.

Schneider, R. L., Lester, L., & Ochieng, J. (2008). *Advocacy, Encyclopedia of Social Work*. Oxford: Oxford University Press.

Seebaran, R., & McNiven, C. (1979). Ethnicity, multiculturalism and social work education. *Canadian Journal of Social Work Education, 5*(2/3).

Weiss, I., Gal, J., & Katan, J. (2006). Social policy for social work: A teaching agenda. *The British Journal of Social Work, 36*(5), 789–806.

Weissman, M. M., & Sanderson, W. C. (2001). *Promises and problems in modern psychotherapy: The need for increased training in evidence based treatments*. Prepared for the Josiah Macy, Jr. Foundation conference, on modern psychiatry: Challenges in educating health professionals to meet new needs, Toronto and Canada.

Werner, E. E. (1990). Protective factors and individual resilience. In S. M. Meisels & J. P. Shonkoff (Eds.), *Handbook of early childhood intervention*. New York, NY: Cambridge University Press.

8

STRENGTHENING 'FIELD' IN FIELD EDUCATION

Structural and functional issues in South Asian social work

Bala Raju Nikku, Bishnu Mohan Dash, and Zia Ullah Akhunzada

Introduction

South Asian social work, like that of the South Asian region, is very diverse, disjointed, and dynamic (Nikku, Udas, & Adhikari 2014). This chapter aims to contribute to the understanding of the role and implementation of field education in South Asia taking Nepal, India and Pakistan as case examples. Formal social work education in South Asia was introduced in 1930s but still struggles to gain its full legitimate professional space in the region.

'Field' in field education

Field supervision (that is, the supervision of students during their fieldwork placement), also known as fieldwork guidance and field education, is one of the most important learning arenas for the professional development of social work students. Hence, fieldwork is considered the 'signature pedagogy' of social work education, and much has been published about its significance by many social work scholars (Dhemba, 2012; Baum, 2012; Nikku, 2010). It is considered a 'signature pedagogy' because it has been a major contributor to the learners' preparation for actual professional practice. Among the key components of a fieldwork supervision, along with instruction, caseload management, and assessment, is the supervisory relationship itself, which plays a vital role in achieving the learning objectives of the field practicum (see Bogo, 2005; Lefevre, 2005).

One of the key tasks for the field education supervisor is to facilitate reflection (from the practice) and to promote a sense of ownership and understanding of fieldwork processes. At the same time the supervisor is expected to instruct, guide, assess, and evaluate the student's competencies required for professional development. Hence, the major challenge for the supervisor is to balance these two dimensions of supervision and maintain a focus on the student's experience rather than the supervisor's own expertise (Nikku & Kadambari, 2016). Further, Lizzio, Stokes, and Wilson (2005) describe the need to find "an appropriate balance between supervisory authority and supervisee autonomy, between evaluation and support and between transmission of required knowledge and the reflective engagement with the supervisees' experience" (p. 240).

The quality of fieldwork supervision and opportunities to practice are important components of social work education, as this provides the best opportunities for social work students to integrate classroom learning into practice. In addition, quality field instruction allows students to test their ideas and values, and hence it helps in self-awareness of the student and compatibility with social work as a career option.

Studies also documented that difficulties between students and supervisors may fester without resolution. The literature indicates that many students cope with problematic supervisory relationships through avoidance tactics remaining silent, getting by, diversion, minimizing complaints, and trying to cover up problems (Hutt, Scott, & King, 1983). Leaving supervision with unfinished goals that have not been discussed or worked through may have negative consequences for undergraduate social work students, who by definition are at the beginning of their professional development, and hence it is very crucial to help these troubled students attain a measure of psychological closure (Beike & Wirth-Beaumont, 2005). This will enable them to stop dwelling on the distressing event and move on with their professional development (Baum, 2012).

A community, an organization, an institution, or a family can be a 'field' in social work practice. It is this *field space* where the integrated action of field training, supervision, and learning takes place, keeping the best interests of both the student social worker (social work trainee) and the service user(s) within the purview of organizational policies and societal norms.

Social work field education in South Asia

In South Asian countries social work as a helping profession itself is seeking societal recognition. The first school of social work started in 1936 in India on the lines of the American model, and fieldwork has always been an integral part of the education. However, the development of social work as a profession and the education has taken different routes in the countries of the region. In this section we briefly present the status of social work education in India, Pakistan, and Nepal to illustrate the structural and functional issues of field education and then suggest ways forward in the following section of this chapter.

Indian context

The Indian Conference of Social Work (ICSW) in partnership with the Council on Social Work Education (CSWE) of the USA, through the Technical Cooperation Mission Programme, United States of America, shaped the Indian social work curriculum in its initial phase of 1940s (Adaikalam, 2014). Later the first and second review committees on social work education, the UGC Model Curriculum, and the NAAC Manual has emphasized greater role for fieldwork training in Indian social work. The Second Review Committee on Social Work Education (1980) prescribed the following objectives of fieldwork education: (1) development of professional skills through learning to use knowledge for the study and analysis of problems and selection of appropriate means to solve them; (2) development of skills in problem solving at micro and macro levels; (3) integration of classroom learning with field practice; (4) development of skills required for professional practice at the particular level of training; (5) development of professional attitudes, values, and commitment; and (6) development of self-awareness and professional ideals.

The University Grans Commission (UGC) provided a model curriculum on social work that is updated or revised once every ten years. The latest model curriculum (2001) is broad based and listed courses to be offered at the undergraduate and post-graduate level. As per the curriculum, a minimum of 15 hours of fieldwork is required per week. This has a weight of 40 per cent in social work education. The model curriculum has listed nine learning opportunities with specific objectives to develop and enhance professional practice skills among learners with a view to helping them acquire and practise skills. Some of the important objectives of the fieldwork practicum are as follows: (1) to develop the ability to observe and analyse the social realities; (2) to understand the characteristics of social systems and their dynamics; (3) to develop a critical understanding of the application of legislation, legal processes, and social policy; (4) to develop an understanding of organizational structures, resource management, and day-to-day administration for human service programmes, both developmental and welfare; (5) to develop the capacity to integrate knowledge and practice theory by participating in intervention; and (6) to enhance writing skills to document practice appropriately (UGC, 2001).

In order to achieve these objectives the UGC Model Curriculum (2001) has prescribed various fieldwork components, viz. orientation programme, agency visits, structured experience laboratory, rural camp, study tour, workshops for skill development, concurrent practice learning, summer placement, and block placement for effective fieldwork training in social work education.

The National Assessment and Accreditation Council (NAAC) has developed a *Manual for Self-Study of Social Work Institutions* which is the outcome of the proceedings of the National Seminar on Standards for Assessment of Quality in Social Work Education organized by the Tata Institute of Social Sciences during 11–13 November 2003. The manual gives an overall curriculum structure and allocates credits, hours, and marks for each component of social work education. It has set the standards for teaching-learning and evaluation, curricular aspects, research, consultancy and extension, infrastructure and learning resources, student support and progression, and organization and management of the social work institutions. The objectives for fieldwork as per the NAAC manual are as follows: (1) observation and understanding of the interaction between human behaviour and the social, economic, and political systems and systemic marginalization of vulnerable groups at the micro level; (2) development of critical self-awareness about one's attributes, values, and sensitivities with reference to the ideology of social justice and human rights and ethical requirements of social work profession through experience; and (3) learning and practise of social work methods and skills for the prevention and amelioration of social problems at micro and macro levels, administration of non-profit organizations and documentation, monitoring- and evaluation of one's social work intervention (NAAC, 2005).

The NAAC has prescribed a minimum of 15 hours for the fieldwork practicum, and marks for the fieldwork practicum should comprise at least one third of the total marks. The fieldwork practicum components suggested by NAAC are similar to the components listed by the UGC Model Curriculum (2001). The NAAC also suggested that the fieldwork manual covering the aims and objectives, components, role of faculty advisors, format for process and summary recordings, administrative rules, code of conduct and ethics, marks/credits, assessment criteria and procedure, and so on be distributed to all students and fieldwork supervisors at the beginning of the year.

Fieldwork education in India reflects a disappointing and sad state of affairs due to the unattended structural and functional issues. The theoretical curriculum is designed and well developed, but the consequent fieldwork exposure and practice in these domains is negligible due to the disconnect between the theory and practice. For example, theory courses taught on rural development, crime and correctional administration, personnel management, labour welfare, and industrial relations are adequate and well developed, but fieldwork exposure in these fields is very weak and suffers from number of limitations. So the student's fieldwork learning experience is adversely affected as they are not able to link to theory.

There are many other problems with fieldwork training across the Indian schools of social work (of which there are more than 600 currently), and these have been discussed and documented. These problems begin with the placement of students and end with the evaluation of the fieldwork performance. Finding suitable agencies, lack of competent professionals both in the schools and the agencies, the content of fieldwork and its suitability to the agency settings, the evaluation of the students' performance in fieldwork, etc., are a few noteworthy problems with the fieldwork setting in India (Lawani, 2002, p. 43).

The major problems of field instruction in India are found to be non-availability of field placements, lack of involvement of agencies in students' training, poor curricula design of field practicum and methods of assessment, non-availability of qualified agency-based field instructors, and lack of proper linkages between classroom teachings and realities in the field (UGC, 1980, pp. 56–58). In line with these observations, Professor R. R. Singh's writings reveal a very disappointing situation. He finds fieldwork is devoid of both conviction and commitment. Almost everything connected with fieldwork looks imperfect – for example, the goals are not precisely defined; faculty–student ratio is so large so as not to allow required supervision; non-observance of a minimum number of days of fieldwork; irregular and indifferent supervision of students, both individually and in groups; uncorrected or casually corrected records; inflated work hours; unplanned field placements; mismatch between the learner's capability and field assignments; inconsistencies in awarding grades or marks due to fear or favour; and deployment of students in institutions, settings, and organizations with little opportunities to learn. It is no wonder that problems in fieldwork abound and solutions are rarely explored. The situation in some of the lesser-known institutions of social work is such that fieldwork there is not even a ritual. The overarching reality of fieldwork education in general and lesser-known institutions in particular is best summed up by an informed academic on the subject (Singh, 1985, p. 179).

In addition to these issues, the lack of a uniform fieldwork programme among the schools of social work in India is also one of the important impediments in fieldwork education in social work. Some schools have three days a week concurrent fieldwork and others two days a week. Accordingly, some departments have introduced summer, placement, block placement, and rural camp, along with concurrent fieldwork, but others have opted for either one or two programmes as part of the field-work programme. Accordingly, some schools have an adequate students–teacher ratio to guide fieldwork programmes closely, whereas others have few teachers who supervise a large number of students. The lack of established norms of fieldwork and lack of clear-cut modules for fieldwork affect the quality of fieldwork education in India (Dash, 2017).

There are also departments without a proper agency to provide adequate fieldwork opportunities to trained students. However, the critical commentaries on the pattern of fieldwork being followed in most schools/departments of social work in the country suggest the 'marginality' and not the 'centrality' of practical-professional learning (Srivastava, 2005).

Dash (2017) further mentions fieldwork supervision/individual conferences is gradually becoming a routine in a number of schools of social work, particularly in those places where a teacher is expected to supervise about 20 students in addition to carrying out their duties. One of the problems for both for the agency and faculty supervisor is the amount of time given to the learners. Due to these structural and functional limitations Indian social work is still struggling to become a human rights profession of the 21st century (Nadkarni and Sinha, 2016).

Fieldwork education in Pakistan

Like in the Indian system, the role of fieldwork in social work teaching and discipline is indispensable and has played a vital role in the nurturing of Pakistani social workers. When Pakistan divided as a separate country from united India in 1947, few schools of social work in Pakistan developed their social work curriculum and training tools according to the country's new needs and culture. To this end, the universities offering social work degrees continued their focus on the role of fieldwork and continued to send students to conduct independent fieldwork to gain practical insights in the dynamics of society and social work practice. The students doing fieldwork are trained to use different intervention approaches and test their applicability and suitability in the Pakistani context. They are guided by external and internal supervisors. The internal supervisor is normally a faculty member of the department, whereas the external supervisor is in charge of the organization where they are placed for fieldwork. The Higher Education Commission (HEC) of Pakistan is the main regulatory body at the central level and has provided a comprehensive curriculum based on consultations and discussions with the social work academia across the country at universities offering a social work degree programme.

The latest attempt regarding revising the curriculum of social work education in the country was made in 2015. The objectives of the fieldwork as per the 2015 revised social work curriculum of HEC are (1) to know the historical background of the agency/organization; (2) to learn about the purpose, mission, vision, main objectives, and main areas of activities of the agency/organization; (3) to learn the NGOs and community based organisations registration process; (4) to study the socio-economic conditions and problems of individuals, groups, and communities under supervision of the agency/organization; 5) to learn various functions and skills, that is, planning the organization, motivation, mobilization, leading, coordination, controlling, decision making, evaluation, report writing and proposal writing, etc., through conducting welfare-oriented activities with coordination of agency/organization. The 2015 revised curriculum further enlists different special areas of interest for fieldwork. The areas include special education, zakat and usher (poverty alleviation), medical social work, parole and probation (criminology), forestry based social organizations, government social welfare institutes, local government, non-governmental organizations, psychiatric social work, drug addict rehabilitation, and child welfare and protection. Apart from these areas a growing number of students have also now started opting for other areas like women empowerment and welfare, disability services, labour welfare, rural and urban development, disaster management, and population welfare. Students practically learn and gain insight in these areas through active physical participation and observation. The HEC has put special emphasis and specified the guidelines in the curriculum for carrying out the fieldwork. The minimum requirement for fieldwork per the HEC is 150 to 170 hours in a single semester in any one of the areas. For the convenience of students and organizations, the departments are usually sending the students once or twice a week in addition to some block fieldworks. These students in different semesters, starting from fifth in the BS programme and third in the master's programme, are placed for fieldwork in these agencies in either individual or group settings. To assess students' performance, the following criteria have been formulated by the HEC: (1) schedule two days a week/block placement; (2) orientation visit to the agencies; (3) submission of reports to the supervisor; (4) supervision by academic and field agency supervisor; and (5) presentation by the student to the class, faculty, and the agency supervisor. Each department must nominate a faculty member to coordinate fieldwork activities and liaise with other members of the faculty and finalize the student's placement.

The assignments for the fieldwork require application of social work methods (i.e., casework, group work, community organization, social administration, and social research). The fieldwork coordinator is the focal person for all field-related activities. The HEC revised 2015 curriculum has enlisted these duties as follows: (1) establish rapport and keep in contact with the field supervisors; (2) organize field seminars and extend support and guidance to the students; (3) coordinate evaluations and presentations of the students; and (4) arrange transportation.

Structural issues

In practice, fieldwork is deemed crucial to social work. However, its value is compromised due to structural normative issues. The structural issues stem from general apathy towards fieldwork by the universities in general, and to social work departments in particular. The departments of social work, except for a few in large universities, were started as a periphery to other departments without any independent status. Most universities have ignored the social work discipline, and only few universities are offering different programmes of social work. Analysis of each university reveals that the social work department is mostly the least bothered with in terms of budgetary allocation, trained human resource, and physical infrastructure. Consequently, fieldwork activity has suffered a lot due to this lethargic attitude. The universities are lacking different facilities for the students of fieldwork. They are often not offering any transportation facility – as a result the students need to travel to distant areas on their own. The organizations are not in proximity to the universities. The students placed with NGOs suffer a lot more because most of the project offices of the NGOs are in the rural backward areas. This mobility problem has also affected the number of students choosing to study social work. Women especially are opting for subjects other than social work. For instance, in the Khyber Pakhtunkhwa province of Pakistan, different departments of social work other than the University of Peshawar failed to attract students. Most of these universities are in the far-flung districts with a low level of facilities. The average female student intake in the University of Malakand and Kohat University of Science & Technology, for example, is almost five students per year, which is very low. One of the major reasons in addition to a lack of proper facilities for carrying out the field practicum of social work is females in conservative Pakhtun culture can't move freely on their own. Hence, they are reluctant to join social work.

A dearth of fieldwork placement agencies is another problem faced by the social work departments in general, and by the departments of smaller universities in particular. The departments are experiencing problems in finding the right agency for their students. There are a very small number of public-sector organizations where students can be placed. The available ones are mostly overburdened, while the NGOs, due to their short-term projects, are unable to accommodate students at regular intervals because they keep on changing their project domains. Moreover, the public- sector organizations lack skilled staff members who can supervise the students and inculcate the true spirit of field practicum. They are not professional social workers in the strict sense because most of them hold degrees in a subject other than social work. Students in these less-professionalized institutions are not welcomed, which creates resentment among them.

Functional issues

The functional issues in the field practicum start with the non-availability of a comprehensive manual. It is a sad reality that none of the departments of social work across Pakistan have developed a field practicum manual, which is considered a cornerstone document. The only available document is the 2015 revised curriculum of HEC. The stakeholders of the field practicum are unaware of their role and responsibilities in the absence of this manual. This whole process of fieldwork is running on a trial-and-error basis because there are no proper guidelines. The modalities between the department and fieldwork agency are unclear, which obstructs the students in achieving their goals and they have to suffer. In addition, the field practicum is not a well-researched and discussed area of academic debate in Pakistan. There is rarely any study conducted on this very important aspect of social work.

Another issue relates to the internal fieldwork supervisor. The supervisor, who is also a full-time faculty member of the department, is usually too busy to spare time for supervision. He or she has many students and must teach their own courses as well. It is very difficult for him or her to give proper time to each student during the semester. It is also observed that some of the internal supervisors do not maintain proper communication with external supervisors. Hence, the objectives of the field practicum are seldom achieved. Furthermore, the external fieldwork supervisor, in most cases, is not aware of the philosophy of this practice. Consequently, the reports of the students are not up to the standard. In addition, social work is a value-based subject and demands strict adherence of the same from its professionals. However, the professionals working in different public- and private-sector agencies do not follow the principles and values of social work in totality. As a result, the students placed to them mostly fail to internalize these.

It was also stated in the interviews with social work colleagues that outlines of different courses of social work in Pakistani universities have become obsolete and need to be thoroughly revised to place Pakistani social work so that is not only nationally coherent but also useful for the region and relevant in the global context. The current social work courses have yet to be made contextual with Pakistani society; thus, they are not on par with the modern-day needs of Pakistani society, which is going through many cultural, economic, and political transitions. Hence, the students find it difficult to adjust and are losing their interest in the fieldwork.

There is also a lack of seriousness on part of the supervisors relating to the final evaluation of the field practicum. The evaluation is considered more like a formality, and hence pedagogical issues need to be addressed.

Field education in Nepal

Field preparation builds professional understanding, skills, and integrity so that social work graduates are prepared to meet their responsibility towards their clients, organizations, and society at large (see Shulman, 2005). The analysis presented in this section is based on the review of teaching materials and field education evaluation methods in Nepal in general, and at Nepal School of Social Work in particular. In addition, the section benefits from the first author's personal teaching experience and key interviews with selected social work colleagues from four affiliated colleges that are offering a bachelor level of social work education. The common expectation from the Social Workers Association of Nepal is that students, faculty, and practitioners are expected to acquire the following core competencies from their field practicum placements during their four years of study. Among other competencies, they should be able to (1) identify themselves as professional social workers and conduct themselves accordingly; (2) apply social work ethical practice principles to guide professional practice; (3) apply critical thinking to inform and communicate professional judgments; (4) Engage, assess, intervene, and evaluate with individuals, families, groups, organizations, and communities; (5) carry out research to influence policies and inform practice; and (6) advance and lobby for the protection of human rights through social, economic, political, and cultural justice. However, based on field evidence we argue that many structural and functional issues have yet to be addressed to meet the goal of nurturing competent social workers in Nepal.

There are issues with the curriculum standards. In addition, the primary job of the faculty supervisor (field liaison) is to see that students' practicum experiences are educational. But due to the severe crunch of trained social work faculty in departments of social work, the faculty supervisors are not able to fulfil their roles. According to the data collected during 2016, on average a department of social work hosts about 10 to 80 students, and only one to four fieldwork supervisors are employed, meaning each faculty member will have about 20 to 30 students under his or her supervision at any point. The faculty interviewed mentioned that they also have to teach at least two to four social work subjects, and hence there is practically no time left for them to do their individual research or do any quality fieldwork supervision. They do not have time to visit field placements, though it is expected and will influence the learning outcomes. It is evident that in Nepal, too, there exist similar issues discussed in India and Pakistan.

Ways forward

Social work educators throughout the South Asian schools of social work do recognize the crucial role that field education plays in the overall social work education and practice. The insights from India, Pakistan, and Nepal suggest that there are number of structural and functional issues yet to be addressed to achieve quality outcomes. Further attention and support from the regional and international social work organizations, curriculum development centres and other NGOs, civil society, and government agencies are needed to develop best practices, which then can be included in social work training. Most often the quality of fieldwork training, both within the schools of social work and in the 'field,' offered to the student leaves much to be desired. We recommend inclusion of the Socratic method in social work field education, which may offer better results given the lack of resources leading to structural and functional issues.

Socratic case: the dialogue method of teaching and field education

The Socratic method is a relevant framework for actively engaging students with the critical thinking process. The Socratic teacher is not 'the sage on the stage.' In the Socratic method, there are no lectures and no need for rote memorization. The Socratic teacher/supervisor is rather 'the guide on the side.'

In the Socratic method, the classroom and fieldwork experience is a shared dialogue between teacher and students in which both are responsible for pushing the dialogue forward through questioning. The 'teacher,' or leader of the dialogue, asks probing questions in an effort to expose the values and beliefs which frame and support the thoughts and statements of the participants in the inquiry. The students ask questions as well, both of the teacher and each other. The inquiry progresses interactively, and the teacher/supervisor is as much a participant as other students in the classroom or fieldwork supervision.

In this method of teaching and learning, the inquiry is open-ended. There is no pre-determined argument or terminus to which the teacher attempts to lead the students. In practising the Socratic method, there is no use for PowerPoint slides. Without a lesson plan, the group follows the dialogue where it goes.

The Socratic social work teacher/supervisor does not do not possess all the knowledge or the answers, nor is he or she 'just testing' the students. The teacher is also a participant in the dialogue and must always be open to learning something himself or herself. It follows from this that the

STRENGTHENING 'FIELD' IN FIELD EDUCATION

Socratic professor does not seek deference to his or her authority. Nor does he or she create a cult of personality by seeming aloof, cold, and distant. Instead, the Socratic teacher knows his or her students' names, and the students know each other's names. When this method is applied, the teacher and students, who are co-learners, experience a productive comfort and not panic and intimidation.

We conclude that the Socratic method is a dynamic format for helping social work students take genuine intellectual risks in the classroom and in the field to learn about critical thinking and resolve ethical dilemmas that are common in day-to-day social work practice.

References

Adaikalam, F. (2014). Contextualising social work education in India. *Alternativas. Cuadernos de Trabajo Social, 21*, 215–232.

Baum, N. (2012). Reflective writing assignment to help social work trainees work through poor supervisory relationships. *Social Work Education, 31*(1), 110–124.

Beike, D., & Wirth-Beaumont, E. (2005). Psychological closure as a memory phenomenon. *Memory, 13*, 574–593.

Bogo, M. (2005). Field instruction in social work: A review of the research literature. In L. Shulman & A. Safyer (Eds.), *Supervision in counselling: Interdisciplinary issues and research*. New York, NY: The Haworth Press.

Dash, B. M. (2017). Revisiting eight decades of social work education in India. *In Asian Social Work and Policy Review, 11*(1).

Dhemba, J. (2012). Fieldwork in social work education and training: Issues and challenges in the case of Eastern and Southern Africa. *Social Work & Society, 10*(1).

Hutt, C., Scott, J., & King, M. (1983). A phenomenological study of supervisees' positive and negative experiences in supervision. *Psychotherapy: Theory, Research, and Practice, 20*, 118–123.

Lawani, B. T. (2002). *Social work education and field instructions*. Pune, India: Centre for Social Research and Development.

Lefevre, M. (2005). Facilitating practice learning and assessment: The influence of relationship. *Social Work Education, 24*(5), 565–583.

Lizzio, A., Stokes, L., & Wilson, K. (2005). Approaches to learning in professional supervision: Supervisee perceptions of processes and outcome. *Studies in Continuing Education, 27*(3), 239–256.

Nikku, B. R. (2010). Social work education in Nepal: Major opportunities and abundant challenges. *Social Work Education: The International Journal, 29*(8), 818–830.

Nikku, B. R., Udas, P., & Adhikari, D. R. (2014). Grassroots innovations in social work teaching and learning: Case of Nepal School of Social Work, Chapter 2. In Nikku, B. R. & Hatta, Z. A. (Eds.), *Social work education and practice: Scholarship and innovations in the Asia pacific*. Australia: Primrose Hall Publishing Group.

Nikku, B. R., & Kadambari, P. (2016). Teaching and practice of family social work: Insights from Nepal School of Social Work. *The Indian Journal of Social Work*, 77(4), 479–490.

Nadkarni, V. V., & Sinha, R. (2016). Transforming social work education in India: integrating human rights, *Journal of Human Rights and Social Work*, 1(1), 9–18.

NAAC-National Assessment and Accreditation Council (2005). *A Manual for self-study of social work institutions*. Bangalore: The National Assessment and Accreditation Council.

Shulman, L. S. (2005). Pedagogies. *Liberal Education*, 91(2), 18–25.

Singh, R. R. (1985). *Field work training in social work education*. New Delhi: Concept Publishing House.

Srivastava, S. P. (2005). Social work education in India: A critical over view. In S. Singh (Ed.), *Teaching and practice of social work in India* (pp. 50–62). Lucknow: New Royal book Company.

University Grants Commission-UGC. (1980). *Review of social work education in India: Retrospect and prospect universities, review of the second review committee*. New Delhi: University Grants Commission.

University Grants Commission-UGC. (2001). *UGC model curriculum: Social Work Education*. New Delhi: University Grants Commission.

9

EIGHT DECADES OF FIELDWORK TRAINING IN INDIA

Identifying the gaps and missing links

Sanjoy Roy and Bishnu Mohan Dash

Introduction

Fieldwork practice has been recognized as a core component of social work education ever since its inception. Fieldwork education provides opportunities to try out first-hand social work practice roles, to develop curiosity and a critical approach to theory and practice, and to examine one's professional identity (Savaya, Peleg-Oren, Stange, & Geron, 2003, p. 298). In support of that assertion Fortune, Mccarthy, and Abramson (2001, p. 111) agree that fieldwork practice is an essential part of education for social work practice and helps students integrate theoretical concepts learned in the classroom into actual client situations within an agency setting (Panos, Panos, Cox, Roby, & Matheson 2002, p. 421). In support of all this, Schiff and Katz (2007, p. 789) state that fieldwork training has been long acknowledged as a major component of social work education.

Fieldwork, as generally understood, is a way to translate knowledge through certain skills and techniques into action. The concept of 'fieldwork' given by M. N. Srinivas (1979) is quite comprehensive and clear, and says fieldwork is an educationally planned and professionally guided programme of interaction of a student with the real situation. The term fieldwork may be stretched to describe both experience and advanced training in the use of knowledge, attitude, and understanding the situation and refinement of skills. The *Dictionary of Sociology and Related Sciences* defines fieldwork as "[a] social survey or process of collecting primary data from a population distributed geographically." In the sociological context, this is quite true, but fieldwork in social work education is quite different. A widely used definition of fieldwork is one by

151

Hamilton and Else (1983), cited in Dhemba (2012, p. 2) who view it as "a consciously planned set of experiences occurring in a practice setting designed to move students from their initial level of understanding, skills and attitudes to levels associated with autonomous social work practice." Fieldwork practice may be defined as a learning process whereby students are instructed by field instructors to develop their professional expertise in accordance with the objective and aims of the institution (New Dictionary Social Work, 1995, p. 26). According to Kirke, Layton, and Sim (2007, p. 15) fieldwork practice in social work education forms the practical component of a social work curriculum. It is an integral part of the education of social work students and is instrumental in developing professional behaviour and acculturating students into the profession. Fieldwork training has been described as an essential bridge from classroom to service delivery settings. According to Kirke et al. (2007, p. 15) fieldwork practice provides an opportunity for students to connect theoretical education and fieldwork practice.

Social work, being a goal-oriented professional education, aims at helping students acquire deep knowledge of the theory and the technical skills for achieving social work objectives. When we used to talk of fieldwork in social work, basically we meant supervised fieldwork, and by that we meant a method by which a social worker, in the beginning, learns how to translate his or her knowledge into practice. This beginning stage later becomes a habit of the learner, as soon as he or she acquires skills and techniques in the work situation. Kasake (1986, p. 55) also observes that fieldwork is an instrument of socialization because it prepares the student for a future role as a social work practitioner. He further asserts that "a meaningful fieldwork placement is one that enhances the student's understanding of the social work profession and the nature of the problems the profession addresses itself to." Learning therefore takes place at various levels, that is, intellectually, emotionally, and practically.

Fieldwork in social work education is a guided interaction process between a student and the actual and practical life situation in which social work as a profession has an abiding and deep concern and which needs to be remedied, improved, or changed for a fuller and more complete development of human-environmental potential (Singh, 1985, p. 43). In support of this, Schiff and Katz (2007, p. 794) state that fieldwork practice has long been acknowledged as a major component of social work. It is in field practice that knowledge learned in the classroom is assimilated in real-life situations, which concurrently and eventually shape the professional identity of the student social worker. In social work fieldwork practice, students can put into practice what they learned in the classroom, which is to integrate theory with practice. Field learning occupies a central role in the curricula of social work schools around the world. Indeed, a glance at the history of social work education reveals that, since the foundation of the first schools of social work until today, field placement learning has been at the heart of social work education, and approaches to field learning and the criteria used to evaluate students' learning and performance vary across schools and countries (Doel & Shardlow, 2005; Bogo, 2010; Doel, Shardlow, & Johnson, 2011; Reamer, 2012 cited in Papouli, 2014). But why is field learning such a fundamental component of the social work educational process (Papouli, 2014)?

Importance of fieldwork in social work education

Fieldwork training could well be considered learning through doing. Dewey's idea of learning through doing has had a primary influence in the concept of fieldwork. Fieldwork is seen as an integrating factor which acts as a balancing force between theory and practice. It has a great significance in the training programme of social work education. It blends theory with practices, facilitates fusion of thinking with doing, combines philosophy with action, and integrates understanding about people with methods of helping them. Its techniques draw heavily on scientific knowledge about people and social phenomena. It is functional in nature and technical in process. It involves an educational process that fosters learning in students. It is an integrated approach that goes concurrently with classroom instruction.

By the end of the 19th century, social work gradually evolved from the apprenticeship method with the launching of the first social work training programme in 1898. This was a summer school established at the New York City Charity Organization Society. Six years later, in 1904, the society established the New York School of Philanthropy, which offered eight months' training in social work. Further to these developments, George (1982), cited in Dhemba, 2012), explained that Mary Richmond, an early social work practitioner, teacher, and theoretician, advocated for complementing field learning with academic education. Royse et al. (2007) who observes that early in social work education, students spent about half of their academic time in field settings.

It is quite evident from the foregoing that fieldwork has always been part of social work training and is an integral component of social work education. As Hepworth, Rooney and Larsen (2002) observe, fieldwork engages the student in supervised social work practice and provides opportunities to marry theory and practice.

Teigiser (2009, p. 139) agrees that one of the key goals of fieldwork training is to enable students to apply the theories and skills they have learned in the classroom to agency practice and to use their practicum experiences to enhance classroom learning. Furthermore, Allison and Turpin (2004, p. 125) maintain that fieldwork experience is the major avenue through which integration of theory into fieldwork practice occurs. Fieldwork training contributes to student development in several ways. It provides unique opportunities to apply and test the theories and facts learned in formal settings and to acquire new knowledge. It also allows students to learn and refine practical skills by working with actual clients. Many practical and procedural skills, such as assessing, are best learned through direct experience. As the social work curriculum is based on both theory and practice, the provision of sound theory is as critical as fieldwork experience. It is vitally important for social work students to acquire, in a classroom environment, practice principles, values, and ethics and the scientific basis for practice. Equally important is the need to apply the theoretical content covered in the classroom to real-life situations as part of a student's preparation to become a professional social worker. It takes more than academic fitness but also evidence-based knowledge, field-tested skills, and a wealth of hands-on experience to become a fully backed social worker. As Shardlow and Doel (1996, p. 6) observe, "[T]hese two contexts for learning about social work practice, class and fieldwork need to be integrated, complementary and mutually consistent." They further point out that the challenge for the student and agency supervisor "is to make this a reality."

Spitzer et al. (2001, p. 79) emphasize that fieldwork practice plays a critical role in modelling a professional culture of social work by providing initial opportunities to engage the student social worker in applied use of their newly acquired knowledge, skills, and abilities. As such, the experience should be systematically patterned and modelled to allow for progressive exposure to the characteristics and demands of contemporary practice. Beyond its substantive importance, fieldwork practice is worthy of sustained attention because it affects so many individuals in social work.

> Field work in social work is carried out in and through social welfare agencies and communities, where the student learns skills and tests out knowledge according to an educational plan. The whole programme is student and field specific. Field work training is supervised practice of social work under the guidance of a trained social work educator, or field personnel. It has been defined as an educationally sponsored attachment of social work students to an institution, agency or a section of community, in which they are helped to extend their knowledge and understanding, and experience the impact of human needs. Such an experience is deliberately arranged on a whole or part time basis.[1]
>
> (Tippa & Mane, 2018, p. 1)

Fieldwork implies both training and education. The distinction between the two is that whereas training is repetitive and skill oriented, education is more broad based, and it is imparted with a perspective. It consists of knowledge of different situations and is a creative, innovative, and dynamic process. It fosters development of intellectual and emotional processes and attitudes. Fieldwork practice is designed to help students integrate theoretical concepts learned in the classroom into actual client situations within an agency setting (Panos et al., 2002, p. 421). In social work field practice, students develop practice skills, translate theory from the classroom into the reality of practice, and test their ability to be professional social workers. In support of all this Schiff and Katz (2007, p. 789) state that fieldwork training has been long acknowledged as a major component of social work education.

The fieldwork programme provides opportunities for the learner to apply the theoretical knowledge taught in the classroom appropriately in different practical situations. It could serve a kind of social laboratory where the students are taught to test their theoretical knowledge and skills against practical situations of social living.

The benefits of field learning for students not only relate to their professional development but also to their personal development. Field learning in practice settings can contribute to students' personal development in a number of ways; during the fieldwork experience, students come into direct contact or interact with different categories of individuals, groups, and professionals, as well as people with different personalities, cultures, and philosophies with whom they are likely to work later in their professional lives. Through this interplay, social work students have hands-on opportunities to discover new ideas or think about themselves and their own values, prejudices, and attitudes towards others, while learning to manage emotions and feelings within real-world agency settings.

The assumption that social work students receive enough training to achieve minimal levels of competence is dubious at best. Data continue to accumulate regarding the ineffectiveness of social work practice and other traditional forms of inter-personal helping. Currently, the data that document the acquisition of various inter-personal skills through social work is far from established (Siddiqui, 1987). The quest for achieving the desired 'professional competence' should inevitably commence from arriving at an operational definition of social work. This requires identifying the task of social work and its boundaries of practice (Brewe & Lalit, 1980).

Objectives of fieldwork

Because the integration of learning into practice is a central goal for all professions, the question of how to bridge the gap between theory and practice and between the classroom and the fieldwork practice is one which has preoccupied social work education since its very beginnings in universities (Clapton et al., 2008, p. 334). During the field practicum, social work students are moving from class-based learning to learning by doing, which marks their entrance into the world of the profession and the demands of learning through work. So field learning is regarded as the missing link between theory and professional practice (Parker, 2007). The whole process resembles a theatrical rehearsal, as students are gradually prepared to play the role of the future social worker. At the final stage of fieldwork practice, social work students participate in a 'prova generale' before entering the professional arena.

Fieldwork is recognized as a major and vital component in professional social work education because of its implications for professional practice. Social work, being goal-oriented and intervention-oriented professional education, aims at helping social work trainees acquire and internalize deep knowledge of the theory and the techniques for achieving social work objectives. The social work trainee must learn every practical aspect within his or her two years of a post-graduate training programme. Further, they must acquire an understanding of the principles, concepts, policies, and processes which constitute the profession of social work. Through the fieldwork programme the social work trainee is prepared to be a competent professional social worker. The main objective of fieldwork in social work education is to provide opportunities to the students to learn and practice the professional skills in the field that are taught in the class. A trainee social worker while in the field tries to interpret and diagnose the situation against the background of the knowledge and understanding, and this helps him or her adjust to the situations. Thus, fieldwork aims at developing students' capacities and capabilities as real-life workers. Direct contract and touch with the people help students grow in their knowledge about people and their problems providing them with emotional maturity, power of judgment, and stability in action.

The Second Review Committee on Social Work Education (1980) mentioned the following objectives of fieldwork:

1 Development of professional skills through learning to use knowledge for the study and analysis of problems and selection of appropriate means to solve them.
2 Development of skills in problem solving at the macro and micro levels.
3 Integration of classroom learning with field practice.
4 Development of skills required for professional practice at the necessary level of training.

EIGHT DECADES OF FIELDWORK TRAINING

5 Development of professional attitude, values, and commitment.
6 Development of self-awareness and a professional ideal.

The main objectives of fieldwork are:

1 Develop professional skills through learning how to utilize knowledge in light of the facts, analyse the problem, and select the appropriate means of problem solving.
2 Develop problem-solving skills for micro-level (individual, family, small group, community, etc.) and change at the macro level in social institutions and process.
3 Provide concurrent opportunity for the integration of classroom learning into field practice and vice versa.
4 Develop skills requires for professional practice at the necessary level of training.
5 Develop a professional attitude involving impartiality, a lack of judgement, and objectivity.
6 Develop professional values and commitments, such as respect for human dignity and worth and the right to participation and self-determination compatible with the good of society.
7 Develop awareness of self and the ways in which psychological and cultural factors affect the perceptions and responses to others.
8 Develop the professional ideal.

Social work education at the master's degree level should include classroom teaching with the core domain of the social work profession including theory and practice, supportive domain of human growth and socio-political bases, inter-disciplinary domain, and elective domain as suggested in the UGC Model Curriculum (UGC, 1980).

According to a second Review Committee (1980), India has focused more on the practice setting than on methods. Thus, fieldwork helps students assimilate theory and the consistent application of its practice. The students are able to develop an understanding about the client, the problem, and the process to solve it. Concurrent fieldwork also helps students to know the status, structure, functions, programmes, and process of the agency where he or she is placed. The student learns and recognizes the necessity of mastering technical skills and the attitude to achieve the broader goals of social work with the perspective of the course content covered in the classroom. This learning by doing with the feedback of theory, though, makes the students put more concentrated efforts into practice. But the content of fieldwork at different levels and in different fields should be determined in accordance with the goals of social work education and of fieldwork as identified by the schools.

Field education in India: emerging concerns

The Report on Curriculum Development (1988) submitted to the University Grants Commission by the Tata Institute of Social Sciences has also mentioned under-nutrition, malnutrition, ill health, deteriorating ecological environment, lack of access to opportunity, social conflict, poverty, bad housing, etc., as major problems that ought to engage the attention of professional social workers in India. The report pleads for change in retarding institutional structures and stresses the need to develop knowledge and skills which enhance the potential of people for their own development. In this connection, the report lists out developmental, promotive, remedial, and rehabilitative tasks for professional social workers. The report recommends that fieldwork practicum in the schools of social work should provide opportunities to develop and enhance a variety of skills, including analysis of social realities and participation through social intervention.[2]

Thus, problems of poverty, food supply, nutrition, population growth, and environmental degradation in developing countries call for a commitment to a need-oriented, self-reliant, environmentally sound, and peaceful socio-economic process and harnessing of energy to meet the basic needs of target groups.[3]

All the schools of social work use institutions and communities for providing fieldwork experiences to students at the undergraduate and post-graduate levels. Open community placements, with or without any agency-based programmes (and with micro-action groups) were started by a few schools in the mid-1960s. These were followed by others in the 1980s. The range of fieldwork placements has varied from a unit, institution, area, target group, and social or environmental policy issue to micro-action groups and legislative work. All these varieties of placements, however, have not been utilized by most of the schools of social work. Although the courses have included social development aspects to an extent, the pattern of fieldwork has remained traditional and in some cases confined merely to sporadic visits. Even the traditional approach has not been followed rationally and systematically in terms of the selection of suitable cases or situations, exploration and partialization of problems, appreciation of dynamics, and initiation of action on the basis of proper assessment followed by the evaluation of its impact, as well as of the educational experience in this process. This has happened because any useful reported activity in the area of placement has been regarded as fieldwork by some without any regard for its orientation, approach, and application of knowledge and skills. It is also worth noting that although the contents of fieldwork or assignments have been worked out, reading lists have not been provided. They are neither insisted upon nor supplied at different stages of field learning. It has perhaps been assumed that students will automatically apply theoretical knowledge imparted in the classroom. The Report on Social Work Education in India (1988) has provided some reading lists, but more needs to be done in this area, and it suggested that the first-year post-graduate students would gain experience by working with the victims of circumstances (i.e. migrant workers, street children, etc.) and second-year students would work with victims of the self (i.e., drug addicts, cases of family discord, etc.). This model assumes that the second-year work assignments would be more complex than the first-year assignments. Because the theory courses would not always conform to the demands of the field, and there would always arise the necessity for teaching by the supervisor, the option of community or agency placement, work with victims of self or of circumstances with a developmental focus (which includes the curative, preventive, and promotive aspects), and even the matters of ecology, policy, and law (social welfare and alliance with micro-action groups) during the same year or every other year should be kept open by the schools. Field assignments in one or more of the areas mentioned could be structured based on progression in a student's learning and in response to an emergent problem or social initiative in the region where a school is located. Identification of assignment-related reading materials at different phases of fieldwork should, however, be made as much a requirement as they are for theory courses. This will make supervision more focused and meaningful and provide more occasions for reflection and reflective action both by the supervisor and the supervisee.

Major challenges

Fieldwork in social work education faces several challenges. Although the primary responsibility for addressing these challenges lies with the social work department or unit, there are issues that need the intervention of central administration at the training institution. Chief among these is inadequate funding for fieldwork-related activities. Second is the lack of a clear learning content for fieldwork. Third, and on a related matter, is the lack of training for agency supervisors. In order to develop fieldwork to its fullest potential and to enhance the quality of learning, it is necessary to adopt the following measures. Social work is a relatively new profession which came to prominence in the early years of the 19th century. According to Parton (2000), social work "is still seen as [a] newer, younger, less developed" science, which needs much research and analysis (p. 450, cited in Hend Al-Ma'seb, Anwar Alkhurinej, Mohammed Alduwaihi, 2013).

However, several studies have discussed the relationship between theory and practice in the social work profession and have concluded that there is a gap between theory and practice (Al-brathen, 2010; Aldamigh, 1998; Clapton et al., 2008; Parton, 2000; Sheldon, 1978 cited in Maseb et al., 2013). This gap has been the subject of considerable debate recently.

Clapton et al. (2008) found the division between theory and practice becomes apparent when social work students go to the field where they must apply what they have learned in school. Usually, students find that what they learned in school "came to be unhelpfully counter-posed. What was highlighted was the apparent split between the classroom and the field" (Clapton et al., 2008, p. 335). Clapton et al. (2006) found that the schools of social work do not train their students adequately for field placement, although field placement is supposed to be "designed to bridge the gap between the theoretical world of academe and the real world of professional practice" (Fernandez, 1998, p. 173).

The beauty of the concurrent fieldwork arrangement lies in the simultaneous and immediate application of theory learned in the classroom into practice. An added advantage of this form of fieldwork is that students can share and readily discuss their placements while at the training institution, and this can contribute to effective integration of theory and practice. However, a major limitation of this arrangement is that students must be attached at agencies within proximity of the training institution. Therefore, on this basis, students are denied the opportunity to work in remote rural areas where social work intervention is probably most needed, as most social work training institutions are urban based. Furthermore, this arrangement may not work well, as the student has to report to both his or her training institution and the agency supervisor. In support of this view, Hall (1990, p. 31) states that,

> the disadvantage is the possibility that the fieldwork experience becomes more fragmented and students are unable to do justice to either theory or practice because of the overlapping expectations of workplace and school.

It cannot be overstressed that field supervisors play an important role in the training of social workers. They are partners in the training process with a responsibility to manage the transition from the classroom to the field, and this requires support and continuous dialogue between the training institution, the agency supervisor, and the agency. It is probably in recognition of this fact that the IASSW and IFSW (2006) spell out the need for training institutions to provide fieldwork manuals and orientation to agency supervisors. This enables them to appreciate the expectations of their role; it also ensures that students are given the maximum opportunity to develop professional knowledge and skill.

Lack of visitation by school supervisors

Although school supervision visits provide opportunities for students and agency supervisors to get guidance in pursuing the objectives of the placement and to assess their performance, students reported that such visits were sporadic at one of the institutions. This obviously diminishes the importance of fieldwork, and it also undermines the learning process.

Highlighting the importance of supervision visits by school supervisors, Raphael and Rosenblum (1987) observe that even the planning of these visits has an energizing effect on the placement. They assert that:

> Knowing that a faculty member who represents the School will be coming on a specific date to review progress stimulates the field instructor and student to assess their progress. The heightened energy available at such times should be consciously used to facilitate change for educational purposes.
>
> (1987, p. 158)

Burden of Americanism

Professional social work came to India from the West, namely, the United States and UK. Today field education in India evidences the profound influence of American ideas. Consequently, our fieldwork education continues to remain out of context with our social realities without having an indigenization of literature. We hardly have any evidence to suggest that fieldwork has responded to any of the critical social problems in a visible manner.

Unchanging pattern of fieldwork

The unchanged pattern of fieldwork is a marked weakness of social work education in the country. The present pattern of fieldwork has remained traditional and there is a lack of any linkage between the classroom theories and the realities of the field. Many schools of social work have failed to develop fieldwork programmes based on reality.

Lack of linkage between theory and practice

Parker (2007, p. 763) notes that there is a lack of integration between social work theory and social work practice. In addition, Coulshed and Orme (2006, p. 7) argue that there is indeed a continuing tension between theory and practice, pointing out that students and practitioners alike have protested that it was necessary to forget theory once in practice.

Lewis and Bolzan (2007, p. 136) agree that social work has always been characterized by a tension between the theoretical understandings that underpin its knowledge base and the daily practice of social work, which is heavily influenced by the context in which it is situated. One of the key goals of field education is to enable students to apply the theories and skills they have learned in the classroom to agency practice and to use their practicum experience to enhance classroom learning. However, there is often a lack of connection between theories learned in the classroom and field experiences (Teigiser, 2009, p. 139). The effectiveness of fieldwork practice is enhanced when the students, university-based educators and supervisors, and agency-based supervisors work in harmony and continuously communicate goals and expectations regarding social work students' integration of theory into practice.

The shortage of qualified and experienced agency supervisors was found to be a common problem. Invariably, qualified and experienced social workers should handle practical training in social work. Sherer and Neta (2005, p. 316) point out that agency-based supervisors play a role in socializing students to the profession and in transmitting key knowledge, values, and skills. They also are responsible for coordinating student involvement in fieldwork practice between the university and their local agency.

Social work educators do not work as practitioners

We, as the educators, practitioners, and student learners, acknowledge social work as a profession like medicine, law, engineering, etc. The professors/educators of medical colleges or universities practise their profession by visiting hospitals along with the medical students; professors/educators of engineering colleges are involved in practice; and professors/educators of law colleges also practise their profession, update their knowledge, and enhance their competencies to deal with the contemporary social issues. On the other hand, in social work, the holistic view on teaching, practice, and research is a huge absence. The truth is that most social work educators are content with conventional classroom teaching and are seldom found in the practice and research domains.

Declining fieldwork in the mushrooming schools of social work

Notwithstanding the fact that the number of social work schools, institutions/departments of colleges, and universities have been mounting slowly but steadily during the last few decades and rising rapidly over the last decade or so, the quality of professional social work education, practicum, and its standards have diminished. As a result, there is a serious harm to the professional status and image of social work. Innumerable departments/ institutions of social work mushroom every day. Professional social work is being commercialized today, and issues of superiority, credibility, and ethical standards are compromised by diverse stakeholders. Field education in these institutions has become a kind of formality.

Lack of uniformity in field education

Another serious issue in social work is the lack of uniformity in curriculum and standards of practice among professionals in different settings of social work. Despite earlier efforts made by social work educators and social work associations, sill social work still does not have a Council for Social Work Education. In the absence of a national council, there is no proper system of accreditation of social work institutions, standardization of social work education, and learning and practices of practitioners.

Absence of fieldwork manuals

It is imperative that schools of social work develop their own fieldwork manuals, covering the teaching and learning content for fieldwork. This is particularly important considering that each institution is unique in terms of the prevailing socio-economic conditions, challenges, and experiences, as well as the social work education curriculum in a given country. Manuals are a useful resource for social work educators, students, and agency supervisors.

Second, there seems to be a lack of interest in fieldwork issues among social work scholars, which partly explains the paucity of literature on the subject. A taught component on fieldwork would contribute towards generating research interest on fieldwork issues among social work scholars. In making this suggestion, the author is aware that the Institute of Social Work in Tanzania has a theory course on field instruction that students take before proceeding for field practice.

There are some departments and colleges of social work education that have only two to three faculty members, most of them from sociology or other social sciences. Few schools or the departments are headed by non-professionals. Due to lack of their academic background and knowledge in fieldwork, they are not properly involved in policy and planning processes.

Lack of qualified and competent agency supervisors

The shortage of qualified and experienced agency supervisors has become a common problem in India. Invariably, qualified and experienced social workers who work in the agency should handle practical training in social work and guide student trainees. There is a penetration of the profession as some of the social welfare agencies are employing workers from other disciplines to carry out social work roles, as this costs them less in salaries compared to professional social workers.

Lack of suitable and appropriate agencies for concurrent fieldwork placement

Now the more stringent problem of fieldwork practice is to find out the good number of agencies that actually practise social work. Everyday new social welfare agencies are mushrooming in the name of social work. Therefore, concurrent placement becomes an extra burden on the social work department to place students. On the other hand, students also are not able to use theoretical understanding in the practice.

Financial support for students in fieldwork practice

In India, most of the students in social work institutions do not get fieldwork allowances where they must travel a lot to do their fieldwork practice. Students have raised the issue several times. Students wondered how they were expected to apply themselves seriously in such a situation when it is very costly to stay in metro cities to complete their study.

Inadequate fieldwork methods to deal with the varied social problems today

The effect of globalization has really manifested in a lot of global social problems today. It is difficult to deal with these problems with limited social work methods. Even the social action method is not practised in most of the countries in the world, neither are proper casework methods used, especially in India (or this happens only rarely). The problems are multifarious and multi-dimensional, and social work methods are sometimes incapable of dealing and coping with these situations. For example, the social work profession still is not perfectly equipped to deal with issues around the homosexual community, communalism, terrorism, or corruption in India or with international problems like global migration, asylum migration, global terrorism, inter-fostering adoption, etc. Therefore, according to us, the key to finding solutions to these problems is perhaps re-thinking; to search for new methods of social work with varied models such as developmental social work, legal social work, international/global social work, advocacy social work, etc.

Less recognition

Recognition is another challenge in social work as well as in fieldwork practice when students go for fieldwork. The general perception of the community is that social work can be practised by anybody who is motivated to help the needy, and it does not require any specialized education and training. Most of our students in the field feel that, in India, social workers are not accepted as professionals until recently, and hence the importance of their work gets diminished.

Fieldwork agency does not practise social work values and principles

Many of the social welfare agencies or social service agencies do not act according to social work values and principles which are followed in the classrooms. It may be because of the limited ability of social work schools in India to influence the structure and work patterns of the social services.

As highlighted by Subhedar (2001, pp. 51–52) these problems are:

1   Well-established agencies do not allow students for fieldwork training in their agencies. Even if they do allow them, they do not provide enough time.
2   Many social welfare agencies do not have well-set programmes, qualified and experienced staff, good standards of services, etc., which otherwise provide a rich learning experience to the students in the agencies.
3   Many social welfare agency workers feel that students are sometimes quite critical about the workers' service towards the community, and thus create problems; thus, the real practices are not demonstrated to the students. Complete or relevant information in such cases is not divulged to the students in the agencies. This hesitation or fear is one of the major problems of the agencies.

Students often do not incorporate social work values and ethics in practice when they deal with clientele. Sometimes they don't even follow the processes of social work methods and its processes. Say, for example, a student deals with a client in a hospital; they will not follow the stages of the casework process of social study, social diagnosis, treatment and feedback, and evaluation. However, the reality at social work training institutions, as Kaseke (1990) observes, is that fieldwork is marginalized when compared to its academic counterparts. Kaseke asserts that "there is very little written on this subject matter, thus leaving social work educators, students and field supervisors without any meaningful and comprehensive guide to field instruction." Mupedziswa (1997) also corroborates this view, contending that "social work institutions need to recast their fieldwork in order to give it equal importance to academic instruction."

Notes

1 Hegerty, J. E., *The training of social welfare.*
2 Tata Institute of Social Sciences. (1988). *Social work education in India: A Report* (p. 28). Mimeographed: Tata Institute of Social Sciences.
3 Kurian, P. (1990, January 6). Rational energy strategies. *Economic and Political Weekly, XXV*(2), 35.

References

Al-brathen, A. A. (2010) *Articles in social work.* Amman, Jordan: Dar Alfiker.
Aldamigh, S. (1998, March). Practice licensing: Reasons and importance to enhance the effectiveness of social work practice. In *Eleventh Scientific Conference.* Holwan, Egypt.
Allison, H., & Turpin, M. (2004). Development of the student placement evaluation form: A tool for assessing student fieldwork performance. *Australian Occupational Therapy Journal, 51*, 125–132.
Bogo, M. (2010). *Achieving competence in social work through field education.* Toronto, ON: University of Toronto Press.
Brewe, C. & Lalit, J. (1980). *Can social work survive?* London: Temple Smith.
Clapton, G., Cree, V. E., Allan, M., Edwards, R., Forbes, R., Irwin, M., . . . Perry, R. (2006). Grasping the Nettle: Integrating learning and practice revisited and re-imagined. *Social Work Education, 25*(6), 645–656.
Clapton, G., Cree, V. E., Allan, M., Edwards, R. R., Irwin, I. M., MacGregor, W., . . . Perre, R. (2008). Thinking outside the box: New approach to integration of learning practice. *Social Work Education, 27*(3), 334–340.
Coulshed, V., & Orme, J. (2006). *Social work practice, an introduction* (4th ed.). New York, NY: Palgrave Macmillan.
Deborah, P., & Valentine, D. P. (2004). Field education: Exploring the future, expanding the vision. *Social Work Education, 40*(1), 3–11.
Dhemba, J. (2012). Field work in social work education and training: Issues and challenges in the case of eastern and southern Africa. *Social work and Society, 10*(1). Retrieved from Fieldwork in Social Work Education and Training: Issues and Challenges in the Case of Eastern and Southern Africa on November, 12, 2018
Doel, A. M., & Steven, M. S. (2005). *Modern social work practice: Teaching and learning in practice setting* (p. 273). Farnham: Ashgate Publishing Ltd.
Doel, A. M., & Shardlow, S. M. (2005). *Modern social work practice: Teaching and learning in practice settings.* Burlington, VT: Ashgate.
Doel, M., Shardlow, S. M., & Johnson, P. G. (2011). *Contemporary field social work: Integrating field and classroom experience.* Thousand Oaks, CA: Sage.
Fernandez, E. (1998). Student perceptions of satisfaction with practicum learning. *Social Work Education, 17*(2), 173–201.
Field Learning in Social Work Education: Implications for Educators and Instructors. *Field Scholar, 4*(2), (Fall).
Fortune, A. E., Mccarthy, M., & Abramson, J. (2001). Student learning processes in field education: Relationship of learning activities to quality of field instruction, satisfaction, and performance among the MSW students. *Social Work Education, 37*(1), 111–124.

Hall, N. (1990). Social work training in Africa: A fieldwork manual. *Harare, Journal of Social Development in Africa*, p. 31.

Hepworth, D. H., Rooney, R., & Larsen, J. A. (2002). *Direct social work practice: Theory and skills*. Pacific Grove, CA: Brooks/Cole.

IASSW & IFSW. (2006). *Global standards for the education and training of the social work profession* (pp. 170–191). IASSW. Retrieved June 10, 2016, from www ifsw.org

Kasake, E. (1986). *The role of field work in social work training*. In Social development and rural field work, proceedings of a workshop held in Harare, Harare Journal of Social Development in Africa.

Kaseke, E. (1990). Foreword. In N. Hall (Ed.), *Social work training in Africa: A fieldwork manual*. Harare: Journal of Social Development in Africa.

Kirke, P., Layton, N., & Sim, J. (2007). Informing field work design: Key elements to quality in field work education for undergraduate occupational therapy students. *Australian Occupational Journal, 21*, 14–21.

Lewis, I., & Bolzan, N. (2007). Social work with a twist: Interweaving practice knowledge, student experience and Academic theory. *Australian Social Work, 60*(2), 136–146.

Maseb, H, Alkhurinej, A., & Alduwaihi, M. (2013). The gap between theory and practice in social work. *International Social Work, 58*(6), 819–830.

Mupedziswa, R. (1997). Training social workers in an environment of economic reforms: The mother of all challenges? *Social Work/Maatskaplke Werk, 33*(33).

New Dictionary of Social Work. (1995). Cape Town: CTP Book Printers.

Panos, P. P., Panos, A., Cox, S. E., Roby, J. L., & Matheson, K. (2002). Ethical issues concerning the use of video conferencing to supervise international social work field practicum students. *Social Work Education, 38*(3), 421–437.

Parker, J. (2007). Developing effective practice learning for tomorrow's social workers. *Social Work Education, 26*(8), 763–779.

Parton, N. (2000). Some thoughts on the relationship between theory and practice in and for social work. *The British Journal of Social Work, 30*(4), 449–463.

Raphael, F. B., & Rosenblum, A. F. (1987, March). An operational guide to the faculty field liaison role. *Social Casework: The Journal of Contemporary Social Work*, 156–163.

Reamer, F. (2012). Essential ethics education in social work field instruction: A blueprint for field educators. *Field Educator, 2*(2). http://fieldeducator.sim mons.edu/article/essential-ethics-education-in-social-work-field-instruction/.

Royse, D., Dhooper, S., & Rompf, E. (2007). *Field instruction: A guide for social work students*. Boston: Pearson Educational Inc.

Savaya, R., Peleg-Oren, N., Stange, D., & Geron, Y. (2003). Congruence of classroom and field instruction in social work: An empirical study. *Social Work Education, 22*(3), 297–308.

Schiff, M., & Katz, P. (2007). The impact of ethnicity and phase in training on Israeli social work student's satisfaction with the field instruction. *Social Work Education, 26*(8), 794–809.

Second Review Committee. (1980). *A review of social work education in India: Retrospect and prospect*. New Delhi: UGC.

Shardlow, S., & Doel, M. (1996). *Practice learning and teaching*. London: Macmillan Press Ltd

Sheldon, B. (1978). Theory and practice in social work: a re-examination of a tenuous relationship. *The British Journal of Social Work, 8*(1), 1–22.

Sherer, M., & Neta, P.-O. (2005). Influence of teachers' field instructors' and students' views on job analysis of social work students. *Journal of Social Work Education, 41*(2), 315–328.

Siddiqui, H. Y. (1987). Towards a competency based education in social work. *Indian Journal of Social Work, 48*(1), 23–32.

Singh, R. R. (Ed.). (1985). *Field work in social work education: A perspective for human service profession*. New Delhi: Concept Publishing Company.

Spitzer, W., Holden, G., Cuzzi, L., Rutter, S., Chernack, P., & Rosenburg, G. (2001). Edith Abbott was right: Designing fieldwork experiences for contemporary health care practice. *Social Work Education, 37*(1), 79–90.

Srinivas, M. N. (1979). *The field worker and the field*. New Delhi: Oxford University Press.

Subhedar, I. S. (2001). *Field work training in social work*. Rawat Publication.

Teigiser, K. S. (2009). Field note: New approaches to generalist field education. *Journal of Social Work Education, 45*(1), 139–148.

Tippa, N. G., & Mane, S. R. (2018). Problems and prospects of field work training in social work education: A Review. *Innovare Journal of Social Sciences, 6*(1), 1–2. Retrieved July 25, 2018, from file:///C:/Users/Win7/Downloads/23065-Article%20Text-129479-1-10-20180622.pdf.

University Grants Commission. (1980). *Review of social work education in India, retrospect and prospect*. New Delhi: UGC.

University Grants Commission (2001). Third Review Committee Report of Social Work Education.

10

LEARNING SOCIAL WORK PRACTICE SKILLS

Reflections from communities, NGOs, and universities

Swapan Garain

For a helping profession, the competency of the practitioner is an essential component for both immediate and long-term remedial intervention. The skill development orientation needs to start as part of the university[1] education, as a core component under the mentorship of experienced professionals. The graduating students must be adequately skilled to be ready for practice before leaving the protective environment of the university. The practice skills are required to be complemented by an appropriate knowledge base and a conducive attitudinal perspective on the part of the young professionals (Ramachandran, 1986)

Among the helping professions, social work takes a prime slot as a multi-faceted, inter-disciplinary approach to working with the clientele at the individual, couple, family, small group, community, and institutional levels. As a helping profession, social work is concerned with working systematically to enhance their wellbeing and better adaptation to society. It is an academic as well as a practice-based professional discipline that integrates values, theory, perspective, and practice. Like other professions, social work is also based on specialized knowledge, core principles, and appropriate skills. It helps individuals restore or develop their competency for social functioning. Social work aims at enhancing or creating societal conditions and resources that support the needs of individuals and groups. At the macro level, social work aims at promoting social change, enhancing the pace of development, and improving community integration. The primary goal of the social work profession is to improve the quality of life for the individuals and in society at large (Dasgupta, 1967; Ranade, 1975).

In view of the wide and challenging spectrum of issues and interventions, beyond the established protocols found in other professions, the social work profession calls for human-centric skill, attitude, and knowledge building, leading to comprehensive competency development on the part of the social workers (Yelaja, 1970).

Social workers help the needy to cope up with their problems such as poverty, addiction, physical and mental illness, unemployment, and disability. They take an integrated view of a problem or situation, including aspects of individual versus collective, economic versus social, emotional versus rational, and the like. They uniquely look at different aspects of a problem, keeping in mind the social work values, human rights, social justice, respect for equity and diversity, and collective responsibility of the client and of others. They provide direct assistance as a service provider (i.e., a counsellor, therapist, trainer), as well as indirect help by mobilizing or facilitating access to external facilities or resources. They help prevent crises and help people cope up more effectively with the stresses of everyday life. Considering the clients' internal struggle, the social workers help them develop their inner resources (like interpersonal relationships, family system, etc.) for empowerment and/or bringing changes in the situation or context that impact them. The social workers enhance clients' ability to use their own resources and those of the community to address their problems. They apply their knowledge about development dynamics, appropriate interventions, and methods to assist clients in reaching their full potential. They work with and help the poor, deprived, disadvantaged, underprivileged, vulnerable, displaced, destitute sick, addicts, those with special needs and abused children, youth, women, and the elderly. The social worker is indeed a resource person for someone seeking any type of help (Government of India, 1955, 1978, 1987).

In general, social workers, irrespective of the settings, fields of work, target population, and level of position in the organizational hierarchy, are required to develop relevant competencies for carrying out some of the following typical tasks:

1 Planning, organizing, and conducting meetings, consultative dialogue, and interactive sessions with the target groups, community leaders, experts, and resource providers for promoting the cause of its target population or issues of interest.
2 Interacting with individuals, families, and groups to assess their needs, issues, and situations.
3 Conceiving project ideas for intervention for addressing the needs of the target population.
4 Advising, recommending, and sometimes deciding on a solution from available alternatives, and developing a road map for realizing the objective.
5 Formulating project proposals with or without revenue models.

LEARNING SOCIAL WORK PRACTICE SKILLS

6 Appraising project proposals.
7 Raising financial and non-financial resources for carrying out ongoing activities and initiating new projects.
8 Initiating dialogue, liaising with, and making referrals to resource persons and representatives of resource organizations to access services and facilities for the needy.
9 Offering counselling, guidance, and information support to the target population.
10 Conceiving, organizing, and/or conducting training programmes for capacity building of the target groups.
11 Designing a project monitoring plan.
12 Supervising work of the subordinate staff, interns, and volunteers and preparing them for greater responsibilities.
13 Communicating and reporting to superiors about the tasks assigned to them.
14 Preparing and maintaining accurate reports and records of tasks, activities, events, interventions, projects, etc.
15 Attending to queries, correspondence, and requirements for communicating/reporting to funding agencies and from other external sources.
16 Evaluating completed and sponsored projects.
17 Calling and conducting/chairing meetings of committees.
18 Participating in meetings of staff, committees, and forums within the organization.
19 Serving in a multi-disciplinary team of experts that is engaged in complex or new areas of intervention.
20 Carrying out advocacy for promoting interest in a cause.
21 Undertaking research, documentation, and publication on issues or causes engaged in.
22 Fulfilling statutory compliances on behalf of the organization.
23 Networking with partner organizations, technical/resource agencies, and other organizations engaged in similar issues.
24 Representing the organization in external committees and forums.

Successful execution of tasks and efficient service delivery by a social worker depend on the level of skill competency acquired and practised in some of the following areas:

1 Community-based need assessment
2 Ability to conceive project ideas based on needs assessment
3 Formulating a project proposal
4 Appraising a project proposal
5 Fundraising skills
6 Programme development skills

7 Preparing monitoring project/activity/task/centre plan
8 Project evaluation
9 Conceiving, planning, organizing, and conducting training programmes
10 Report writing skills
11 Drafting letters for government and funding agencies
12 Counselling skills
13 Inter-personal skills
14 Good communication skills
15 Event management skills
16 Leadership/initiative taking skills
17 Case management skills
18 Computer and Internet skills: Word, Excel, PowerPoint, web surfing, email
19 Advocacy skills
20 Social networking skills
21 Team work / team building
22 Negotiation skills
23 Problem-solving skills
24 Observation skills
25 Planning skills
26 Writing skills
27 Skills in drafting minutes of meetings
28 Policy analysis skills
29 Costs and benefits analysis skills
30 General administrative skills
31 Management information system skills
32 Reading and referencing skills
33 Organizing skills
34 Coordination skills

Attainment of overall effectiveness of a social worker depends on the level he or she acquires the following competency traits:

1 Ability to make a judgment and make a difficult decision under pressure
2 Ability to work independently
3 Analytical mind
4 Critical thinking
5 Effective listening
6 Empathy
7 Flexibility to adapt to changing situations
8 Genuine desire to improve the quality of interventions
9 Language skills
10 Legal frame of mind
11 Mediation ability

12 Multi-tasking ability
13 Patience
14 Resilience
15 Service orientation
16 Social perceptiveness
17 Staying calm during a crisis

The personality traits required for an effective social worker seems to call for high level of consciousness, maturity, and self-development.

The onus for skill development of the social work students remains with the educators and the university. However, human relations related skill development for social workers requires personal interest and involvement. This is the cornerstone in acquiring the appropriate level of skills required for a social work practitioner.

Building core competency in the form of knowledge and practice skills among the social workers in the formal university education system requires identification and consensus on a minimum skill set, standardization of the process of skill development, and ensuring availability of competent faculty to impart skill training (UGC, 1980; Datar et al., 2010).

Perspectives of the applicants

Admission in the social work courses at the diploma, bachelor's, or even at master's level do not require any prior training, education, or experience in social work or related fields. In order to enrol for a master's degree in social work, the applicant must have at least a three or four year bachelor's degree in any discipline. This refers to three or four years of undergraduate study after ten years of schooling and two years pre-university study. Similar general rules apply for bachelor's or diploma-level admission. Although this is a requirement from the point of view of the university, as per laid down university admission rules anywhere in the country, a pattern in applicants' choices in relation to their gender, age, and ethnicity has been noticed. The ranking of the university, level of entry, specializations or electives offered, and medium of instructions, among others, also influence the choice of the applicants and help shape their perspective. Furthermore, the applicant and their parents can complicate the decision-making process. Reflections from the personal experience of the teachers often challenge some common place assumptions about the social work profession, and the motivations and dilemmas that social work course applicants encounter in choosing a university, applying for admission, selection process, and during their classroom and field training. There are many competing factors that affect the choice(s) made by applicants to become social workers. The perspectives of the applicants potentially have far-reaching implications for social work education and training (Christie & Kruk, 2007).

When seeking higher education, there is a general trend among the applicant community for bachelor's degrees in arts, science, commerce, agriculture, law, management, mass media, engineering, medicine, and allied subjects. The career prospect is the broad guiding force. In view of increasing unemployment, competition, and poor conditions of work in general, an applicant considers the status of campus placement as a primary factor when selecting a master's-level course in social work. For an average as well as below-average student from a professional stream (like engineering, law, agriculture, etc.) and for most students from other BA/BSc/BCom streams, social work education from a good university is considered a better means to land in a job.

The applicants seeking admission in the university mostly have an expectation of a well-paid job and career. The selection of the course is the first step for higher education in general. However, an applicant exploring a career in social work has an obvious choice to go for a MSW degree. The MSW is the universally recognized degree across the globe. In some countries/universities, it may be called MA in social work instead of MSW. At the next stage, considering the job prospect and personal aptitude, an applicant looks at the choice of a university based on its reputation, faculty, intellectual resources, physical infrastructure, cost of education, regional/linguistic orientation, and chances of getting in. Reference from an alma mater or the presence of any senior from his or her current university also plays a role in choosing the university. In addition, the availability of a particular specialization at the MSW course in a university is a critical factor in the selection process. This is in fact a conscious decision for a better career opportunity to study social work in a chosen university.

Research studies on the students from social work courses in Canada, United Kingdom, and Northern Ireland reported on the complexity of the decision-making processes. Some of the factors that affect the choice to become a social worker may be related to their gender, age, and ethnicity, among others. After admission, the students deal continuously with the aspects of motivation, career aspirations, concerns, and disincentives of being a social work professional. These findings will have impact on the redesign of the social work curriculum to address expectations of the prospective employers in terms of attracting and retaining social work graduates (Christie & Kruk, 1998; Wilson & McCrystal, 2007).

A small percentage of students opt for a career in social work, either due to emotional reasons or as a conscious decision to help the needy and underprivileged. The reasons for being drawn to a career in social work may vary from having experienced hardship to being helped by a social worker in the past. Hence, they became interested in helping others to overcome their problems. Sometimes, one may have specific interest to work on problems and issues of street children, domestic workers, pavement dwellers, addicts, alcoholics, cancer patients, or the elderly. It may not be a factor whether they belong to very rich families or poor families. Rather, the common factor is often some moving personal experience or encounter in their own life or in the life of someone else that left a deep imprint. Irrespective of the varied reasons for choosing a career in social work, most individuals cherish being in the social work profession, as they help others overcome their problems to live a better life.

Unfortunately, the expectation, selection, and decision on a course of study and university is often not based on any in-depth self-exploration, online research, or dialogue with one or more practising or working social work graduates. The applicants usually depend on the general recommendation of others, like teachers, peers, alumni, and family members about the reputation of the university in terms of campus placement and career prospects.

Applicants in general look forward to a well-paying job and a better career after completing a master's degree course in social work.

Expectations of students

On joining a university, students' immediate expectation relates to the course curriculum. From the point of competency building in the students, the expectations can be grouped into inputs from classroom teaching, different internships or fieldwork as part of the curriculum, voluntary internships, possible foreign university exchange programmes, and other extra-curricular academic activities during their two years with the university. Participation and expectation of the students in the curriculum requirements range from a bare minimum of being eligible for the degree to getting the maximum benefit from all possible institutional resources. On an average, most students expect and strive to get better grades/marks in academic assessments. Every effort begins and ends with this goal.

Competency building is seen to be low in the mind of the students. Completing the requirements of the coursework and internship is the only thing in the mind of the students in the first year. With the beginning of the second year, the job placement starts to become a priority until a job offer is made or until the graduation ceremony.

Competency development on the part of the students is a slow process. It has two dimensions: social work skill building and overall self-development. Both depend on the interest, capacity, and efforts of the students in participating in the academic requirements of the MSW course. Social work skill building is complemented with creating a knowledge base and developing an attitude appropriate for social workers. The fulfilment of academic requirements aims at contributing to social work skill building. However, there is no benchmarking or assessment of level of skill building before the students graduate.

During study, the students in general are found to be short-sighted with regard to becoming social workers. The immediate concern is to get a well-paying job upon graduation. The pay packet is the top most criteria, followed by the nature of the recruiting organization, place of posting, and nature of job, mostly in that order. Mid-term expectations, on the two- to five-year horizon, namely, the status of the employing organization and the nature of job responsibilities, are also found to be of some concern in the mind of social work professionals. For example, when switching to another job, the social work professional's eye is on a corporate CSR[2] job, funding organizations, consulting firms, and large established NGOs.[3] In terms of job stability, social work professionals look for government organizations, international funding agencies, big corporations' or multi-national corporations' (MNCs) CSR jobs.

In terms of job responsibilities, the social work students become choosier about the job content, particularly being concerned about the level in the hierarchy, autonomy, flexibility, financial authority, and the domain of work. Graduating students are generally not particular about the nature of job responsibilities and are willing to settle for any type of job within the broad social work domain if offered an attractive and competitive pay. For mid-career professionals, the social work students think a job that will provide opportunities to develop and apply specific skills and acquire domain knowledge competency in certain areas of one's interest for a long-term career. The nature of job responsibilities rotates around the skill and domain knowledge requirements of the job. When considering long-term career perspectives, the social work students remain concerned about their area of interest, the location of the position in the organizational hierarchy, and the financial health of the employing organization. Skill component is kept aside by the graduating students while thinking about a job.

Perspectives of universities/institutes

The university education system is not considered an ideal place for acquiring practice skills in any discipline. Thus, an independent, autonomous, private, and affiliated institute in most disciplines, in every country, are considered the best institutes for higher learning. Few institutes are found to be centres for excellence from the practitioners' point of view. Course curriculum is considered a necessary requirement to develop a knowledge base in the mind of the students about the systems, processes, and likely outcomes (UGC, 1980). However, practical training alone can help develop the basic skills in students. Realizing this, some of the disciplines have made mandatory provisions for parallel, actual, and relevant institutionalized service centres for field training of the students. For example, a college for training doctors must have an attached hospital with approved specifications of licenced doctors, hospital beds for patients, diagnostic laboratories, etc. Similarly, a college for hotel management students functions with an attached licenced hotel. For certain other skill-based courses, the institute, instead of creating in-house facilities for practical training, procures access to third-party facilities. A college of pharmacy or biotechnology uses the laboratory of a pharmaceutical company for laboratory and practical training of its students by entering a memorandum of understanding with the company. In another set of disciplines that may not necessarily require a client interface for offering live services, like engineering, architecture, web design and animation, film production, and advertising courses, the institutes create in-house laboratories and simulated workstations for practical work training. In brief, the university/institute appreciates the need for practical training for a certain level of required skill development of the students, under the supervision of faculty members, before graduating them from the university.

Institutionalized social work education in India started more than 80 years ago (Gore, 2011; Pathak, 1975; Manshardt, 1967). Since its inception, social work education has primarily followed the American model (Mandal, 1989), and this influence can be seen in the curriculum, reading material, and method of teaching and training. Throughout the history of social work education in India, both the faculty and the students wanted to go to America for higher studies, faculty/student exchange programmes, and for conferences. The continuing impact can be seen in classroom instruction, field training, and practice orientation. The debate on student competency building in clinical approaches of American and European curriculum vis-à-vis developmental approach of the developing countries continues.

Some leading universities attract international students as well as facilitate local students to go abroad for higher studies or place them in international agencies for internship or employment. Thus, the curriculum is geared to some extent to include an international perspective by way of offering courses in international social work, guest lectures on global issues or international exchange programmes for students. The purpose is to develop student competency in international social work and global citizenship with a sensitivity towards social, economic, religious, linguistic, and cultural diversity (Das & Anand, 2014; Manohar, 2010; Yip, 2005; Cox, 2000). The lack of competent in-house faculty to build an appropriate curriculum in international social work may self-defeat the purpose itself by taking the perspective to a self-satisfying domain. Otherwise, the course will end up being offered with the 'given competency of the instructor faculty' instead of what it actually entails. This will compromise the desired competency building on the part of students.

The essential perspective on the part of the university is to enable students to appear for the qualifying examination of the university and/or of the licensing authority and qualify to be a practitioner in the concerned discipline.

With regard to graduating students with social work degrees or diplomas, skill development calls for training in live human laboratories in individual, group, community, or institutional settings (Nair, 1981). It is a very complicated, challenging, and sensitive environment that calls for a lot of prior preparation and planning, in addition to close on-site supervision by a trained professional, in order to avoid – but sometimes address – the negative, damaging, or irreversible impact on the client(s). The university assigns experienced in-house faculty members or a qualified practitioner from the agency itself to supervise the student's field training. The university typically assigns a student for field training in a non-government social work agency with or without community outreach activities, village or slum communities, or institutional settings like a hospital, prison, old age home, counselling centre, etc. Rarely the university may have its own facility for field training of its students, except some demonstration or field action projects for accommodating a very small number of students.

The university education in social work, like in many other practising disciplines, strictly follows the curriculum requirements of coursework and practical/field training, including hours of classroom teaching and specified hours of practical/fieldwork training, attendance, compliance of assessment requirements including written and oral examinations, and minimum qualifying marks for awarding the degree, diploma, or certificate. Even for the curriculum with practical/field training components, the concern of the university largely remains focused on admitting students, conducting classes, offering practical/field training opportunities, conducting qualifying assessments, and providing university certification to graduating the students. The students' skill competency development is overshadowed by an ultimate concern with fulfilment of minimum qualifying requirements to be eligible for the degree (UGC, 1980; Patel, 1972).

Skill building as part of the university curriculum is low on priority. The standardization of the type of skills and level of competency to be acquired is mostly non-existent in the university curriculum. Hence, the assessment of social work skills acquired by the graduating students is merely rudimentary and lacks any form of standardization (Nagpaul, 1986).

It is viewed that the students, after graduating, will learn on the job. Thus, the university is often found to be gearing towards providing campus placement to graduating students. The students, finding jobs through on-campus placement, off-campus placement, or on their own efforts shortly after graduating, is considered an indicator of a good social work school.

Expectations of field placement agencies

Learning social work practice skills takes place in the field placement agencies and in the communities. Besides classroom learning of domain knowledge, the social work students are required to develop practice skills through real-life learning experiences in the form of internships in a variety of community-based organizations such as self-help groups, community resource centres, day care centres for children and the elderly, pre-schools, counselling units, shelters for homeless, community kitchens, state agencies, human services non-profits, and similar organizations. Some students also opt for field experiences in their own communities. Even in case of placement in an open community, anchoring with a social work agency is critical for getting an entry point into the community, as well as for critical intervention. Thus, the field placement agencies and the rural and urban communities assume significance in the development of practice skills among social work students (Garain, 2016; Garain, 1993; Datar et al., 2010).

The field placement agencies and their communities are the most resourceful entities for learning, as well as making a difference in the lives of the disadvantaged, deprived, and underprivileged (Garain, 1993). These agencies and communities constitute the social laboratory that creates the essential opportunities for the social work students to gain exposure and experience in working with issues concerning individuals and groups, constituting the target population of social workers, such as:

1 Abused and neglected
2 Aged and elderly
3 Children, particularly those at risk
4 Chronically ill
5 Communities: villages and slums
6 Economically disadvantaged
7 Internally displaced
8 People with learning disabilities
9 People with mental health conditions
10 People with physical and mental disabilities
11 Poor
12 Refugees
13 School drop-outs
14 Socially underprivileged
15 Those with inadequate housing and the homeless
16 Those with issues of cultural competencies and diversity

17 Unemployed, under-employed
18 Unskilled, semi-skilled
19 Vulnerable population
20 Women: disadvantaged, deprived, destitute
21 Young offenders

In the fieldwork laboratory setting, the social work students get to diagnose, experiment, and practise social work skills in working with individuals, groups, communities, and organizations (Datar et al., 2010; Singh, 1985).

The field placement agencies have their own ongoing problems of funding constraints, shortage of human resources, infrastructural inadequacy, limited consumables, infinite needs of the clientele, and at times credibility issues too. Most agencies operate under all sorts of constraints and look for support from every possible sources. In this context, assigning social work students for fieldwork training is often welcomed by the agencies, as the students act as an extra helping hand at the front line assisting the paid social workers of the agency. In order to get more out of the trainee social work students, the agencies put forward their requirements and expect its fulfilment by the social work institute. Considering the requirements of the agency, the community, and the clientele, the agency may seek students with specific language competency, gender, number of students to be assigned, regional/ethnic belongingness, educational background, and prior experience. Once the student is placed for fieldwork training in the agency, the students are expected to follow the agency schedule and adhere to agency rules and requirements, the same as its paid employees. Most agencies do not have prescribed rules for engaging volunteers, interns, and students. The students are called upon to share the burden of the agency staff and assist them in carrying out their responsibilities. It is viewed that the students will learn while doing the work. Here, the role of the fieldwork faculty supervisor assumes significance for the learning of the students. While the fieldwork agency contact person assigns the tasks to the students in the agency or community, the faculty supervisor mentors learning of the student in carrying out the assigned tasks. In the process, the students fulfil the academic requirement of learning practice skills as guided by the faculty supervisor. The students also contribute to the agency by delivering completed tasks. In order to optimize student learning, the faculty supervisor needs to maintain a good working relationship with the agency and its contact person. At times, conflicts arise around the expectation of the agency contact person from the students, particularly about certain tasks assigned. For example, the students are asked to assist in routine administrative work like sorting and filing documents, which is seen by the students as of no learning value. Inability of the students to actually secure funding from external sources for agency work or events is another area that creates discomfort.

In addition to a social work degree and the corresponding fieldwork training experience, it is helpful for a student's profile to include exposure and experience working with certain emerging issues that may not be covered in the curriculum. This can be gained through volunteering or internship with actual work experience in the field. Many a times, the agencies pay some honorarium to the intern. The interested students undertake such voluntary internship, outside the curriculum requirements, during university vacations (Garain & Komal, 2016).

The field placement agencies also expect the social work institutes to place students for voluntary internship during vacations, which is not part of the compulsory curriculum requirement. As mentioned, students do undertake voluntary internships during vacations for extra exposure in the area of their interest and to build their resume, keeping an eye on campus placement. The students often prefer to go for paid internship in the agencies rather than in the ones where the university places the students for fieldwork.

Expectations of graduating students

Social work practice skill is the core determining component of a successful social worker. Most students seeking admission into a post-graduate programme in social work do this based on self-motivation. The motivating factor could be an inner urge to be in a helping profession or just to prepare oneself for better career opportunities. Either way, learning social work practice skills is important to attaining one's goal.

In the selection process comprising a range of assessment tools, the ultimately selected candidates display an inner urge and motivation to work among the needy, deprived, and the disadvantaged. In order to prepare for the admission process and to enhance their chances for selection, many applicants undertake internships and volunteer among the disadvantaged sections of the society prior to admission. It becomes significant to convince the admission panel that the applicant feels for and has fair understanding about the disadvantaged sections of the society and their issues. During the admission/selection process, the selected applicants are believed to have succeeded in expressing and displaying in front of the selection panel their expectation from the social work course, their ability to learn the skills to help the needy and helpless, their interest to give back to society, and their level of motivation to derive personal satisfaction from the helping profession.

Upon admission, as the course progresses, one can see the gradual changes in their expectations. From the second year onwards, most of the students become focused on job opportunities and campus placement, abandoning their pre-admission disposition and concern for the society. One can see the sea change in their motivation and expectation, contrary to the pre-admission mind-set. There is nothing wrong in being career oriented. However, the switch is deceptive and worrisome for the profession. The worry is about getting the wrong people in a helping profession. Imagine someone acquiring a medical degree and converting the skill to a money-making business. One can clearly feel the difference between the expectations expressed at the time of admission compared to the expectation expressed by the graduating social work students.

Becoming the alumni of the best-known universities is the primary goal, followed by the desired programme of study in that university. It is like getting into the best available university and then using the name of the university as a launching pad in one's career. People in society refer to themselves as alumni of the university without detailing the course of study completed. Being an alumnus of a much-sought-after university lends a measure of prestige.

Developing competency in social work practice skills is found to be a low priority for students. The desire to get the degree with the highest possible grade is the primary concern while attempting to complete the given curriculum requirements. A social work degree is seen as a vehicle to pursue a career, earn a livelihood, and get recognized in the society. Not many qualifications provide this unique combination of making good money, getting job satisfaction, and earning respect in society, as provided by a career in social work.

It is a different career to pursue in social work, unlike the commonly travelled studies and careers in medicine, engineering, architecture, or management. In contemporary times, a large number of students in reputed social work institutes are found to be holding basic eligibility degrees in a much-sought-after professional course like medicine, engineering, architecture, agriculture, physiotherapy, management, law, or mass communication. At times, the students enrol and complete such courses in order to fulfil the desire of their parents or due to peer pressure and then switch to social work courses as a personal choice. There are also instances of students from a professional course deserting halfway through to enrol in a course in social work. These students form a separate segment of those who display motivation and sincerity in getting the best out of the curriculum and attain a better degree of competency in terms of skill development than the rest of their classmates. A well-paid job and so-called good career are low in their frame of mind. Such students look for something beyond money from a career in social work.

Expectations of recruiters

Although different recruiters may have different specific need-based expectations from a social worker, a certain degree of skill competency, domain knowledge, personality traits, and attitude are always highly

LEARNING SOCIAL WORK PRACTICE SKILLS

valued by all prospective recruiters. A master's level degree in social work is the most desired qualification for an entry level job in a social sector organization. Some recruiters and recruiting organizations also hire graduating students from related social science disciplines such as sociology, psychology, counselling, rural development/management, mass media, education, or home science. At times the recruiters also settle on undergraduate/ bachelor's level qualifications for field/community level job profiles with or without experience. However, a master's level degree is considered a requirement for most positions in social sector organizations.

The social workers are found to be engaged in every facets of community life and engaged in wide range of organizational entities, both in not-for-profit and for-profit sectors. In order to understand the recruiter's expectations about skill competency on the part of the social workers, it will be useful to look at the nature and range of organizations that employ professionally qualified social workers:

1 Cells for senior citizen, women, and children at police stations
2 Chambers of commerce
3 Child development agencies: day care centres, adoption agencies, children's homes
4 Community-based organizations: mahila mandals (i.e., women's groups), youth clubs, famers clubs, self-help groups
5 Community division of international clubs: Rotary, Lions, Giants, Inner Wheel clubs
6 Community mental health centres: clinics, day care centres, homes, outreach programmes
7 Consultancy and intermediary organizations in the social sector
8 Corporate social responsibility (CSR) division of companies
9 Correctional division in prisons and under-trial facilities
10 Correctional programmes and facilities
11 Counselling and social service division of physiotherapy clinics
12 Counselling centres for general counselling, career counselling, therapy
13 De-addiction and rehabilitation centres for drug and substance addicts, alcoholics, smokers
14 Foreign/international funding agencies
15 Government development agencies and departments: funded, sponsored, and run by the government
16 Health and hospital organizations: social service departments in hospitals, nursing homes, outreach health centres, community/rural health posts, preventive/curative health care programmes
17 Hospices
18 Human resource department of companies
19 Inter-government bilateral aid programmes/agencies

183

20 Legal aid agencies: legal aid clinics, legal firms, family courts, and other courts
21 Market research organizations
22 Media centres: print and electronic media companies, advertising agencies
23 Mental health institutions: clinics, day care centres, homes, community outreach units
24 Networking organizations
25 Night shelters
26 Non-government funding agencies in India: public charitable trusts
27 Office of elected representatives/political party offices
28 Private practice by social worker: self-employed/freelancing/independent practitioners
29 Recruitment firms: head hunting/placement agencies
30 Rehabilitation and resettlement division of real estate and infrastructure companies
31 Schools: for counselling, work education, crafts, recreation, sports, extra-curricular activities
32 Senior citizen centres: day care centres, non-institutional and outreach services, old age homes, post-retirement homes
33 Social advocacy organizations
34 Social enterprises
35 Social-sector research agencies
36 Social service department of local self-government in rural and urban areas: panchayat, municipality
37 Universities, colleges, and academic institutes: for teaching, research, administration, social protection office, counselling, campus placement work
38 Vocational and skill training centres
39 Youth organizations

It may be seen in this list that most of the recruiting organizations for social workers are engaged in direct service delivery to the clients, as individuals or in small groups, through institutionalized as well as non-institutionalized or community outreach facilities. A few of those are of residential in nature, but most of the agencies are non-residential activity centres. Most of the programme of activities in which the social workers are engaged are primary settings for social work practice, whereas a few are secondary settings. In brief, it may be stated that most employed social workers are likely to be supervised by professionally qualified social workers in the primary setting organizations. The primary setting organizations, as well as the social work unit in the secondary setting agencies, will provide a hospitable environment to the social workers for practising social work skills while performing their duties.

In continuation with understanding the nature of recruiting organizations, the following section provides the typical designations offered to the social workers at different levels of the organizational hierarchy in various settings, as follows:

1 Administrator
2 Advocacy Officer
3 Case Worker
4 Community Relations Officer
5 Community Social Worker
6 Community Worker
7 Consultant
8 Coordinator
9 Counsellor
10 Development Officer
11 Documentation Officer
12 Evaluation Officer
13 Field Officer
14 Fundraising Officer
15 Liaison Officer
16 Manager
17 Medical Social Worker
18 Membership Officer
19 Monitoring Officer
20 Officer
21 Partnership Officer
22 Planner
23 Policymaker
24 Programme Assistant
25 Programme Associate
26 Programme Manager
27 Programme Officer
28 Project Assistant
29 Project Associate
30 Project Manager
31 Project Officer
32 Public Health Officer
33 Public Health Social Worker
34 Research Assistant
35 Research Associate
36 Research Fellow
37 Research Officer
38 Researcher
39 Resource Officer

40 School Social Worker
41 Social Researcher
42 Social Worker
43 Supervisor
44 Trainee
45 Trainer
46 Training Officer
47 Volunteer Officer
48 Welfare Officer

(Note: The terms manager, coordinator, officer, and worker may be used interchangeably depending on the size and nature of the organization).

The range of designations offered to the social workers reflect the nature and scope of work of the recruiting organization. The nature of work assigned to a social worker largely is reflected in the designation. At times, the significance of the post in the organization depends on the depth in the hierarchy of the organization, being a tall or flat type of organization.

Irrespective of the designation, most social workers are required to do a certain amount of both client interface work and administrative work. As they go up in the organizational hierarchy, the non-client interface administrative work increases. In view of the nature of the work, it is pertinent to note that the non-government social-sector organizations, particularly the small NGOs, are starved of funds to carry out activities. They look at social workers with a hope to be able to help them in accessing funds from available sources. The medium and large NGOs expect the graduating students, being fresh out of university, to be able to conceive new need-based projects, help formulate project proposals, and help in ongoing project execution. They are not looked at as valuable for fundraising by their recruiters. The corporate and government recruiters look for smart, knowledgeable, and competent workers. There is one common expectation among all the recruiters, that is, on joining the organization, the social worker must be able to assume responsibility and start delivering quickly. The corporate and large NGOs may have an induction period, and the small NGOs and the government organizations may allocate a day or two for introduction, induction or orientation purposes.

Most recruiters, irrespective of nature or size of the organization and location of the desired position in the hierarchy, look for core competency in the form of domain knowledge and basic skills required for executing social-sector projects and activities. Although the domain knowledge requirement may differ from organization to organization, core skill competency is a basic common requirement for all recruiters for job performance (Nagpaul, 1988). All the recruiting organizations expect the social work graduates to have a basic level of skill competency at least in the following areas:

1 Needs assessment
2 Conceiving project ideas
3 Writing project proposals
4 Fundraising
5 Project review reports
6 Organizing training programmes
7 Conducting community meetings
8 Writing reports
9 Drafting letters
10 Counselling
11 Computer and Internet
12 Social networking

The recruiters, in general, expect the social workers to have some degree of domain knowledge in the following areas:

1 Government policies for education, health, housing, women, children, and NGOs
2 Laws applicable to NGOs
3 Basic rights of women, children, the physically and mentally challenged, scheduled castes, scheduled tribes, minorities, and other indigenous populations
4 Government schemes for women, children, the physically and mentally challenged, scheduled castes, scheduled tribes, and minorities
5 Government organizations and ministries for supporting not-for-profit and charitable initiatives
6 Prominent NGOs working for women, children, the physically and mentally challenged, scheduled castes, scheduled tribes, minorities, drug addicts, and alcoholics
7 Prominent NGOs working on skill development, community health, livelihood, and education
8 Prominent non-government funding agencies at the local and national level
9 Prominent foreign funding agencies operating in the country

As most of India's population reside in the villages and in slum communities, most community-based organizations and the programme of activities operated and/or sponsored by the government, corporate, and non-government organizations are focused on these community settings. The recruiters expect the graduating students to be equipped with the necessary competency skills to conceive, design, and develop required tools; collect field data; and prepare village studies reports with a plan of action for intervention (Lipton, 1978; Mukherjee, 1963).

In view of increasing cross-border as well as global exchange of knowledge, funds, volunteers, and technical expertise, the recruiters value and look for social networking skills in the prospective employees, the social workers. Due to advances in technology and globalization, the problems are becoming more complex. This has brought a focus on the expectation of social networking skills on the part of the graduating social workers. Such emerging expectation has impacted the curriculum structure of social work education in India as well and called for developing appropriate perspectives among the social workers. The perspective, values, curriculum structure, mode of imparting knowledge and skills, and the standards for social work education have been undergoing changes in the domain of cultural diversity, social networking, virtual volunteering, social business for economic empowerment, computer skills, social protection and affirmative action for the minorities, etc. (Alphonse, George, & Moffatt, 2008; Das & Anand, 2014).

Overall, the recruiters look for honest, dedicated, passionate, dependable, loyal, and career-oriented social work employees. They expect the social workers to commit to stay on the job in the organization for a certain period, say at least for two years.

Expectations of clients

Social workers are expected to connect the clientele/beneficiaries with agencies that provide services, resources, and opportunities to the needy individual, his or her family, and the members of his or her community.

The clients expect the social workers to represent and advocate by mobilizing efforts on behalf of them as individuals and their communities to resolve their problems in accessing resources, facilities, and government benefits and to protect them with regard to issues of human dignity, social exclusion, inequalities, social injustice, exploitation, and violence.

The clients seek help from the social workers to get relief in a personal crisis, to secure material and financial assistance, to access government facilities and benefits from schemes, and to find references for reaching out to external resources (Nagpaul, 1988). They look at the social workers to be resourceful to address and resolve all of their problems. Although the clients normally do not expect material or financial help from the social worker personally, they expect the social workers to do the work for them. For example, a slum dweller may approach a social worker for help in procuring a ration card for the family, government proof of dwelling for their hut, electricity connection for their home, water connection for the community water tap, community toilet, sewerage cleaning, municipal garbage collection, starting pre-primary school in the community, admission for their children to the neighbourhood school, sponsorship for skill training for their children, medical clinic for the community, etc. The social workers are expected to do the necessary paper work, follow up, and get the services. It is taken for granted by the clients that the social workers have the required knowledge, skill, and attitude to assist them. It is usually found that the social workers resort to a directive approach to assist or facilitate addressing the problems of the clientele. The directive approach is chosen over the non-directive approach on the grounds of expecting quicker results, through norms and procedures prescribed by the social worker.

Whether or not the client consents to participate in the process directed by the social worker, clients expect and want to participate and express their opinion at every stage of the process to attain the desired goal. The client also expects the social worker to maintain confidentiality about the case and the client's information. The client expects the social worker to be resourceful and get them access to material and financial resources, although they have little concern about the social worker's inter-personal skill competency.

Career path of social work employees

Graduating social work students look for opportunities to work through organizations. This gives them an institutionalized system, a secured environment, fixed pay, and minimum or no risk or challenges to work. The social workers are not trained to be risk taking, which is a critical attribute for an entrepreneur. Although the social work graduates opt for a job in an organization, mostly spending their entire work life as an employee, the career path may vary. The underlying factors contributing to different career paths may include personality attributes, the competency level acquired in the university, career goals, and the effort put forth in the job.

A graduating student is equipped with rudimentary skills; incomplete information about applicable government rules, policy, and laws; and inadequate domain knowledge. Most of them may have had no prior exposure to or experience with social-sector organizations and projects, except doing some ad hoc internship or volunteering somewhere. However, they come with a certain degree of theoretical knowledge and exposure to social-sector projects/organizations, as well as energy, dynamism, fresh ideas, and the urge to earn a livelihood. It is a challenge for the employing organization to guide, mould, and train them while they learn on the job. On-the-job learning in the first job after graduating from a social work institute creates and builds the actual foundation for a successful career in social work.

The nature of the job pursued by a social worker during his or her career is an important aspect in the career path. The nature of the job can be categorized into four areas: (1) skill-oriented service delivery, (2) managerial, (3) conceptual and research based, and (4) strategic and policy based. Skill-based service delivery jobs are often located at the operational level and are field based and client or beneficiary centric. They are designated as trainee, field assistant, co-worker, social worker, case worker, counsellor, field officer, and project officer, among others. In the organizational hierarchy, the skill-based jobs are positioned at the grassroots level, sometimes lower and, at the most, the middle level in the hierarchy. This is typically a line function in organizational structure. The managerial jobs refer to coordinating or running a major project, division, or the organization itself. This is a line function at the middle and senior level of the organization. The job designations may include supervisor, coordinator, programme officer, project manager, administrator, centre or area in charge, assistant/deputy director, and director or executive director. Conceptual and research-based job contents relate to positions concerning visualizing, conceiving, analysing, designing, and developing ideas, projects, programmes, events, and interventions for providing support to the policy makers, administrators, fundraisers, and operational staff of the organization. Such positions are located at the middle and senior levels of hierarchy, and it is a staff function. Social workers holding conceptual and research positions enjoy a high degree of autonomy and a flexible work environment. Typically, they are designated in one of the roles mentioned earlier. The head of the organization is normally found to be accommodative and flexible in deciding their designations. Strategic and policy based job positions may be a line function or a staff function in an organizational structure. However, they are invariably located at the middle level or higher level in the organizational hierarchy. Such a position may also be consulting or advisory in nature. The nature of the job in strategic and policy centric positions relates to either (1) being head of an organization or of a major division, or (2) providing decision-making support services to chief functionaries and senior executives, as well as board members of the organization. The job typically may involve directing the organization or advising in macro-level decision making in the organization. The strategic positions may be designated as project manager, administrator, director or executive director, consultant, advisor, policy analyst, executive assistant, etc.

The skill oriented and managerial jobs of a social worker are operational and line functions in an organization, whereas research, strategy, and policy based jobs are advisory and supporting in nature and do not involve decision-making and executing responsibilities in the mainstream organizational structure. Sometimes, the position of the head of an organization may refer to the strategic and policy making functions and hence constitute operational and executive position.

The career path of a social work employee is largely in the track of skill-based, operation, decision making, and executive function in an organization. They move up the organizational ladder, starting from entering the organization with a skilled job and going up to managerial and strategic positions. Some may go horizontally in the organizational structure and opt for an advisory, consulting, non-executing function.

The career path of a social worker may also be classified as field based or office based. The skill-based service delivery jobs are mostly field based, whereas the managerial, research, strategic, and policy jobs are primarily office based with certain level of involvement in the field. The nature of the job can be grouped into primarily executing, coordinating, managing, directing, and advising, mostly progressing in that order in terms of one's seniority, competency, and hierarchy in the organization. The extent of involvement of a social worker in any of the classifications in conceiving, initiating, planning, organizing, coordinating, staffing, budgeting, fundraising, resource allocating, communicating, reviewing, documenting, reporting, policy making, controlling, leading, directing different aspects of the tasks/activities/projects/centres/ divisions/organization will differ according to operational manual and by-laws of the organization.

The career path that evolves in an organization for a social work employee will also depend on the nature of the organization. A small grassroots community based non-governmental voluntary organization is likely to be very informal, and hence a social work employee may have to perform any and all types of responsibilities as the situation demands. For example, one may have to draft a letter or proposal, type it, print it, and then go to post office to send it. He or she may also have to receive a representative of the funding agency, accompany him or her on a site visit, give a presentation, and negotiate the terms. The situation is very different in a large NGO, a company-sponsored foundation, and in a government organization. The organizational structure is very formal and at times rigid, and the nature of job responsibilities may be highly structured and specialized with a clear monitoring mechanism. A graduating student with limited skill competency cannot afford to be choosey and thus he or she takes the available best-paying job at the first instant. For the first job, many graduates start work in a small local NGO and then switch to medium or large NGO in few years' time. Then in early mid-career, they look for avenues to join a government organization or a CSR job for better pay, better work environment, and job security. Although the option to get into a government job is constrained by an age limit, efforts to switch to a better job in large or good NGOs and corporate CSR continues mid-career and later. If not content with the nature of job or the career path, some of the social workers take to freelancing and advisory jobs with a flexible and honourable work environment.

Career path of practising social workers

Graduating social workers are not equipped to practise. The curriculum does not adequately prepare them to feel confident to initiate anything on their own. At best, they can carry out tasks assigned and supervised by a practitioner. Yet there are few areas suitable for a new social work graduate to assist a practitioner. The social work degree is still seen as an academic qualification with a certain level of exposure in terms of field practice. Therefore, most graduating students look for job placement, while a few acquire further knowledge and skills through higher studies. Independently practising social workers are normally senior level and experienced professionals who have started their practice after long years of working in an organization. Such practitioners prefer working on their own, with or without setting up a firm or organizational entity. Sometimes, they do engage one or two juniors or interns from social work institutes. Social work as a practising career for a graduating social work professional or a young professional has crippling limitations, and it is challenging to start and get foothold.

The absence of a system for issuing licenses to social workers in most countries has added further constraints in getting trained social workers to practise and receive value for it. In the absence of a licensing authority in the country, a qualified social worker may practise as a freelancing professional on his or her own, with or without seeking membership of a body of social workers. However, membership of an association of social workers does help one to stay affiliated and share a common concern for practising in annual seminars or other meetings of the members and practitioners.

Options available to a qualified social worker to practise can include a gradual movement from interning or assisting under a practitioner or a practising firm to starting one's own consulting entity. As a first entry point to practise, a social worker may join as an intern or a junior assisting a practising social worker or a team of social workers in a consulting firm. At the second level, after acquiring confidence and competency to practise, one moves to become a consulting practitioner in a firm. At the next level, a senior social worker may start his or her own practice as a freelancer. The final stage of a practitioner could be to start his or her own consulting practice firm in order to consolidate and expand the practice in an organized manner.

Given the social work curriculum among the countries, the generic social work curriculum can be grouped into two different practice points of view: clinical and developmental. Broadly, the social work curriculum in developed countries largely focuses on the clinical approach, whereas the curriculum in developing countries is built around a developmental approach addressing the human needs that arise out of poverty, ill health, illiteracy, unemployment, and related aspects. Because the social work degree is considered the basic degree in social work to enter the profession, the generic social work curriculum exposes the students to the basic skills of casework, counselling, trainer, group worker, facilitator, communicator, organizer, and researcher, among others, irrespective of being clinical and development focused (Datar et al., 2010; UGC, 1980).

At the higher level, the social work course with specialized curriculum helps concentrate understanding and focused skills pertaining to the domain of specialization. The traditional available specializations in the social work curriculum are community development, medical and psychiatric social work, family and child welfare, criminology and correctional social work, and social policy and social welfare administration (UGC, 1980). The students enrolling in a particular specialization for a social work degree receive concentrated course work and fieldwork practice in the related domain in the final year of study. Such students graduate with a comparatively clear focus for their career path in that specialized domain and develop practice skills accordingly. In later years of their career, some of them may end up practising in their specialized domain, whereas some may even shift their area of concentration. The course curriculum does play a critical role in building a mind-set among the students in terms of developing the basic practice skills in a particular field of social work (Datar et al., 2010).

The career path of practising social workers is largely dependent on the functional specialization acquired during training, as well as personal specialization attained on the job after graduation. The career path of a social work graduate in the initial years depends on the level of functional specialization acquired through classroom lecture and practice-based learning as part of the university curriculum. The course curriculum in general, and the learning infrastructure at the university in particular, are expected to ensure a certain minimum level of attainment of functional specialization on the part of a graduating student. However, lack of standardization of learning inputs and outputs in the education system can be seen in the wide gap in the attained skills, and this is reflected in the acquired functional specialization in the graduating students (Nagpaul, 1986). A visible indicator is the wide gap in the pay packages received by the graduating students in terms of campus placement. Enhancing functional specialization competency in the graduating students is a challenge to be faced by the students as well as the social work institutions if they want to achieve recognition for the social work profession.

Once in the field, social workers over the years choose to focus on a specific field of practice and acquire knowledge, develop the necessary competency skills, and become oriented to the appropriate attitudinal perspective. This is personal specialization. The level of competency acquired over the years through field practice determines the degree of personal specialization of a social work professional. This is purely individual centric and stays with the person wherever they go in their career. There is limited possibility of codification and standardization.

Typically, a practising social worker may be operating in one or more domains of counsellor (with options for expertise as marriage counsellor, career councillor, academic councillor, etc.), trainer, advocacy expert, consultant, researcher, among others.

Career path of social work entrepreneurs

Entrepreneurship is equated with business in social sciences and even more in the social work discipline. Social workers entering the domain of entrepreneurship is a recent phenomenon. By and large, social work practice in the West and in developed countries mostly has a clinical approach, focusing on casework, counselling, mental health, and other intra and inter personal relationship skills. The social work profession in Asian and African countries mainly caters to addressing the basic necessities of the poor and disadvantaged with a limited focus on clinical and rights-based approaches.

The social work practice skill sets differ in two different contexts. The former focuses on self-awareness, empathy, inter-personal relationships, coping with emotions, coping with stress, effective communication, and such other clinical social work practice skill sets in order to diagnose and treat psychological, emotional, and behavioural issues so as to assist clientele in functioning better in their social environments. Their psychosocial and inter-personal skills aim at actualizing potential competencies into desirable behaviours and promoting mental wellbeing that leads to a healthy and productive life.

The social workers in Asian and African countries require development oriented practice skills of needs assessment, critical analysis, project formulation, project appraisal, intervention strategies, project monitoring and evaluation, fundraising, creative thinking, problem solving, and participatory development of the beneficiaries in order to help people solve and cope with everyday problems (Datar et al., 2010). Thus, a bottom-up approach from the grassroots level to policy making is critical for social work practitioners in Asian and African countries.

Daily realities, people's perspectives, and policy interventions in the Asian and African countries are likely to be similar in other developing and less developed countries elsewhere. The expectations and perspectives are very different in the Western and European countries.

In both clinical as well as developmental settings, one common ground could be developing entrepreneurial skills in social workers. The social workers with entrepreneurial skills can deliver significant impact in their interventions across different settings. Anneke Krakers researched the business opportunities in social work and developed a method to transform social workers from employees to entrepreneurs (seen in Social Work Helper, 2016). Considering the under-valuation and under-payment of social workers everywhere, she looked at the aspect of entrepreneurship, marketing, branding, packaging, pricing, and promoting services offered by the social workers in a variety of contexts. An entrepreneurial social worker will be better equipped and thereby create more value for self as well as for the clientele who are needy and economically disadvantaged. Besides, a social worker with a business enterprise can grow the business, earn more money, and help others even more. Social workers need to overcome the mental block about negative associations with the word money. It is not about being greedy, but rather about getting value for the services offered and thereby fulfilling one's family responsibilities. The business of a social worker will help create long term wealth in terms of personal security and enable the social worker to have the freedom and confidence to help others.

There are examples of some successful business tycoons in every country turning into philanthropists. Some of the biggest contributions to charity come from business leaders like Azim Premji, chairman of Wipro; Bill Gates, chairman of Microsoft; and Warren Buffett of Berkshire. However, there are very few examples of social workers becoming successful entrepreneurs. Entrepreneurship holds the key to transforming the quality of life of the vast segment of the target population of the social workers. Social entrepreneurship, infusing a business with a social work perspective, is gradually emerging as a method of social work intervention (Garain, 2010). The social work curriculum in many universities, in both developed and developing countries, is focusing on developing social entrepreneurship competency in social work students through coursework, internships, and project work. This has the potential to change the landscape of social work intervention and contribute to enhancing the practice skills of social work professionals.

Conclusion

Social work as a discipline has still not received its due place as a profession. It has remained just an area of study in higher education, although it has earned identity as a discipline. But a lack of standardization of practice skills and codification of protocols for practitioners have been serious limitations. Each stakeholder has distinctive expectations from the discipline, but none has contributed seriously in addressing the limitations and codifying it as a discipline. The applicants and the students look at social work as a lucrative career option to study in a premier university, land in a good job, and earn fame and money. However, they contribute little in terms of self-adhering to given values, code of conduct, and principles of the profession. Self-interest serves as the only concern in their work life. In the same line, the provider of social work education, the universities, are largely concerned with fulfilling academic requirements, as with any other education path. The institutes, including the faculty or the universities, have done little over the decades to go beyond its campus to reach out to other stakeholders and promote the cause of the profession. The only contribution has been in organizing seminars and presenting papers for enriching one's personal profile or university report. The employing organizations have validly had little concern or interest, in the absence of any efforts on the part of the social workers or the alma mater university, about the status of the social work discipline. Lastly, the much-needed social work practice skills need to be organized, and a sustained support is required to standardize, codify, and enforce these to aid in positioning social work as a profession.

In the global arena, there is a wide gap among developed countries and rest of the world in the codification of social work practice skills and therefore the status of the social work discipline as a profession. Only a few developed countries have given statutory recognition to social work as a profession and provided licensing for social work practitioners. The social workers and the social work discipline in rest of the world are far behind in even developing a consensus on a set of common practising skills.

Notes

1 University refers to and includes institute, college, center, and department.
2 CSR refers to corporate social responsibility, philanthropy and community relations division of a business.
3 NGO refers to not-for-profit, private, voluntary, secular, non-governmental, charitable organizations.

References

Alphonse, M., George, P., & Moffatt, K. (2008). Redefining social work standards in the context of globalization: Lessons from India. *International Social Work, 51*(2), 145–158.
Christie, Alastair & Kruk, Edward (1998). Choosing to become a social worker: motives, incentives, concerns and disincentives, *Social Work Education,* 17:1, 21–34.

Christie, A., & Kruk, E. (1998). Choosing to become a social worker: Motives, incentives, concerns and disincentives. *Social Work Education, 17*(1), 21–34.

Cox, D. (2000). Internationalizing social work education. *Indian Journal of Social Work, 61*(2), 157–173.

Das, C., & Anand, J. C. (2014). Strategies for critical reflection in international contexts for social work students. *International Social Work, 57*(2), 109–120.

Dasgupta, S. (Ed.). (1967). *Towards a philosophy of social work in India.* New Delhi: Popular Book Services.

Datar, S., et al. (Eds.). (2010). *Skill training for social workers: A manual.* New Delhi: Sage Publication.

Garain, S. (1993). Training grassroots level workers in empowering the rural poor: Experiences of an Indian NGO. *Indian Journal of Social Work, 54*(3), 381–392.

Garain, S. (2010). Social entrepreneurship: Towards an emerging method of social work intervention. In P. Ilango (Ed.), *Professional social work in India: Contributions to welfare and development* (pp. 17–35). New Delhi: Allied Publishers.

Garain, S., & Komal, S. (2016). Experiential learning in training social workers. In B. M. Das & Sanjoy Roy (Eds.), *Field work in social work education: Contemporary practices and perspectives.* New Delhi: Atlantic Publishers.

Gore, M. S. (2011). *Social work and social work education.* New Delhi: Rawat Publications.

Government of India. (1955). *Social welfare in India.* New Delhi: Planning Commission.

Government of India. (1978). *Report of the second review committee for social work education, retrospect and prospect.* New Delhi: University Grants Commission.

Government of India. (1987). *Encyclopedia of social work in India* (Vols. I, II, III, IV). New Delhi: Ministry of Welfare.

Lipton, M. (1978). Village studies and alternative methods of rural research. In B. Dasgupta (Ed.), *Village studies in the third world* (pp. 15–26). New Delhi: Hindustan Publishing Corporation.

Mandal, K. S. (1989). American influence on social work education in India and its impact. *International Social Work, 32,* 302–309.

Manshardt, C. (1967). *Pioneering on social frontiers in India.* Bombay: Lalvani.

Mukherjee, R. (1963). On village studies in India. *Indian Journal of Social Research, 4*(2), 1–14.

Nagpaul, H. (1986). *Highlights on the paper on the diffusion of Americanism: A case study of social work education in India and its Dilemmas.* Paper presented at the XI world congress of sociology (18–22 August), New Delhi.

Nagpaul, H. (1988). The profession of social work in contemporary India. *Indian Journal of Social Research, 29*(4), 339–354.

Nair, K. (Ed.). (1981). *Social work education and social work practice in India.* Madras: Association of Schools of Social Work in India.

Patel, I. (1972). *The learner in social work education a social work educator's view.* Curriculum development and teaching: Proceedings of the South East

Asian seminar for social work educators, School of Social Work, Bombay University, Institute of Social Service.

Pathak, S. H. (1975). A quarter century of professional social work in India. In S. D. Gokhale (Ed.), *Social welfare-legend and legacy* (pp. 170–192). Bombay: Popular Prakashan.

Pawar, M. (2010). Looking outwards: Teaching international social work in Asia. *Social Work Education, 29*(8), 896–909.

Ramachandran, P. (1986). *Perspective for social work training*: 2000. A.D. Bombay: TISS (mimeograph).

Ranade, S. N. (1975). Social work education in India. In S. D. Gokhale (Ed.), *Social welfare-legend and legacy* (pp. 193–203). Bombay: Popular Prakashan.

Singh, R. (Ed.). (1985). *Fieldwork in social work: A perspective for human professions*. New Delhi: Concept Publishing Company.

Social Work Helper. (2016). *Social workers discover how entrepreneurship increases their impact*. Retrieved May 7, 2017, from www.socialworkhelper.com/2016/09/22/social-workers-discover-entrepreneurship-increases-impact/

UGC (University Grants Commission). (1980). *Review of social work education in India: Retrospect and prospect*. New Delhi: UGC.

Wilson, G., & McCrystal, P. (2007). Motivations and career aspirations of MSW students in Northern Ireland. *Journal Social Work Education, 26*(1), 35–52.

Yelaja, S. A. (1970). Towards a conceptualisation of the social work profession in India. *Applied Social Studies, 2*(91), 21–26.

Yip, K. (2005). Asian challenges to globalisation of social work education. *Indian Journal of Social Work, 66*(1), 49–66.

11

NON-INSTITUTIONAL AND COMMUNITY-BASED FIELD PLACEMENT IN SOCIAL WORK

Experiments with inquiry-based learning and participatory action research

Bipin Jojo and Ronald Yesudhas

Introduction

Field education is an integral part of the social work curriculum, providing learners the opportunity to apply what they learn in the classroom and in real-life situations both in structured agencies and in communities. It consists of both placements (in the form of an internship) with supervision provided by social work educators and professional social workers working in the field. Unlike institutional placements, non-institutional and community-based field placements offer both a broad work scope and space for creativity and innovation. Normally local communities, community-based organizations, and informal action groups support schools of social work to offer such placement to students genuinely interested in creating social change and inclusion.

This chapter documents experiments in institutional and community-based field placement through utilization of inquiry-based learning (IBL) and participatory action research (PAR). In the IBL method, the supervisor facilitates the learning process of students by helping them generate questions, investigate, construct knowledge, and reflect. PAR, on other hand, offers an action-enabled research where student social workers work alongside people in identifying, collecting, and analysing data to help them take control of their lives. Though both methods seem similar, IBL and PAR are different in their orientations in terms of the students' placement and learning perspective. The two cases provided by the authors give an account of utilizing both methods in fieldwork placement to the fullest use. The authors encourage the schools of social work in India to move towards participatory, empowering, and emancipatory methods while going for non-institutional and community-based field placements. This would increase students' interest in reading and research and will eventually help involve people and communities in changing their own lives.

Fieldwork: definition and aims

Social work is a helping profession. The main goal of social work is to help individuals, families, groups, and communities enhance their individual and collective wellbeing. It aims to help people develop skills and enhances the ability of individuals, groups, and communities to use their own resources to resolve social and developmental problems. The values of human rights and social justice are crucial to social work practice.

The International Federation of Social Work (IFSW) defines social work

> as a practice-based profession and an academic discipline that promotes social change and development, social cohesion, and the empowerment and liberation of people. Principles of social justice, human rights, collective responsibility and respect for diversities are central to social work. Underpinned by theories of social work, social sciences, humanities and indigenous knowledge, social work engages people and structures to address life challenges and enhance wellbeing.
> (http://ifsw.org/policies/definition-of-social-work)

From the definition it is clear that social work is a field-based practice profession, and thereby it is clear that it has 'field' moorings. French social scientist Pierre Bourdieu finds field as a setting in which agents and their social positions are located. The position of each agent is a result of interactions between specific rules of the field, the agent's habitat, and the socio-economic and cultural capital of the agent.

Fieldwork is an integral part of social work education. It is often referred to as the flagship or unique aspect of social work education. According to Subhedar (2001), fieldwork is the vital link which "provides an opportunity to the students to apply their theoretical knowledge taught in the classroom appropriately in different practical situations" (2001, p. 23). The UGC Review Committee on social work education in 1978 outlined the important objectives of fieldwork in the social work curriculum, which includes the following:

- Development of professional skills through learning to use knowledge for the study and analysis of problems and selection of appropriate means to solve them.

- Development of skills in problem solving at the macro and micro levels.
- Integration of classroom learning with field practice.
- Development of professional attitudes, values, and commitment.
- Development of self-awareness and a professional ideal.

Though fieldwork is the core of social work education, there are seldom any authentic textbooks on the subject in India. The Department of Social Work, University of Delhi, organized a two-week-long faculty development workshop on fieldwork in 1981. Dr R. R. Singh, the director of the workshop, did a painstaking task of defining fieldwork based on the workshop participants' (social work educators') feedback/definition development exercise. Accordingly,

> field work in social work education is a guided interaction process between a student and the actual life situation in which social work as a profession has an abiding and deep concern, and which needed to be remedied, improved, or changes for full development of human-environmental potential.
>
> (Singh 1985, p. 43)

One must keep in mind that the learning goals in fieldwork must be arranged sequentially from simple to complex. However, the overall aim is to provide opportunities for applying the knowledge and the information gained in the theoretical background to daily reality. This learning experience should provide an opportunity of working with communities, groups, and individuals/families and managing organization tasks. At the end of fieldwork, student should possess the following capacities:

- Understanding both the agency and the clients as systems.
- Developing knowledge about administrative procedures, programme management, and utilizing these skills in practice.
- Developing skills of problem-solving processes and practice-based research.
- Acquiring skills in communication: writing client records, documentation of agency records, correspondence, and public relations skills.
- Using instruction to learn to practise.
- Developing as a professional.

Components of fieldwork

There are six important components of fieldwork. They are orientation, rural camp, concurrent placement, block placement, study tour, and summer/winter internship.

Orientation

Students choose social work programmes for various reasons, such as passion for an issue, personal challenges, parental pressure, etc. Hence, it is important to give proper orientation to the field and fieldwork.

Orientation can be organized right in the first month of the fieldwork or can be spread across the semester or during the first year of the BSW or MSW programme. Some of the aspects of orientation include the following:

- Input on various aspects/concepts related to fieldwork such as agency, community, client, activities, methods, supervision, report writing process, etc.
- Agency visits
- Community visits
- Screening documentary films on social development issues
- Exercises to understand self and others
- Debriefing/reflection exercises, etc.

Rural camp

The second important component of fieldwork is the rural camp. Generally, rural camp is organized once in the academic programme (normally it is held for a week just before the fourth semester of the BSW programme and second semester of the MSW programme).

Rural camp can be organized in three ways. In the first model, the fieldwork secretariat/committee chooses a remote village and students live in groups of 20 to 30 in the selected village for a week to 10 days. They cook and share food, eat, and sleep in the villages. Emphasis is given on observing/studying the social systems, economic systems, and political systems in the villages.

In the second model, the fieldwork secretariat/students choose a remote village, and the students live in groups of six to ten and work closely with the people in preparing a village development plan, utilizing techniques of participatory rural appraisal/rapid rural appraisal. They finally present the plan to the village panchayat, which can be pursued by the panchayat later. This can normally be done in a week's time. In both the first and second model, students spend the entire week in the chosen village only.

In the third model of rural camp, the fieldwork secretariat/students choose an anchoring agency which will provide accommodations and food along with orienting them to the rural realities in the region. There could be multiple village and agency visits. This will help the students understand the work done by different agencies for rural development.

Concurrent placement

Concurrent placement is the most popular form of fieldwork practicum done by the students. In this model, students go to the field for two days and spend the rest of the week attending theory classes. This kind of placement offers close supervision by the faculty advisor/field instructor. Normally, concurrent placement is the norm during the first year of the MSW programme, and the first and second years of the BSW programme.

Block placement

During the senior years (MSW second year and BSW third year) at the social work department/college, students take block placement for four to five weeks' duration. During this time, there is plethora of opportunities for the students to get fully involved in the work of the agency. There is more space for creativity and less supervision by the faculty advisor/field instructor. This helps the student evolve into an independent professional.

Study tour

A study tour is organized for the final-year students to understand the work of different agencies on a select thematic area or in general. Exemplary organizations throughout the country can be visited, and their models are studied by the students. This helps them have a comparative perspective in future professional practice.

Summer/winter internships

Though not compulsory, the students, on their own or with the help of the career guidance and placement cell of the departments, can explore short-term internship opportunities. This gives them real-life work experience. It also helps them understand the job market situation and fine-tune their skills.

Other innovative aspects

There are several other innovative aspects which are experimented with by different schools of social work, such as urban immersion, international immersion, skill development workshop series, etc. With social work becoming a global profession, the demand for social workers with global experience is increasing. These innovative aspects of fieldwork can help students gain confidence and develop skills to deal with the ever-demanding world of work.

For the junior students, fieldwork agencies are allotted based on aspects such as distance from the residence, language ability, etc. However, for the senior students, their fieldwork interests are considered while working on placements. Students with an interest in working with individuals, groups, and families are placed in institutional and traditional settings. Students who show keen interest in non-traditional aspects are placed in non-institutional setups, such as in the communities.

Non-institutional, non-traditional, and community-based fieldwork

Conventionally, social work practice is located within a 'structural-functional' frame. The agency setting such as a psychiatric ward, prison complex, or child guidance clinic where a client–social worker relation is clearly defined is called a traditional setting. A traditional social worker uses micro practice to the fullest use and could use mezzo practice skills to a certain extent.

On the other hand, not all problems are individual or group based. Most of the problems have a basis in the socio-economic conditions prevailing in the society. Hence, social work intervention is largely required in non-traditional, non-institutional areas, such as the community, where utilization of alternative spaces is required. These non-traditional settings centre around public spaces (like community halls, buddha vihars, etc.) where community members gather socially. These spaces are rooted in the cultural heritage of the community.

Delgado (1999) describes non-traditional settings as informal centres which reach out to the communities that need help. He argues that such informal centres allow social work service to be based on the community's own strengths, while developing the community's capacity to help itself with assistance from professionals. These non-institutional forums play influential and very active roles in helping community residents in need. It engages local people and professional social workers to plan services with the communities.

Communities offer numerous characteristics that can be built upon for services and organizing. The idea is that by organizing around an existing collective identity or shared experience, there is a higher possibility of cohesion, as social capital plays a major role, and it turn it may lead to increased effectiveness of organizing. In the long run, non-traditional settings provide access to multiple generations of people living in the same community.

Now, let's talk about the term 'community.' As we know, this term is ambiguous. It means different things to different people. However, by looking at the context of the evolution of the term, we can narrow down its meaning. Two eminent functional sociologists, namely Ferdinand Tonnies and Emile Durkheim, argued that modernism has resulted in the decline of the traditional community. They also argued that traditional organic communities are replaced by a more atomized, individualistic, and superficial form of society. Thus, in their perception, community is a 'value.' It is not just a collection of individuals, but rather represents individuals who are part of a larger commune, which has meaning for them and for others. There are three major types of communities, namely geographic community, identity-based community, and community of interest. Corresponding to each type of community, appropriate field-work placement is offered to students opting to work in the community and non-institutional settings.

As the name suggests, a geographic community has physical boundaries by which it can be located. A geographic community is also known as a neighbourhood. Each neighbourhood has unique characteristics, such as caste, religion, region, language, etc. Within a neighbourhood itself, there could be people from diverse social strata and caste groups. As a social worker, it is important to understand different social groups and the space they occupy within the neighbourhood. Fieldwork placement in a geographic community is done by placing a group of three to five students in a neighbourhood. Usually, the local community-based organizations and social centres anchor the students.

Identity-based community is the second type. Such communities are formed on common identifiable characteristics such as having the same culture. Identity can be based on age, caste, religion, sexuality, etc. Community of identity may or may not be geographically bound. Fieldwork placement in a community of identity is done placing students with LGBT or with Dalit communities, etc., for example.

Community of interest, the third type, is present contemporaneously in different geographical spaces. Individuals may be connected to their interest community at the local, national, regional, or global levels. Fieldwork placement in the community of interest is done by placing students with environmental groups or other new social movements and social action groups which are involved in creating global cultural changes in the communities.

Experimentation is mostly avoided in higher education institutions offering social work education programmes. However, in the non-traditional, non-institutional, and community-based fieldwork settings there is lot of scope for experimentation and innovation. The evolution of inquiry-based learning and participatory action research has strengthened the cause. The two cases presented next illustrate this point.

Case 1: junior students and inquiry-based learning

IBL is an innovative instructional model. It is closer to the academic approach in field instruction (Royse, Dhoopa, & Rompf, 2012).

Professor Miriam Freeman in the College of Social Work, University of South Carolina, is a pioneer in using inquiry-based learning in social work education (Besley et al., 2007). In this method, the faculty advisor/field instructor facilitates the learning process by helping students generate questions, investigate, construct knowledge, and reflect (Besley et al., 2007). Inspired by the initiative of Professor Miriam Freeman, a few social work educators in India have started to use IBL in their field education programmes.

The first job for an educator is to develop a step-by-step process of facilitating learning among students using IBL. Justice et al. (2007) provide a framework of inquiry which was used by the authors. One important precondition for the excellence of this model is that the students should select an issue of their choice in the fieldwork practicum. It should not be thrust on them externally. It is appropriate to use IBL for supervising the BSW first-year and MSW first-year (junior) students.

In the experimentation done by the authors, a small cohort of three BSW students of the College of Social Work, Nirmala Niketan, Mumbai, was involved. The students in the cohort were from different geographical, cultural, and social backgrounds. Their abilities were also different. However, they chose a slum community as the area of work. The fieldwork committee placed them in an NGO working in a slum in the Malad area in Mumbai. The committee allotted the second author as field instructor to guide them. After an informal chat with the students, the field instructor understood their specific area of interest, namely 'water and sanitation conditions in slums.' He explained to the students his plan to use IBL for the fieldwork course. The students agreed to participate in the experiment. Once the learning plan was agreed to, the safety policy was reviewed by the students. This helped the students understand the safety protocol to follow during instances of stress, harassment, and human rights violations. The stages of the progress of the students are summarized next.

During the first fieldwork seminar, the students came with the proposal to study and understand the water and sanitation issues in the slums of Mumbai. The students were not used to reading scientific literature. Hence, they were initially bored after reading few articles. After motivation from the field instructor, the students took it as a challenging assignment and began to read the relevant literature. During the second fieldwork seminar, they came up with a brief review of the literature. The field instructor helped the students ask curious questions based on their readings. During the third fieldwork seminar, the students deliberated on the method which could be used in the study. They were not exposed to different methodologies at the undergraduate level. Hence, the field instructor oriented them to qualitative and quantitative research paradigms. Finally, based on the research questions, the qualitative methodology was found to be appropriate. The field instructor suggested the students use semi-structured interviews for the study.

Data collection was done in four phases. In the first phase, a list of key community informants was created. In the second phase, an interview guide was developed. In the third phase, data were collected from the participants who consented for the study. In the fourth phase, data were analysed thematically by the students. The findings were presented in the fourth fieldwork seminar. During the final fieldwork seminar of the semester, the students began to synthesize their findings. With a little bit of support from the field instructor, they were able to discuss their new discovery in relation to the questions investigated. Finally, the students not only published their research but also gained meaningful insight into the community with which they worked (Ronald, Lalit, Josy, & Impana, 2014). The following benefits were experienced:

- The students got an academic overview of the fieldwork situation. This is very important for the first-year students. As observed by many authors, many first-year students get lost in the field because they do not know what to observe and how to build rapport. Both these challenges are addressed in the IBL methodology.
- Second, IBL developed a research mind-set in the students. This helped them see the problem from a larger perspective.
- Third, students developed sensitivity towards the social problems of the local communities, as they see the issues of the people first-hand, rather than just read about it in books. This helps them appreciate social work values and develop the skills necessary for social work practice for the senior years in the respective social work programmes.

Case 2: senior students and participatory action research

Senior students (MSW second year, BSW second and third year) not only observe but also do constructive field intervention in the communities. Hence, PAR can be used both as an educational pedagogy and a critical tool for social work intervention in the field. PAR encourages students to analyse peoples' social problems and work in partnership with the poor to solve their issues.

PAR is a self-reflective and collective inquiry that social work students and community members undertake to understand and improve local situations in a way they find suitable. The main methodological concepts in PAR include *experience, critical reflection,* and *praxis*. PAR methodologists affirm that experience can be the basis of knowing and that experiential learning can lead to legitimate forms of knowledge (Baum, MacDougall, & Smith 2006). Another important concept in PAR is critical reflection. Freire's concept of 'praxis' is also important, as PAR sees that action and reflection must go together so that praxis cannot be divided into a preliminary stage of reflection and a subsequent stage of action.

There are many models in PAR. The community action model proposed by Lavery is closely related and useful to social work. This model is vital from the point of view of students' intervention in the field. The community action model involves a five-step process, namely (1) finding areas of concern, (2) research, (3) analysis, (4) planning action, and (5) implementation.

The authors did an experiment on the PAR methodology with a cohort of three MSW students of the College of Social Work, Nirmala Niketan, Mumbai. The students in this cohort were from different geographical, cultural, and social backgrounds, as in the case of the previous experiment. The students chose two areas, namely children and the slum community, as the area of work. Thus, the fieldwork committee placed them in a child rights NGO working in a slum in the Govandi area in Mumbai. The committee allotted the second author as a field instructor. Unlike the junior students, these senior students had the necessary interest, skills, and abilities. The process of utilizing PAR in the study context is explained next.

In the first stage, the fieldwork students, field instructor, agency contact persons, and the people in the community meet to analyse and identify the socio-economic forces that create problems in the community. This is a crucial step where the key issues challenging the community are identified.

In the second stage, the core team involved more volunteers (youth) from the community to design a participatory action research project. The objective of the project was to determine the root cause of child abuse in the community and outline the necessary steps to develop a child-friendly neighbourhood. Multiple methods such as surveys, unstructured interviews, and case studies were used in data collection.

In the third stage, results were drawn, and the core team prepared a preliminary report. The students met all the community volunteers and involved them in analysing, as they needed to acquire the skills to present the findings. This exercise gave the community volunteers not only confidence but also provided a feeling of ownership of the research.

In the fourth stage, the fieldwork students, field instructor, agency contact persons, and the key people in the community came together to develop an action plan. This included an awareness meeting in the community, a campaign in the slum level, and forming a pressure group to address the issue. In the fifth and final stage, the community took full control of the action. A brief evaluation exercise was conducted at end of the fieldwork by the core team.

The following benefits are derived from the PAR methodology:

- First, PAR is consistent with the code of ethics and core values promoted by the International Federation of Social Workers. The code clearly states that social work, as a field of study, and social workers, as responsible individuals, have an ethical responsibility to develop knowledge and use it for the advancement of social justice (Barbera, 2008). PAR in that sense helps the professional social work students develop local knowledge and challenge existing structural issues.
- Second, PAR allows social work students to work in partnership with people. Thus, it brings people into the centre of the debate. It also empowers people. Thus, one can see that 'partnership' and 'empowerment,' the critical concepts of social work practice, are integral to PAR (Barbera, 2008).
- Third, in PAR, the expertise and knowledge of groups and communities with whom the social work students intervened is honoured, respected, and utilized (Cassano & Dunlop, 2005). Thus, the social work value of respecting the community and their knowledge is adhered to by PAR.

Conclusion

From the presentations, one must be clear that IBL and PAR are two innovative methodologies used by social work educators to train the students in community-based field placement and facilitate their growth as full-fledged professional social workers. As discussed earlier, in the IBL method, the field instructor/supervisor facilitates the learning process of students by helping them generate questions, investigate, construct knowledge, and reflect. PAR, on other hand, offers an action-enabled yet research-driven fieldwork where student social workers collaborate with people in identifying, collecting, and analysing data to help them take control over their lives.

IBL and PAR can be well integrated into a BSW and MSW fieldwork practicum. It is not very difficult. The key to success is to motivate social work students, field instructors/supervisors, agency contact persons, and, above all, the departmental colleagues. Once departmental support and institute approval are obtained, one can enlist the help of fieldwork supervisors and the local community.

The role of the agency contact persons and the community people is pivotal in the successful use of IBL and PAR. If they provide support, the models discussed in this chapter can be successfully implemented. The students will be empowered to find areas of concern, develop research-oriented questions to collect data along with people, analyse, and plan an action with the community. The faculty advisor, field instructor, and supervisors can easily facilitate the process. The department and university's role, by extension, will also be justified through such innovative experiments in community-based fieldwork placements.

References

Barbera, R, A. (2008). Relationships and the research process: Participatory action research and social work. *Journal of Progressive Human Services*, *19*(2), 140–159.

Baum, F., MacDougall, C., & Smith, D. (2006). Glossary: Participatory action research. *Journal of Epidemiology and Community Health*, *60*(10), 854–857.

Besley, J., Caicedo, J., Crews, T., Freeman, M., Friedman, D., & Weinberg, J. (2007, October 23). *An exploration in to the inquiry based learning by an interdisciplinary group of USC faculty.* Retrieved from www.sc.edu/cte/inquiry/doc/ibl_exploration.pdf

Cassano, D, R., & Dunlop, J, M. (2005). Participatory action research with South Asian immigrant women: A Canadian example. *Critical Social Work*, *6*(1). Retrieved from http://www1.uwindsor.ca/criticalsocialwork/participatory-action-research-with-south-asian-immigrant-women-a-canadian-example

Delgado, M. (1999). *Social work practice in non-traditional Urban settings.* New York, NY: Oxford University Press.

Justice, C., Rice, J., Warry, W., Inglis, S., Miller, S., & Sammon, S. (2007). Inquiry in higher education: Reflections and directions on course design and teaching methods. *Innovative Higher Education*, *31*, 201–214.

Ronald, Y., Lalit, P., Josy, A., & Impana, S. (2014). Water and sanitation in Mumbai's slums: Education through inquiry based learning in social work. *The Qualitative Report*, *19*(45), 1–10.

Royse, D., Dhoopa, S., & Rompf, E. (2012). *Field instruction: A guide for social work students.* New York, NY: Pearson Educational Inc.

Singh, R. (1985). *Field work in social work education: A perspective for human service.* New Delhi: Concept Publishing Company.

Subhedar, I. (2001). *Field work training in social work.* Jaipur: Rawat Publications.

12

DEVELOPING SOCIAL WORK PRACTICE THEORIES
Some alternative ideas and approaches

Indrajit Goswami

Background

Since its inception in social work education, fieldwork has been mostly viewed as an obligatory component and has hardly been considered a strategic tool. After its long eventful journey through several evolutionary and revolutionary changes, social work is now at a juncture, where the whole world is undergoing rapid transformations due to disruptive technological innovations, rapidly changing lifestyles and aspirations of people, technology-driven changes in commerce and economy, and the vivid influence and impact of social media on thought processes and behaviour of people. Irrespective of their habitats, the functional and social-exchange modalities of people are a stake due to unprecedented changes in politics, governance, and product and service delivery systems. There have been instances where people, especially those who are still socially and economically backward, experience ambiguity, uncertainty, and helplessness. Several macro-level changes are happening without considering the real-life inconsistencies and sufferings of those who are still living at the mercy of governments, bureaucracy, and political leadership.

It wouldn't be fair and just to be myopic and think that we can still afford to maintain a status quo in social work education. The pace of development and transformation in the domain of social work education and practice, including the fieldwork practicum, has not yet witnessed any major breakthroughs so that it could emerge as one of the most deserving career options amidst other leading professional courses. Recently, a 'great place to work institute' survey for 2017 (Manzar, 2017)) found NGOs are ahead of the corporate sector in providing a positive and engaging employee experience with comparatively modest remuneration benefits than it could afford earlier. Many other positive push factors could have taken social work education to a new height, provided the opportunities had been tapped and integrated strategically with its systems and mechanisms. On the contrary, business/management education has flourished despite the economic slowdown due to its very professional approach and corporate connections. Unlike other professional disciplines, social work still can't establish itself as one of the most deserving professional disciplines due to a semi-professional outlook and lack of innovation. In the contemporary data-driven society, evidence-based credibility is one of the powerful attributes to get recognition of social work as a full-fledged 'service profession.'

Right from the beginning values and ethics have played a central role in shaping the structure, function, and scope of social work education and practice. However, it is evident that a greater amount of time and more resources in social work education have been used in classroom teaching but not in field education, especially in field training and grooming of professionals. The review of social work literature from the early part of the 20th century reveals that primarily it was all about understanding the values and moral purposes of the profession (Pumphrey, 1959). Later, in 1970s and 1980s, social work scholars, practitioners, and field instructors encountered issues related to ethical and moral dilemmas, and there had been recorded evidences of conflict between our duties and obligations (Hardman,1975; Teicher, 1967; Timms, 1983; Loewenberg & Dolgoff, 1982; Reamer, 1982,1993). Several mechanisms, such as introduction of specializations, field seminars, and statements on applied and practical ethics, were brought in to practice to overcome those 'dilemmas' and 'conflicts' (Rowan & Zinaich, 2002; Bogo, 2010; Doel et al. 2011; Royse et al. 2012), but despite few incremental changes, no significant improvements or transformations have happened.

It is evident that the majority of social work theories are constructed on the fundamental concept of 'the relationship' (Baldock & Prior, 1981) and that is a transactional relationship through verbal communication between the social worker and the client. It is expected that the trainees or students at social work schools will undergo rigorous training to become sensitized to establish, execute, govern, and utilize 'the relationship' effectively for the benefit of the people. The situation or context demands that social workers need to be self-aware and conscious about their language, values, ethos, personal likes and dislikes, preferences, and other social and cultural orientations. However, it is hardly known to us what exactly happens during the social interactions between a social worker and the clients. In addition, there is dearth of literature which could throw light on such interactions. Are we serious in strengthening the 'fieldwork' component? If so, we cannot afford to ignore or neglect the development of transactional skills among students. Also, it is important to appreciate that in the contemporary and emerging societies, the scope of the transactional/relationship competency of social workers extends beyond verbal communication and includes other competencies, such as patience, tolerance, gender sensitivity, adaptability, managing diversity, digital competencies, etc.

The development of transactional/relationship skills among students might have suffered due to a continuing misfit between textbook theories and actual practice (Curnock & Hardiker, 1979; Hardiker &Barker, 1981; Lewis, 1982; Corby, 1982). What is more important: 'theory-led practice' or 'practice-led theory'? The debate is still alive, because there is hardly any concrete research evidence to reach a conclusive solution on the issue. However, we cannot wait until the debate ends. We need to explore alternatives, first to save the discipline from becoming obsolete, and then, to revive the practice components of learning, especially fieldwork, through some emphatic initiatives. We are aware that theories in social work have been borrowed from other social science disciplines and are not derived from social work practice. Even if we principally accept that, we still have two more primary sources of knowledge to explore: (1) values, ethics, and ideology and (2) drawing insights through practical experiences and use of narrative research, phenomenology, grounded theory, ethnography, and other qualitative research methods. Experts cannot deny that practice many times has to adapt to structural constraints, which are subject to the mismatch between the 'agency missions and objectives' and 'professional goals and values' of social work education (Loewenberg, 1984). Such a mismatch might have been widened further after 'corporate social spending' was made mandatory by law in India. Living amidst these disrupting opportunities and emerging challenges definitely requires more innovative thinking and creativity to find and create a space for survival and career advancement. We should not be sceptical and ignore that there are immense social and professional advantages in belonging to an ideological or intellectual camp. Ideologies should not be overlooked as a source of knowledge for professional practice (Rees, 1979; Curnock & Hardiker, 1979). Students should never be stigmatized for defending their own ideology or even value system. An excessive scientism and objectivity may not find solutions for all situations. It's worth citing an example here. Although she was not a trained social worker, Vatsala Srivastava has been successful in transforming the lives of hundreds of women through her online project 'Bindi Bottoms.' The idea for her project came about through her ideas and passion for rediscovering herself. She believed in storytelling as a powerful tool for transformation and female empowerment.

Similarly, the values and ethics for social work cannot develop solely within the subject itself as a form of learning the 'right things to do.' If possible, we need to explore the scope of application of 'nudge theory' in the study of fieldwork practice (praxeology). We need to create an inclusive learning atmosphere where a variety of ethical idealists could profess different approaches for doing the right thing. We must create options to leap beyond 'ethical idealism' through incorporating other contemporary and rational beliefs and ideologies related to productivism and progressivism. The model of education to inculcate social work values and ethics among students need not be bureaucratic, but rather more organic so that students get enough space to understand, sensitize themselves, and align their values and ethics with that of the profession. Although we claim that we have a system in place to impart values and ethics training to students, most of the social workers in practice face value conflicts with clients (62 percent), conflicts of interest with clients (83 percent), maintaining confidentiality (66 percent), and conflict with agencies (23 percent) (Goswami, 2011).

Dorothy (1956) raised a few questions that are worth exploring: (1) To which culture do social work values belong? (2) Do they belong to the dominant national culture or to the professional culture of social work? (3) Do they belong to the culture of the individual worker or that of an individual client? Undoubtedly, the potential tensions or dilemmas existing between these different cultures and set of values result in many unclear situations for social workers (*ibid*). Our goal here is to think about how to ensure the development of a favourable attitude among students. Let us not just criticize the existing system. Let's find out other possible options to effectively train the millennial students, the future professionals in the making.

Training on self-exploration

Every learning process must go through three stages: (1) reading, (2) listening, and (3) observing and doing. The third stage is a process of direct and independent learning (also supervised at times). The objective here is to lead students to learn through self-realization and self-exploration. As a mechanism, we need to welcome 'mistakes' by students and use those as anchors to sensitize them to raise their self-awareness. It is assumed that such initiatives and activities will facilitate an awakening of the conscious self that may cause the students to take ownership in correcting these shortcomings. Once such habits are formed, the students must learn self-confession. This will help them to explore and find the real cause behind their 'failures.' The process does not involve any hidden agenda; however, sometimes it may invite criticism. It's all about transforming the learning process into an organic system where religion, spirituality, ideology, beliefs, and individual value systems need to be allowed to stay with the individual learners so that they can better find a match between their preferences and professional expectations. If the learning process cannot ensure students' 'continuous happiness,' then it would be unfair expecting them to do well in fieldwork and in practice settings in later life. We know that students in every professional discipline more or less suffer from conflicts between their needs and aspirations. They need adequate guidance and counselling so that they can effectively set their career goals. It's difficult to discuss all the techniques here. Many good books and training modalities are available. We must strive to ensure that while pursuing social work education, every student must take care of (1) making their own families happy, (2) social acceptance, (3) achieving peace of mind, (4) experiencing religious and spiritual harmony etc.

Training on values and ethics

Here, we need to think beyond making academic references in classrooms about social work values and ethical guidelines in the form of a professional code of ethics. This requires a series of planned discourses and activity-based learning to sensitize and train students to naturally accept human values (Gogate, 2011). This may do wonders in developing a habit among students to evaluate their own behaviour rather than making judgments about others. They need to understand the value of self to their families, society, environment (and ecosystem), etc. Further, we need to explore situations and use simulations, where students get opportunities to learn through ethical reasoning to gain a clearer and sharper logical focus on problems and dilemmas. The following three criteria can be used in ethical reasoning (Weiss, 2006):

1   Moral reasoning must be logical. Assumptions and premises, either factual or inferred, used in judgments should be made explicit.
2   Factual evidence cited to support a person's judgment should be accurate, relevant, and complete.
3   Ethical standards used in a person's reasoning should be consistent.

There is no universal definition of what constitutes a morally wrong act in absolute terms. The intent must be to learn about how to develop ethical and moral thinking and take appropriate decisions on ethical issues by following certain ethical principles: (1) relativism, (2) utilitarianism, (3) universalism, (4) rights, and (5) justice. An adequate knowledge of values and ethical guidelines and related skills may better equip a student to maintain an equilibrium between clients' demands/expectations, agency's vision and objectives, and professional standards. In highly disruptive and unpredictable socio-political situations, the knowledge of theories may sometimes fail to guide practice. However, practitioners' wisdom, personal experience, and ethical orientation may prove to be the saviour.

Like management students, social work students also need to learn (1) stakeholder analysis, (2) mapping stakeholder relationships, (3) mapping stakeholder coalitions, (4) developing a matrix of stakeholder moral responsibilities, (5) developing specific strategies, and (6) monitoring shifting coalitions (if applicable).

Ethics content in fieldwork training

Unlike in the West, social work interventions in the East, especially in India, are macro-centric. They are more about the developmental and empowering approach to practice than the clinical. However, there is a need for specific forms of intervention with individuals, groups, and families. Social work educators and policy makers must work together to develop practice theories suitable to Indian situations. Along with field education and training, this requires a specific strategy to incorporate qualitative and action research methods as components in the regular curriculum. We need to critically think and give more weight to learning through a single-case design and incorporate it in our fieldwork and research syllabi. Simultaneously, there is a felt need to indigenize the ethical content in our curriculum. It is unfortunate to note that there still is hardly any common code of ethics for social workers in India, whether among students or educators. Discussion and brainstorming sessions are required to redesign the framework of social work values, ethical principles, and code of conduct. It's worth mentioning here a few recommendations from a doctoral study (Goswami, 2011).

The recommendations

1   Social work educators/supervisors must productively use the fieldwork conference to discuss their ethical dilemmas, decision-making process, and risk management strategies.
2   Agency–institute interactions should be made compulsory and more frequent. Regular workshops, seminars, expert talks, etc., need to be organized so that there is adequate exchange of ideas and opinions between educators, students, and practitioners.
3   Besides social work practice skills, necessary managerial aptitudes should be developed among the students so that they can fulfil the changing expectations of clients, people, and agencies.
4   Thorough field/need assessment is a must before formulating ethical guidelines for social workers in India.
5   The code should not be extremely prescriptive in nature, but it should be more flexible, sensitive, and constantly upgraded or revised.
6   The students must have access to historical case references, current solved case examples, and interpretive guides, etc., to learn and acquire ethical decision-making skills.

Inductive method of theory building

Empiricism and quantitative methods of research have immense importance in social and behavioural sciences. However, social work students need to learn five qualitative approaches to inquiry to facilitate the theory building process and contextualize their practice interventions. For example, case studies that use qualitative research documentation such as audio- and video-taping are more appropriate for studying social work practice. It's true that sometimes the understanding through one case study may not be applicable to another case study. However, an archive with so many case studies may help students understand the uniqueness in each case and its subjectivity. Philosophically the profession believes in the principle of individualization, and so the craze for generalization is not well justified. Although academic theories may be built on through generalizations, the social work practice theories may require inputs both from qualitative and empirical studies. Always, the quantitative logic of descriptive or inferential statistics is not adequate to represent the reality of most social phenomena (Ruckdeschel &Farris, 1981). Even in community social work, it involves engaging in networks and bringing about change through identifying patterns of interactions and interventions in such a way that new patterns develop (Smale, 1983). Methods of interventions need to be developed through a rigorous process of learning, de-learning, and re-learning. Also, we need to change our attitude and accept that sometimes tradition must be replaced by new approaches.

Qualitative research begins with assumptions and the use of interpretive and dialectical frameworks that lead us to ascribe social or human problems to them. The observers must learn and use an emerging qualitative approach to inquiry and collect data in natural settings, being sensitive to the people and places under study. Then, for data analysis, both inductive and deductive methods can be used to establish patterns or themes. The final report or documentation may include the voices of participants, the reflexivity of the researcher, a complex description and interpretation of the problem, and its contribution to the literature (Creswell, 2013, p. 44). The students need to be oriented to four different philosophical assumptions: (1) ontological, (2) epistemological, (3) axiological, and (4) methodological. The preference of the approach over tradition is essential because it involves closer attention to the interpretive nature of inquiry and situating the study within political, social, and cultural contexts. The emerging scenario demands the physical presence of the social work researcher in the field to draw insights through direct observation and interaction with people or subjects.

Goldstein (1986) rightly observed that the social worker's intent should not be only to diagnose or assess objectively but, in collaboration with the individuals (and groups), to begin to make sense of and find meaning within the problematic or chaotic circumstances of their life situations. It's not predominantly the objectivity, but rather the subjective realities that could guide us to work with them.

The changing workplace and changing workforce

Contemporary and emerging technologies are shaping both the millennial students and their prospective employing organizations. This has made organizations comfortable reaching out to people. The 2017 Global NGO Online Technology Report (www.techreport.ngo) summarizes how NGOs worldwide use web applications and email communications, online and mobile fundraising tools, and social and digital media. In the years to come, NGOs will become more empowered to use the Internet to inspire philanthropy and create social change by 2025 (Mint, a English daily from Mumbai, 13 October 2017). Rural areas of India also are expected to transform through governments' 'Digital India' and 'Smart India' initiatives. We have miles to go, but the continuous launch of mobile apps is expected to create an impact on the life of rural populations. Some of those apps, such as Swach Bharat Abhiyan, MyGov, MEAIndia, PostinfoApp, Online RTI, MeriSadak, and ASHA (Accredited Social Health Activists) are very popular (Manzar, 2017). It is expected that technology will transform the way *panchayat*, self-help groups, schools, and hospitals function. The social work institutes must take adequate care so that students get appropriate exposure to the emerging technologies and acquire competencies to use those in their practice.

Conclusion

The time has arrived to rescue social work students and practitioners from their dichotomy of being loyal to professionalism and contributing to developmental activities. A post-modern and liberal society must appreciate an open system of ideas and diverse ideologies. We need to adapt to the changing times and transformations that impact society, culture, and our life behaviour. There needs to be a balance between absolute values and instrumental values; otherwise, we may fail to move ahead. We shall welcome the emerging strategic alliance between and among professional standards, practitioners' ideologies, and agency purposes. It may not be always knowledge and technical skills, but rather practice wisdom that leads to problem-solving competencies of professionals. Hence, it is essential to revisit the modalities of social work education and field training. The social work educators, scholars, and practitioners shall not enjoy a monopoly to determine the future of the profession. We need to incorporate a stakeholder approach to redesign our curriculum, especially the fieldwork practicum, so that the profession and the professionals remain relevant as new scenarios emerge.

References

Baldock, J., & Prior, D. (1981). Social workers talking to clients: A study of verbal behaviour. *British Journal of Social Work, 11*, 19–38.

Bogo, M. (2010). *Achieving competence in social work throughfield education.* Toronto: University of Toronto Press.

Corby, B. (1982). Theory and practice in long-term social work. *British Journal of Social Work, 12*, 619–638.

Creswell, J. W. (2013). *Qualitative Inquiry and Research Design: Choosing Among the Five Approaches* (3rd ed.). Thousand Oaks, CA: Sage Publication.

Curnock, K., & Hardiker, P. (1979). *Towards practice theory: Skills and methods in social assessments.* London: Routledge and Kegan Paul.

Doel, M., Shardlow, S. M., & Johnson, P. G. (2011). *Contemporary field social work: Integrating field and class-room experience.* Thousand Oaks, CA: Sage Publication.

Dorothy, L. (1956). The consistency of culture. *Children, 3*(3), 110–114.

Gogate, S. B. (2011). *Human values and professional ethics.* New Delhi: Vikas Publishing House.

Goldstein, H. (1986). Education for social work practice: A cognitive, cross-cultural approach. *International Social Work, 29*(2), 149–164.

Goswami, I. (2011). *Ethics in social work education and practice in India.* Mangalore: Mangala Publications.

Hardiker, P., & Barker, M. (Eds.). (1981). *Theories of practice in social work.* London: Academic Press.

Hardman, D. G. (1975). Not with my daughter you don't! *Social Work, 20*, 278–285.

Lewis, H. (1982). *The intellectual base of social work practice.* New York, NY: Haworth Press.

Loewenberg, F. (1984). Professional ideology, middle range theories and knowledge building for social work practice. *British Journal of Social Work, 14(1),* 309–322.

Loewenberg, F., & Dolgoff, R. (1982). *Ethical decisions for social work practice.* Itasca, IL: F.E. Peacock.

Manzar, O. (2017, October 27). *Death by data: Digital world.* Published in Mint, an English daily from Mumbai, p. 10.

Pumphrey, M. W. (1959). *The teaching of values and ethics in social work* (Vol. 13). New York, NY: Council on Social Work Education.

Reamer, F. G. (1982). *Ethical dilemmas in social service.* New York, NY: Columbia University Press.

Reamer, F. G. (1993). *The philosophical foundations of social work.* New York, NY: Columbia University Press.

Rees, S. (1979). *Social work face to face.* London: Arnold.

Rowan, J., & Zinaich, S. Jr. (2002). *Ethics for the professions.* Belmont, CA: Wadsworth.

Royse, D., Dhooper, S.S., & Rompf, E.L. (2012). *Field instruction: A guide for social work students* (6th ed.). Boston, MA: Allyn & Bacon.

Ruckdeschel, R. A., & Farris, B. E. (1981). Assessing practice: A critical look at the single-case design. *Social Case Work: The Journal of Contemporary Social Work, 62*(7), 413–419.

Smale, G. G. (1983). Can we afford not to develop social work practice? *British Journal of Social Work, 13,* 251–264.

Teicher, M. I. (1967). *Values in social work: A re-examination.* New York: National Association of Social Workers.

Timms, N. (1983). *Social work values: An enquiry.* London: Routledge and Kegan Paul.

Weiss, J. W. (2006). *Business ethics: A stakeholder and issues management approach* (3rd ed.). New Delhi: Thomson.

13

ESSENTIAL SKILLS FOR FIELDWORK PRACTICE IN SOCIAL WORK

Sayantani Guin

Introduction

Social work is a practice profession. It involves working with people to enhance their social functioning and enabling them to lead an empowered life. To fulfil this goal, social workers need to be equipped with certain skills. Skills are an important component of the social work profession and are taught to social work students during their fieldwork training. This chapter explains the skills needed for social work professionals for effective social work practice.

Meaning of skills in social work practice

The dictionary meaning of 'skill' is the ability to do a job or activity well. The ability to do so is learned through practice, training, and experience. In social work practice, a skill has been defined as a 'specific behaviour' (Shulman, 1999, p. 4) and inter-personal skills (Dickson & Bamford, 1995, p. 85) in helping clients solve problems. Barker (2003, p. 399) explains skills as proficiency in the use of talent, knowledge, personality, and resources. Trevithik defines the term as follows:

> A skill is an action with a specific goal that can be learned, that involves actions performed in sequence, that can be organized in ways that involves economy of effort ad evaluated in terms of its relevance ad effectiveness. Although these characteristics have been described separately, they interweave and overlap.
> (Trevithick, 2012, p. 155)

Skills can be learned, and their effectiveness can be realized during an intervention. In social work practice, a plethora of factors need to be kept in mind, including the setting and whether we are referring to the individual, family, or community.

Types of skills for social work practice

During their fieldwork training social workers are taught to practise a variety of skills. To begin with, a social worker must build rapport with the client, community, or agency staff where he or she is placed. Effective communication through verbal and non-verbal means is essential for this purpose. After rapport building, the social worker is required to work with clients to help them. Many times, interviewing is essential to enable clients to share their problems. During this process, documentation is an essential component which enables the practitioner to record the social work processes and techniques used. The following skills may be considered essential for practice during fieldwork.

Communication skills

Communication is key to any relationship, be it in an office or in personal life. The ability to clearly express one's ideas and to interact with a person defines the success or failure in any relationship. In social work, effective communication with the client is important, as it is through communication that a social worker can make an assessment, undertake interviews, and engage in problem-solving and decision-making activities, negotiate a plan, and evaluate our effectiveness (Trevithick, 2012).

Some of the characteristics of effective communication skills are the following (Sheafor & Horejsi, 2003):

1 **Developing a helping relationship**: Communication involves the ability to develop a helping relationship with the client. Empathy is one of the essential components which the social worker must have in order to understand the client's problem. Being empathetic involves the ability to imagine the situation, understanding the feeling, and transfer those feelings to oneself. Giving due respect and positive regard to the client, regardless of his or her sex, appearance, caste, class, or behaviour, is another skill whereby the client is understood to be worthy to solve his or her problems. Genuineness is where a social worker displays his or her real characteristics and the ability to match what he or she says and does. In cases where the social worker has a negative feeling towards the client, the social worker may exercise self-discipline.

2 **Verbal communication skills**: This is the ability to articulate ideas in a clear and concise manner so that they are understood by the client. A social worker communicates with the client during the helping

process and while exchanging information within the agencies and among professionals. Effective verbal communication involves the willingness to listen, the ability to organize thoughts, and to take the required time to express what is intended to be conveyed. A major aspect of verbal communication is speaking over the phone. Body language and facial expressions are reflected in one's voice. Interjecting with words like, 'yes' and 'ok' at brief intervals while talking will emphasize listening.

3   **Non-verbal communication skills:** This includes messages conveyed through facial expressions, eye movements, gestures, and voice qualities such as tone, pitch, and resonance. Some of the specific non-verbal communication skills include maintaining eye contact; appropriate gestures of greetings, taking into consideration the cultural differences; expressing warmth in the form of smile, a soft and soothing voice, etc.; and appropriate body language, dress, and appearance.

4   **Helping skills:** These skills have a beneficial effect on clients' thinking, feeling, and behaviour. These include getting ready before a meeting with the client, anticipating the client's feelings such as anger or fear, and initiating the client into the helping relationship. Before each meeting, the purpose of the meeting and the role of the worker must be specified. Questions involving the what, where, when, and how of the client's behaviour and situation should be framed to enable the social worker to express their thoughts and feelings. Active listening is another helping skill which involves encouragement, clarification, paraphrasing, reflection, summarization, and maintaining silence.

Observation skills

Observation skills help one understand and analyse a situation. A social worker needs to assess the problem situation during fieldwork. Observation of a client's facial expressions, appearance, tone of voice, postures, gestures, and speed and intonation of communicating can convey a great deal of information regarding the client's situation and state of mind.

Observation may be general or it may be used for a specific intervention. Inviting a colleague in a meeting and observing to gain a different perspective may be an example of using observation as a specific intervention. Observation may also be intentional, which involves seeing with a purpose that leads to action. Some common errors while observing include the following (Trevithick, 2012):

1   Failure to link observation to its significance due to one's own bias and experiences.
2   Failing to link observation to the behaviour and situation of the client.

3 Inability to observe impartially, that is, failure to separate our own judgement of a situation from that of the client's situation.
4 Missing out on important factors that trigger an important behaviour in the client, such as the context and the setting.
5 Inability to express a clear and precise point of the observations made.
6 Inaccurate generalizations of the observation made, viz. observation in a school setting cannot be generalized for a community setting.
7 Improper conclusion based on observation.

Interviewing skills

Interviewing is an important aspect of social work. It is through interviews that the social worker can gather information regarding the problem of the client, assess the problem through discussions, and finally outline an intervention plan.

Interviewing skills consist of five basic skills, viz. observation skills; listening skills; questioning skills; focusing, guiding, and interpreting skills; and climate-setting skills. As discussed, **observation skills** involve an ability to understand the non-verbal behaviour of the client, including the client's body language, opening and closing sentences, shifts in conversation, recurrent references, inconsistencies or gaps in information, stress and conflict indicated by the client, etc. It also involves the ability to validate the client's verbal expressions and provide feedback accordingly. **Listening** skills involve the ability to listen to what the client is talking about and not just hearing without paying attention. The social worker should be open to what is being said without being judgemental and focus on what the client wants to communicate. Interruption during communication for premature evaluation or advice is not advisable during listening. **Questioning skills** involve using appropriate questions during interviewing. Several categories of questions include open-ended questions, closed-ended questions, leading questions, responding questions, etc. Open-ended questions do not require a specific answer and thus enable the client to freely share information and feelings. These types of questions, along with closed-ended questions, are more suitable in developing a social history of the client, as it allows discussion about problems and sharing of life experiences. A leading question is used to explore more about the subject at hand. In a responding question, the social worker asks questions based on the client's responses. There are some questions, viz. answer and agree question, which prompts the client to agree with the worker. **Focusing, guiding, and interpreting skills** involve the ability to paraphrase, summarize, confront, and be silent in order to proceed towards the desired outcome. Paraphrasing and summarizing helps in understanding and clarifying the content of what has been communicated by the worker. Confrontation is the ability to help the social worker face his or her feelings, issues, and disagreement regarding the problem, which if hidden may result in anger, frustration, etc. Being silent is an important aspect in interviewing which helps both the client and the worker to be reflective. **Climate-setting skills** are those skills such as empathy, genuineness, and non-possessive warmth which enable and facilitate the interviewing process. Empathy is the ability to put one's own self into the client's situation and feel what the client is feeling. Being genuine means being truthful so that the client can trust the social worker. Non-possessive warmth involves concern for the client so that the client can make decisions and share both positive and negative feelings.

Documentation skills

Documentation skills in social work are an ability to write reports to describe events and analyse them for better understanding and for deciding on a further course of action. Reports may range from a two-page handwritten note to a bound volume of several dozen pages. Reports document information about the client, the intervention used, and the case study of the client, or it may describe a survey study. These reports are read and referred to by other social work professionals, NGOs, government officials, or the media. An inaccurate, improper, and inadequate report creates misunderstandings. The quality of the report may be improved by applying the following techniques (Sheafor & Horejsi, 2003):

1. Reports should be written keeping the readers in mind. Consider how the report could be understood or misunderstood before writing the report.
2. Reports may be highly organized and formal or may be in an informal, memorandum-type format. The appropriate writing style and format will depend on the readers of the report. For communications within an agency, an informal memo-type report may work, but a more formal report would be appropriate if reports are to be circulated among various agencies.
3. Reports should reflect a well-planned order and organization and should follow a logical structure.
4. Words used in the report should be simple, clear, and direct. Jargon and inappropriate language should be avoided. Words that have different meanings in different contexts should be avoided.
5. Sentences should be short and precise using active voice. Each paragraph may present a different theme.
6. The language should reflect the professional competence and confidence of the writer. Statements which reflect doubt or wishing should be avoided. For example, 'It seems as though' or 'I feel placement is necessary' should be avoided.

7 Revising the draft report after thorough re-reading is a must before finalizing the report.
8 Grammar, spelling, and punctuation should be correct in the report, and dictionaries and computer programmes may be used to ensure there are no grammatical errors.

Documentation skills also include **letter writing**. Letter writing is taught in schools from a young age; however, a social work professional must take particular care when writing letters. Letters are written for various purposes, such as for arranging meetings with experts, for applying for grants, for communicating with the client, etc. A professional letter should be written on letterhead and include the date, address, subject, salutation, body, and signature. Proper titles of the addressee may be written (e.g., Mr, Mrs, Dr). If the letter is confidential, the word 'confidential' may be mentioned on the envelop, which is an acceptable practice in India. To maintain confidentiality, sensitive information may not be shared in the letter. For letters sent to clients, it is important to humanize and personalize the letter. For a complaint letter, the language may be direct and written with authority and clarity. Proofreading of the letter should be done before it is dispatched. A copy of all letters must be kept and a file of communication should be maintained. Letters sent through email should be downloaded and saved in a folder on the computer.

Process recording is another documentation skill where a detailed report is prepared regarding the progress of a case. A process record includes the name of the persons present in a meeting or those involved in the case, the date, time, venue, length, and purpose of the session. The content provides a detailed description of the interaction, viz. the beginning of the session, the exchange of opinions and information during the session, the specific topics discussed, the decisions reached, and the plans made. The mood of the session and how it ended are also recorded. The process record includes the techniques, skills, and activities used by the social worker; the assessment of the clients' problem; the worker's own assessment of his or her performance; the problems encountered; and the strengths and limitations. The plan for the next meeting is also recorded.

Research skills

Research is an important component in social work practice. It involves application of research methods to generate knowledge that is useful for social workers to solve the problems that confront them. Social work research seeks to find answers to questions raised regarding social work techniques, methods, interventions, or effectiveness of treatments. Social work research involves identification of a problem, need assessment, selection of social work research design, pre-intervention measurement, intervention, post-intervention measurement, and inferences. The research skills of the social worker involve the following:

1   Identification of an appropriate research problem: The problem to be investigated should add to the knowledge base in social work, especially to social work theory and practice, and should improve the efficiency of professional social workers through research. Research problems in social work can run the entire gamut of social work profession, including concepts, theories, methods, programmes, services, and problems faced by social workers in their practice.
2   It is a skill to be able to formulate a simple research proposal, apply basic sampling techniques, formulate interview schedules and administer them, analyse the data acquired through them, and finally write the research report. This involves appropriate knowledge of social work methods and techniques and is achieved through practice.

Stress management skills

Social work professionals are constantly engaged with people's problems and issues and how to solve them. Many times, professionals themselves may be experiencing a crisis in their personal lives. They are overloaded with cases and other administrative responsibilities. Social workers often experience stress and burnout. It is important that the professionals themselves practise stress management skills. Some of the aspects which may help social work professionals acquire stress management skills are as follows:

1   **Managing time at work**: Priorities for tasks and assignments may be set while keeping in mind the agency's mission and job description. There should be match between the personal and professional work ethics and values; otherwise, one may get frustrated. Time may be managed by preparing a list of things to do within a certain time frame and then adhering to deadlines. Daily and weekly plans may also be developed. Complex tasks may be handled at the beginning of the day with a fresh mind, after which mundane tasks may be taken up. Delay in completion of work should be avoided. Procrastination and delay in work may be avoided and the habit of learning from mistakes should be inculcated. Keeping up-to-date on information regarding an agency's policy and procedure is important. Meetings should commence and end with the agenda and should not go astray. Papers should not pile up on a desk, and timely cleaning up is important. On-the-job training helps in honing skills and knowledge. Burdening one's self with someone else's work may cause stress and should be avoided.

2 **Controlling the workload:** Taking additional work apart from the work assigned may be a cause of stress at the workplace. It is important to manage one's own workload and learn to say 'no' to additional work. Before committing to additional work, one may take time to decide whether the job can be done along with the assigned task within the required time frame. Any refusal should be conveyed firmly and calmly. Similarly, while asking others for their help, proper explanation should be given as to why help is being asked. In case the other person refuses, such refusal should be considered graciously.

Conclusion

The social work profession consists of a variety of skills. It is through fieldwork that these skills can be learned, practised, and improved upon. This chapter focused on the various skills that a social worker should practise during fieldwork. These include communication skills, observation skills, interviewing skills, documentation skills, research skills, and stress management skills.

References

Barker, R. L. (2003). *The social work dictionary* (5th ed.). Washington, DC: NASW.

Dickson, D., & Bamford, D. (1995). Improving the inter-personal skills of social work students – the problem of transfer of learning and what to do about it. *British Journal of Social Work, 25*(1), 85–105.

Sheafor, B. W., & Horejsi, C. R. (2003). *Techniques and Guidelines for Social Work Practice.* New York, NY: Allyn and Bacon.

Shulman, L. (1999). *The skills of helping individuals.* Families, Groups and Communities, F.E. Peacock.

Trevithick. (2012). *Pamela: Social work skills and knowledge, a practice handbook.* Milton Keynes: Open University Press.

14

USING THE GROUNDED THEORY APPROACH IN FIELDWORK EDUCATION IN INDIA

Binod Kumar

Introduction

The fieldwork practicum is a key curriculum component of the social work programme. Academicians as well as students assume this learning experience as crucial to their transition from student to professional social worker. The researcher assigns a central role to fieldwork education in the training of social work students. The discipline tries to equip students to integrate theory and practice, to empathize with clients, to engage in practice-based learning, and finally to find professional ways to resolve the problems of clients.

Social work education across the world faces the problem in applying the theories of the classroom to the realities of the field. It uses a broad variety of perspectives to devise ways to work with people in their innate environment. Social work, being a practice-oriented profession, witnesses a long-standing focus on the theory, its practice, and research. The challenges in bridging the gap between theory and practice have been a problem in social work, and it is critically important for social work education that we resolve this.

There are few literature vis-à-vis application of grounded theory to the discipline of social work. After a detailed literature review, this chapter tries to give insights into how grounded theory can help in analysing the fieldwork reports of students and consequently reaching a generalized theory after a careful inductive process.

Social work education in India

The changing role of the welfare state in India has been an important backdrop against which professional social work has developed recently.

The notion of charity existed in India from time immemorial; however, the modern conception of professional social work came into being only with the establishment of the Sir Dorabji Tata Graduate School of Social Work in 1936. The areas in which social workers were working are completely different from the Western model; nevertheless, there was no attempt to theorize the models in the Indian context. This lack has limited the application of social work for a long time. However, as the role of the state changes in a post-liberalized era, so is the role of professional social work.

Social work education in India is offered at two levels: one at the graduate and the other at the post-graduate level. The graduate-level course runs for three years, whereas the post-graduate–level course runs for two years. Both these courses comprise concurrent fieldwork apart from the essential practicum at the end of the course. Some institutions offer the specialization at the post-graduate level, whereas graduate courses contain no specialization.

As per the norms of the curriculum, students are expected to complete certain courses, which consist of theoretical classroom learning and essential fieldwork. The students are also expected to produce fieldwork for each day spent in the field. Through these activities, students are expected to acquire the knowledge and skills to assume a professional role and identity through critical and theory-based reflection (Rehn & Kalman, 2016, p. 3). Depending on the themes on which trainees are placed, they gain experiences of casework, group work, or community work. The decision on allotment of agencies is anchored through faculty supervisors, keeping the interests of the trainee in mind. The field supervisor, who is also a trained social worker, and faculty supervisor are responsible for support, guidance, and learning of students through fieldwork practice. The students are supposed to visit their faculty supervisor regularly in scheduled meetings once in a week and on an as-needed basis. In order to facilitate proper learning, the faculty supervisor coordinates with the field supervisor and students on the instruction and activities they engage in. The faculty supervisor also visits agencies or field settings to oversee and understand the fieldwork pedagogy used by the agency to promote learning. The students are also supposed to produce organizational details and narratives witnessed in the field in the form of seminars in addition to the daily reports of fieldwork. At the end of the semester, trainees' recordings and narratives are submitted to the department and evaluated through a mixed model, where the faculty supervisor assesses students and external faculty assess them through viva-voce.

The gap between theory and practice

In order to facilitate learning in social work, the relationship between theory and practice should be collaborative one. However, the current

USING THE GROUNDED THEORY APPROACH

gap between theory and practice in social work has been a subject of considerable debate over years. The flow of knowledge in the discipline of social work must be bidirectional. The unidirectional approach, where the community is seen as the recipient, prevents learning and theorizing the field experiences. In bridging the gap between theory and practice in social work, the grounded theory approach would be helpful, where community is considered the source of knowledge. The trainees can learn from the community where they are placed, and the grounded theory approach can be used as a tool to theorize the learning at the grassroots level. However, we need to un-learn many things which we acquired consciously or unconsciously; learn the newer realities of the field; and re-learn the process and theory in order to make it more effective, robust, and realistic. Moreover, the knowledge gained through the application of grounded theory needs to be tested to evaluate its validity, and there is a need to apply theoretical learning in the field to test its effectiveness.

Aldamigh (1998) agrees that there is a problem with the actual application of theory and research in the field. He also opined that students of social work are not prepared to use and apply classroom learning to the practical situations in the field. Instead, trainees rely on a generic methodology to solve the clients' problems through trial and error. Hence, there is a need to bridge the gap between theory and practice and prepare and equip the upcoming professionals with hands-on tools to solve problems through scientific and evidence-based practice.

This gap has also led to the development of two subcultures in the discipline of social work: theory as the domain of academics and practice as the domain of practitioners within the disciplinary trajectory of social work (Thompson, 2000). Expecting an insulated research model where no other means and methods are applied is impractical. Rather, we need a general framework to resolve clients' problems in the field and that allows the practitioner to be creative and practical in finding solutions. The idea of these subcultures has been dominant in the discourse since Sheldon articulated it in 1978. Moreover, the idea has been gaining support from other academicians. The gap has been justified by the explanation that the social workers are dealing with real-time situations in the field and sometimes they feel incapacitated in the field due to the absence of remedies available. In this context, Sheppard (1995, p. 267) explains, "The precise recreation of meaning and experience of the client is fundamentally an intuitive process." In this situation, the social worker relies on their spontaneous mental acumen, which helps them to be more sensitive towards the client and deal with the problem. But learning from the field application is not coming to the theoretical subculture of social work, as social workers rarely apply grounded theory in the field. Although fieldwork in social work is designed to bridge the gap between the theoretical world of academics and real-world professional practice, unfortunately, schools of social work are not able to adequately prepare students for field practice.

The reasons for this are numerous. Social realities have changed in the field, but we are still using the same methods of intervention. In the Indian context, there is a large disconnect between theory and field realities. There has hardly been any opportunity for Indian social workers to practice casework and group work in institutional settings. The methods of casework and group work are not able to connect with the large populations in India and translate the theoretical underpinnings to evidence-based practice. With the changing realities of the practice landscape, there is a need to adapt the framework in social work so as to make it relevant to these circumstances. The Western conception and methods developed in a specific context, but in the absence of integration of local concerns social work practice has not grown at the same time in India. Local concerns need to be infused in the context of the realities of social work, and then academics needs to develop theories to solve problems. Sometime students complain of having overwhelming and confusing theoretical models in social work; in addition, it is difficult to apply these theories because they were developed in a different context.

Methodology

For the past two-and-half years, I have been teaching social work and supervising trainee social workers. The course of BA Social Work (Honours) runs through six semesters. Each semester, I supervise 12 social work students. Each week, I meet these students for half an hour to discuss their field experiences, their challenges and successes with the agency and clients, how their personal and professional behaviour are changing as a result of their social work study, and finally how they are reconciling with their agencies. As part of the fieldwork curriculum, students are supposed to write four to five pages of fieldwork reports for each day of fieldwork, which happens twice a week. This is called concurrent fieldwork. The report contains the plan for the day, timeline, work done, process recording, observation, analysis, and theoretical underpinnings, if any. As part of the curriculum, students are also expected to present their work to other students and faculty members in a field seminar, which is called a group conference. This enables them to get feedback and suggestions, which has potential to improve the interventions in the field. At the end of the semester, student trainees are evaluated based on their work in the field, report writing, attitudinal changes, professionalism, and finally presentation of knowledge in front of the interview board.

As part of the fieldwork evaluation, the graduate social work students at Dr Bhim Rao Ambedkar College were asked to write narratives at the conclusion of their semester. They were expected to write and reflect on the connection between theoretical learning in the class and field practice. The students were asked to include the methods of intervention adopted, problems identified in the field, ethical dilemmas faced, problematic situations to which they were not able to respond, and their experiences with field education. The researcher consciously chose to keep the answer broad and open to identify methodological gaps. Thus, it was left to the students to include the experiences of fieldwork education in the social work programme. It was also left to the students to reflect on the reasons why they were not able to respond to certain circumstances. In total 36 students were asked write up a one-page report, and the process spanned for three semesters.

In analysing the qualitative data produced by the students, author used the traditional grounded theory open coding process of Glaser's six C's to sort data into causes, contexts, contingencies, consequences, covariance, and conditions (Hall, 2015, p. 89). In order to organize the categories in a cohesive manner, I made subcategories and prepared memos. In order to better understand the write-ups, researcher re-read them several times to try and find newer ideas.

Navigating grounded theory and social work

In response to the extreme positivism in social research, Glaser and Strauss developed the grounded theory approach in 1967. They put forth the innate and inherent differences of social and natural processes and argued that they cannot be dealt with in the same type of subject matter. Glaser and Strauss argued that scientific truth is the result of observation and a consensus of interpretation within the community of observers. They proposed a new theory that could be developed through careful observation of the contrast between daily life and the interpretations of it made by those who participate in this reality. Hence, the use of grounded theory in fieldwork ensures a flow of knowledge from the field to classroom and consequently bridges the gap within the discipline. In this way, Glaser and Strauss struck the balance between extreme empiricism and complete relativism by proposing a middle ground in which systematic data collection could be used to develop theories. They also rejected the traditional positivist notion of falsification and hypothesis testing and instead proposed the organic method of theory building using grounded theory approach. It is most suited to answer some categories of interpretative questions involving inter-subjective experiences. It is less appropriate to use grounded theory to make knowledge claims of an objective reality.

Grounded theory has demonstrated an impressive track record in its application in the applied disciplines, and it has methodologically evolved over time. It has been useful in a broad range of theoretical perspectives and has proved its adaptability to accommodate different philosophical orientations. Although it has been dismissed for its focus on empiricism and inductive processes, it has been used effectively due to its strong focus on subjective-interpretative foci. Accordingly, the grounded theory approach may be used in social work to intersperse the theoretical flow from academics to practice and at the same time from practice to academics to better serve the profession's ethical and functional goals. It offers a route whereby social workers might feel the need for research to further the profession's ethical goals. It is a methodological intervention for local and context-specific research, which has the potential to integrate experiential knowledge. Grounded theory is better equipped to answer the problems faced by social workers, as it offers a chance to emotionally engage practitioners and weave a strong relationship between researchers, policy makers, and service providers to reinforce the theory–practice connection. In context of its applications in social work research, it is important to highlight that the grounded theory methodology takes care of ethical problems. It has the potential to translate and document practice in the field and can repackage and theorize the ground practices for classroom teaching. Finally, grounded theory offers protection by distancing participants from research conclusions by enhancing anonymity. There is an urgent need for research approaches that work to promote the profession if we are to support the development practice cultures that value research.

The application of the grounded theory approach in a pedagogical sense to social work has yielded numerous threads. As mentioned, there are critical gaps in field practice, as students are not prepared enough to deal with the real situations in the field. Instead, students apply generic methods which they are comfortable with in solving the immediate problems. The students also get perplexed with overwhelming theories of social work, and many times they are not able to decide on which methods and theory to apply in the field. The context in which theoretical constructs emerge has also changed. As also mentioned, India transplanted the Western models of social work, which are not suitable to its socio-political and economic realities. Hence, responses of professional social work have largely been limited to certain geographical areas and issues in India, with a few exceptions.

Signature pedagogy in social work education

The term signature pedagogy as used by Shulman (2005) and Gardner and Shulman (2005) to refer a particular approach in higher education to prepare students to practise a profession. As has been characteristic of every profession, professionals are assessed and regulated in their ability to adhere to certain standards. The older professions like medicine, law, nursing, education, engineering, and clergy involve acquiring and demonstrating a certain pattern of knowledge. Social work, like other professions, involves a distinctive educational component and its signature pedagogy. Social work as a discipline has all the attributes of other traditional professions. It is therefore appropriate for the social work discipline to recognize the features of field education, its own signature pedagogy, to support the profession's ethics and ideals. However, there is also a need to recognize and implement fieldwork in social work education in a consistent and cohesive manner before adopting a signature pedagogy.

In order to make fieldwork in social work programmes more like other professional courses like law and medicine, it must be unique in its approach to interventions. If there is a possibility of a generic intervention which non-professional can also practise, then professional social work will not be able to take a signature pedagogy as a mark of distinction of the discipline. In the Indian context, there have been several attacks on the discipline of social work, and many other professionals are occupying the niche space created for a professional social worker in the absence of a signature pedagogy in social work. The Council of Social Work Education (CSWE) has already accepted field education in social work education's signature pedagogy (Boitel & Fromm, 2014, p. 608). This considers fieldwork as an integral component in which core and advanced competencies are to be demonstrated by students to acquire and occupy a professional space. Through adoption of a signature pedagogy, academicians need to reformulate the methods of teaching/learning interaction where students should be able to acquire and demonstrate the distinct knowledge, skills, and values of professional social work.

As social work is a practice- and process-oriented profession, the knowledge, which is process oriented in nature, is difficult to demonstrate in the classroom. Thus, the support and guidance of the field supervisor is important to promote learning process-oriented work in the field. The expert field practitioner has the ability to extract and use information to harmonize the methodological intervention in the field, whereas students have limited knowledge and understanding to combine classroom learning and fieldwork. It has been suggested that social work schools provide a complementary field seminar course for trainees so as to reinforce the transfer of learning. Through this, students would benefit from the experiential learning of field experts, and in turn field experts can take away the theoretical knowledge.

Limitations

The limitations of study lie in the fact that it is based on the narratives of a small group of students of social work from the University of Delhi,

India. Despite its limitations, the study furthers the importance of assuming fieldwork in social work education as a centre stage of learning. The respondents, being social work students at the graduate level, may have limited understanding of questions asked despite the researcher's repetitive efforts to extract relevant information. The responses by master-level students could have made the result more reliable and broadly applicable.

Conclusion

The students' narratives were highly fragmented and non-cohesive, making it difficult to extract information and arrive at a conclusion. However, the narratives clearly demonstrated the gap between fieldwork and classroom teaching. They also point to a gap in the discipline of social work, where the practitioner possesses the field knowledge and academics hold the grip on theoretical teaching and learning. Both subcultures are not converging to add value to the knowledge repository of social work; rather, both are flowing in parallel. In order to designate fieldwork education as the signature pedagogy of social work, it must have consistency and cohesiveness in its implementation. Faculty members need to articulate the need for fieldwork education in social work programmes, and students' field reports and notes should be used to assess the need for theoretical engagement not only with students but also with field supervisors. This will ensure the flow of theoretical knowledge from the field to the classroom. I would like to acknowledge that I did utilize grounded theory in analysing the field reports but did not teach grounded theory to students because the focus of the engagement was field practice rather than theory. However, use of grounded theory in the process of supervising the field education of social work students at the graduate level has been tremendously helpful in expanding the knowledge base not only for students but also for myself.

References

Aldamigh, S. (1998, March). *Practice licensing: Reasons and importance to enhance the effectiveness of social work practice.* Eleventh Scientific Conference.

Boitel, C. R., & Fromm, L. R. (2014). Defining signature pedagogy in social work education: Learning theory and the learning contract. *Journal of Social Education, 50,* 602–608.

Gardner, H., & Shulman, S. L. (2005). The professions in America today: Crucial but fragile. *Daedalus, 134*(3), 13–18.

Hall, J. C. (2015). Utilizing grounded theory to enhance: The education of graduate clinical social work field students. *The Grounded Theory Review, 14*(2), 86–92.

Rehn, M., & Kalman, H. (2018). Social work students' reflections on challenges during field education. *Journal of Social Work, 18*(4), 451–467.

Sheppard, M. (1995). Social work, social science and practice wisdom. *The British Journal of Social Work*, *25*(3), 265–293.

Shulman, L. S. (2005). Signature pedagogies in the professions. *Daedalus*, *134*(3), 52–59.

Thompson, N. (2000). *Theory and practice in human services*. Buckingham: Open University Press.

15

ESSENCE OF COMMUNICATION SKILLS IN FIELDWORK

Saumya

Introduction

Communication skills are essential in every realm of our life, from relationships to employment. Communication can be viewed as a social process and a specific interactional skill of vital importance to the individual as well as society. Social work professionals communicate with clients – an individual, a family, a small group, an organization, or a community – to gain or convey information and make important decisions. It is important for social welfare administrators who manage agencies and organizations, as well as social work educators, to teach communication skills to students. Communication is a two-way process between the social workers and clients or stakeholders that involves getting a message across and understanding what others have to say. It includes both spoken words and non-verbal body language cues. Communication establishes relationships between the social worker and the client and makes organizing possible. Every message has a purpose or objective. The social worker intends – whether consciously or unconsciously – to accomplish the objectives by communicating. Communication is complex process and context related. It does not happen entirely within the limits of a relationship but also in a larger world that affects both the nature of the relationship and the nature of the communication.

Therefore, we can say that communication is a process by which one assigns and conveys meaning in order to create shared understanding. This process requires skills in intra-personal and inter-personal relationships. The literature available on communication skills is usually from the UK, United States, Canada, Israel, and Germany which makes it difficult to draw conclusions and may not be relevant to the Indian context due to socio-cultural differences. The literature available also is in the context of casework and clinical practice, which is predominant in Western countries, in contrast to India, where the focus is on community development. Therefore, it is difficult to generalize and contextualize. There is

238

ESSENCE OF COMMUNICATION SKILLS

hardly any literature in India on the learning and teaching of communication skills, either in theoretical curriculum or in fieldwork, in social work education. The objectives, tasks, or guidelines for fieldwork in BSW and MSW programmes do not specifically emphasize learning or acquiring communication skills. It is perhaps assumed that the student learns and acquires the skills eventually by doing fieldwork and through theoretical inputs in classroom teaching. Or it may be that the student acquires these skills based on their own experiences, inherent qualities, personal thoughts and feelings, socialization, and feedback from the supervisor in individual conferences. Whatever the assumption may be, the curriculum should focus on developing a social work student's ability to engage critically and constructively in interaction with stakeholders, he or she should be able to answer and ask questions coherently and concisely and follow spoken instruction, and should be able to speak according to the context and situation.

Communication skills are not only important in themselves but are an integral part of the development of other skills like inter-personal skills, interviewing skills, counselling skills, or helping skills. In India, we need to incorporate ways of learning and teaching communication skills in the curriculum of social work education to enhance the practice of working with people. Communication skills are required at every step, from rapport building, to need assessment, to decision making.

Types of communication skills

This chapter emphasizes three types of communication skills: verbal, non-verbal, and writing.

Verbal communication skills

This constitutes skills used when one individual engages in face-to-face communication with another, like a social worker with client in casework or as an organizer in group work or community development. This skill includes logical and concise selection of words, skill in providing information – giving factual context-related information, explanations, information about boundaries, and offering opinions and proposals, asking appropriate and sometimes probing questions to gather information, answering questions, responding to the receiver's verbal and non-verbal cues through minimal verbal comments, reflecting back feelings and content, paraphrasing, and giving feedback. Verbal communication should be accompanied by the appropriate voice and facial expressions to convey the intended message. The language should be clear without any ambiguity. The words chosen should not have double meanings or sensitive meanings for any community, as social workers work with people

239

from different social, cultural, and ethnic backgrounds. The information passed to the client/group or community should be easy to understand and process without any overload. Cross (1974) points out that there are role expectations and cultural and social pressures which play an important role in any interaction, and verbal communication skills can be understood against this background.

The social worker should ask appropriate questions or frame them differently in the language understood by the client, listen attentively, and pick up verbal and non-verbal cues to get the required information from the client. Verbal communication skills enable the social worker to engage in and maintain interaction with clients to create and sustain an effective working environment and accomplish goals (Lewis & Gibson, 1977). Effective communication is heavily dependent on effective listening. Active and effective listening is a specific skill that can be consciously developed and practised. It enables us to attach meaning to all the information one receives. Developing effective listening skills involves two specific steps: dealing with barriers that prevent listening, and developing and using listening behaviours. There are various barriers to listening, including jumping to conclusions, hearing what one wants to hear, rehearsing one's response when the other is speaking, and being inattentive. Active listening skills include using behaviours like maintaining an open posture, comfortable eye contact, leaning forward, delaying evaluation, maintaining attention, and 'tuning in' to feelings. One needs to listen more intently in social work conversations than in everyday ones, as one strives to understand the other person's point of view, to piece together the current and past elements of their story, to understand relationships, and to consider one's responses.

Responding skills are not limited to verbal skills. Social workers must understand what the stakeholder has said and respond meaningfully. Besides verbal responses like feedback, explanations, questions, or paraphrases, the social worker responds to the client non-verbally. These skills involve being aware of one's own body language – gestures, facial expressions, tone of voice, appearance, and regulating the same in such a manner that the words and non-verbal cues sent are appropriate for their message conveyed to the other person. It also means being comfortable with oneself and one's role as a primary communicator. It involves repeating, translating, and reflecting.

Non-verbal communication skills

Messages conveyed by means of facial expressions, eye movements, gestures, and voice qualities such as tone, pitch, and resonance are part of non-verbal communication that mainly occurs during a face-to-face exchange. Observing non-verbal behaviours and interpreting them

ESSENCE OF COMMUNICATION SKILLS

accurately may also tell the social worker that what the client is saying in words truly reflects his or her thoughts and feelings. Eye contact plays an important role in non-verbal communication. The eyes reveal much about our emotional state and our sensitivity to and understanding of the immediate situation. The social worker must be alert to cultural differences while using gestures of greeting – what may be acceptable and welcome in one community may be offensive to another community. Body positioning has profound importance in non-verbal communication. It conveys various attitudes and intentions. Leaning slightly towards the client shows interest and acceptance. Facial expressions and other movements reveal a social worker's disapproval of a client, even when the social worker is trying hard to be non-judgmental. Smiling, frowning, nodding, yawning, shaking the head, and lip quivering convey our thoughts and emotions. Crossed legs, arms folded across the chest, and body rigidity usually show defensiveness, whereas arms and hands at the side or in an outreached position suggest openness to others. Tone of voice suggests aggressiveness, control, and strength, whereas a monotonous or flat voice suggests lack of interest. Similarly, dressing is one of the important forms of non-verbal communication. A social worker must give careful thought to his or her choice of clothing and hairstyle. He or she should dress according to what is socially and culturally acceptable, as well as suitable to the occasion.

Writing skills

These skills are used in writing reports, writing case histories, recording minutes of group conferences or meetings, maintaining case records, writing emails, and using social media like WhatsApp, Facebook, Twitter, etc. These skills particularly involve using the right words, clear and simple expression, and culturally and socially sensitive and precise documentation. It requires comprehension and logical interpretation of the message conveyed; making sense of what is spoken; and being able to assess, recollect, and then write.

In the Indian context, all three types of communication skills require a social worker to recognize the client's/stakeholder's ethnicity, gender, religion, and socio-cultural and economic status to be more efficient.

Characteristics of communication

Communication involves creation, transmission, and reception of information. It is a two-way complex process between at least two persons. The two-way dialogue requires processing, listening, observing, speaking, questioning, analysing, and evaluating. Communication involves interaction with the physical, biological, and social environment and an exchange of sounds, words, or written/printed material. It is a process where what is said or conveyed cannot be reversed. It is a learned social skill and requires a vast repertoire of skills. Communication has content and is governed by rules and principles. An effective communicator exchanges ideas, feelings, and values by using appropriate language. The tone, pitch, and volume are in tandem with the communicator's feelings adding to the effectiveness of his or her communication with the client. The social worker gives relevant information by using non-verbal signals to emphasize and support verbal messages. He or she clarifies, solicits feedback, listens, responds, reacts to the messages of client, and conveys understanding.

The social worker trainee during their BSW or MSW programme should be trained during fieldwork in the skills of communication with the client/stakeholders/beneficiaries. Through individual and group conferences, the fieldwork supervisor can explain the basic verbal and non-verbal communication skills. During the fieldwork training the student learns to be empathetic towards the client, have a positive regard towards the people he or she is working with, show appropriate warmth, and be genuine while communicating with the clients. In addition, Toseland and Spielberg (1982) lists ten inter-personal helping skills: empathy; genuineness; respect; concreteness, or the ability to express thoughts and feelings accurately; confrontation, where a client is helped to overcome distortions and discrepancies between thoughts, feelings, and behaviour; self-disclosure; warmth; immediacy; potency; and self-actualization. These skills enhance the communication skills of social workers in dealing with stakeholders even in difficult circumstances.

The student should be made aware of the communication problems which develop under different circumstances. For instance, if the social worker speaks for others rather than letting them speak for themselves or does not listen to what others say; if the client keeps things to himself or herself because of fear of disapproval; or the social worker allows prejudices, stereotypes, and discriminations to affect their thinking; suppresses communication by ordering, threatening, preaching, patronizing, judging, or blaming; or if a person's ethnicity, gender, religion, and socio-economic status affects the communication of the social worker, these become barriers in the communication process. The other problem is when the social worker avoids or cuts off the conversation with the client when they are talking about some painful experiences or situations because either he or she feels unable to handle charged emotions or feels powerless in this situation or uncomfortable. Seabury (1980) lists seven communication problems that are common to a variety of practice situations: double message, ambiguous message, referent confusion, selective attention and interpretation, overload of information, ritual-order incongruence, and regulator incompatibility. He emphasizes that for

ESSENCE OF COMMUNICATION SKILLS

individuals from different regional, ethnic, or racial backgrounds, communication may be difficult. All these problems can have a significant impact on communication. Therefore, fieldwork training and the fieldwork supervisor are important in imparting the necessary communication skills to the social work student. These skills help in developing a professional self and in helping the clients help themselves.

According to Pierson and Thomas (2002), in social work and social welfare agencies, good, clear, accurate communication is essential in several contexts. First, all organizations should provide quality information about services that they offer, which should be widely accessible. This will involve not only a range of languages relevant to their local community but also in electronic, Braille, and perhaps taped formats. Second, all social workers need to develop appropriate communication skills both face-to-face and for written communication – avoiding jargon and communicating in the local language. Third, they need to cater to people with specific communication needs. Finally, communication has a non-verbal dimension. Workers need to be aware of body language and the importance of listening skills. In a diverse country like India, where there are people from different religions, cultures, languages, and geographical terrains like rural, urban, and tribal, etc., it is important to be able to adapt communication skills according to the stakeholder's background not only in terms of language but also gestures.

While communicating, the social worker should remember to use simple and clear language. The social worker should listen when the client is speaking without interrupting. Information should be passed on only based on what is required. The verbal and non-verbal stance of the social worker should support what client has to say; he or she should be interested and listen, maintaining eye contact. If the client behaves inappropriately, for example, he or she is angry, insulting, shouting, etc., the social worker should be tactful and calm. Give the client time to express their feelings and then communicate using right words. The social worker should not assume anything, but rather ask questions to clarify any information or interact further.

Patterns of communication

Communication, whether through face-to-face interaction, sign language, intra-personal and inter-personal means, social media (WhatsApp, Facebook, Twitter, etc.), mass media (radio, TV, newspaper etc.), telephone, emails, and letters, requires speaking, listening, or writing. The five components of inter-personal communication described by Chartier are self-concept, listening, clarity of expression, coping with anger, and self-disclosure (quoted by Mayo, 1979). Therefore, these skills are pertinent in social work education. Another dimension of communication skills involves not just effectively 'communicating to' others; the social worker has also to develop better ways of being someone who can be 'communicated with' (Lee, 1968). This element brings the issues of creating a climate and setting a stage for the communication event, building a positive relationship, and operating from the professional self. The pattern of communication should be based on equal empowerment with the client or stakeholder. In India, social workers work with:

- all population groups (men, women, children, adolescents, youth, middle aged, elderly)
- social groups and institutions (family, community, neighbourhood, workplace)
- social issues (education, health, sanitation, mental health, nutrition, etc.)
- minorities (social, religious, caste, ethnic, sexual), and
- specific situations (intellectual, physical, and social disability; disasters, both natural and manmade; disorganization, including familial, personal, and community; social exclusion; riots and mobilizations; dissent and advocacy)

Therefore, the communication skills required are based on the need for services for general and/or specific population groups or social work interventions, or specific techniques of offering services, with the aim of modifying and improving the strategies and techniques.

The foundations of good communication stated by Sheafor and Horejsi (2003) are:

- A willingness to understand that every human being is unique. Consequently, each person experiences and perceives events and interpersonal exchanges in a unique manner. Thus, a social worker should anticipate some degree of misunderstanding and take steps to minimize problems of miscommunication.
- A willingness and desire to organize one's thoughts and present one's message in a way that will make it easy for others to follow and understand.
- A willingness to listen carefully to other people and to lower his or her defences so that he or she can hear and understand what others say.
- A willingness to take responsibility for one's statements and behaviours.
- A willingness to take the time needed to communicate effectively.

Socio-cultural factors influence the levels of communication with the clients, beneficiaries, and stakeholders in casework, groupwork, or community organization. According to Lindon and Lindon (2000) and

MacLennan (1996), there are different levels of communication between the social worker and the client:

- Ritual: the basic exchange of communication about the general wellbeing between the social worker and client – the initiation of a conversation.
- Facts and information: the exchange of information between the social worker and client where the client may be hesitant or uncomfortable in sharing some personal information. At this level, the social worker requires skills in useful or purposive interactions.
- Thoughts and judgments: this level requires trust and courage between the client and social worker.
- Feelings and emotions: only when the client has enough trust and a sufficient level of comfort with the social worker can he or she start sharing feelings and expressing emotions.
- Peak experiences: this is the level reached when the client shares the relevant experiences and ups and downs in life with the social worker. It is pertinent not to break the communication chain through negative feedback or body language.

Thus, the pattern of communication is dependent on many factors; issues; social, economic, and political situations; client groups; and levels, as discussed.

Communication skills through fieldwork: structuring pedagogy

Social work practice is a highly skilled activity and one that calls for an extensive knowledge base and considerable intellectual abilities. It describes a framework that includes three interweaving features: (1) theoretical knowledge (or theory), (2) factual knowledge (including research), and (3) practice/practical/personal knowledge (Trevithick, 2008). The fieldwork training provides an opportunity for social work students to learn and practise some of the basic skills of face-to-face verbal and non-verbal inter-personal communication. The design and delivery of the fieldwork curriculum should ensure that communication skills are imparted to social work students in a systematic manner through academic and practice settings, either in the teaching of social work methods or the field practicum. First and foremost, the fieldwork supervisor should explain the purpose of communication with the client, stakeholders, and beneficiaries. As stated earlier, unlike Western countries, where the focus of social work is on casework with individual clients, in India, social workers not only work with individual clients but also with groups as well as in rural, urban, and tribal community development. The student should acquire as much information about the client (individual, group, or community) as possible. He or she must be careful in what is communicated and why. The content and manner of communicating should be considered. He or she should be able to anticipate the likely responses of the client. Second, the social worker needs to arrange an appropriate place and time for communication to take place. Third, non-verbal gestures and behaviours, like showing warmth, being welcoming and caring, and establishing rapport and a working relationship by clarifying roles and expectations of the participants in the communication process, need to be established.

The curriculum should specify on understanding the audience – their needs and capabilities – including speaking coherently and precisely in clear and simple language; understanding non-verbal cues; and using lip reading, sign language, and finger spelling with persons who are hearing impaired. The social work student should be able to observe, listen, respond, and question. The fieldwork supervisor should emphasize during individual and group conferences the need to be unbiased, non-judgmental, and empathetic while practising observing skills, active listening, verbal skills, and responding skills.

Lewis and Gibson (1977) note that the social work educator has two major tasks: first, to establish the most important areas of skills to be taught in class and second, to develop an instructional design appropriate to the development of such skills. Day (1977) describes various tools of learning – lectures, group discussion, role-plays, simulation exercises, case records, diagrams, literary and visual arts, and practice in writing reports and summarizing. Lewis and Gibson (1977) argue that existing class and field instruction is inadequate for skill development; hence, they need to be complemented by simulated practice using videotape. Video as a medium for the teaching of communication skills has been used successfully for many years wherein the students observed themselves and benefitted from the practice (Cartney, 2006). However, using videotape, role-plays, or simulation in learning, teaching, and assessment has been debated by several scholars. Some argue in favour of its efficacy, whereas some point out the shortcomings. For instance, videotaped discussion between two faculty demonstrating casework sessions can help students understand speaking and listening skills. The students can observe and then discuss symbolic, verbal, and non-verbal communication processes, choice of words, gestures, body language, facial expressions, body positioning, pace, tone, pitch, interaction patterns, initiation and closing of the interaction, exploring the problem, attitude, etc., which is easier for students to comprehend and learn as compared to learning these skills through textbooks. Through this exercise, they learn to apply concepts and theories. But in this exercise, Rossiter (1995) points out that students forego their own experience of what the simulated client means and instead search for 'what they should say.' In this situation, students are learning to bypass their experience of another person's perspective and to look instead for an external response deemed by experts and teachers to be correct. Rossiter further says that telling people what they should say contradicts the most basic definition of empowerment: that people assume the authority to name their own experiences. Such a pedagogy violates our belief as social workers that learning and change take place in empowering environments. In India, we have still not incorporated the use of videotaped discussions in our curriculum, and we need to reflect thoroughly about choosing this medium to teach communication skills.

Some schools and departments of social work in India have group conferences in the curriculum which provides a platform for social work students to discuss issues concerning fieldwork for 10 to 30 minutes in a group consisting of eight to ten students and four to five faculty members. After the discussion, minutes are prepared by a member of the group, and this role is rotated among the members. This exercise helps them present views coherently, argue and think critically, respond and administer, and understand and assess the accuracy of their listening and recall skills and they learn recording skills. During a group conference discussion, the students can assess the effectiveness of the communication and the arguments which are put forth by members and resource persons. The faculty members and other group members provide feedback on the presentation and chairing of session, as well as recording of minutes in the meeting.

It is significant that one needs to constantly work towards developing effective communication skills. No matter how good and effective a communicator may be, one does face certain barriers from time to time which forces them to work on becoming even more effective in their skills to communicate. Therefore, fieldwork training needs a more formalized structure than the existing one and should be designed in such a way as to emphasize acquiring skills for making any communication effective.

Theories of communication

The author could not gather through a review of the literature any coherent theoretical framework which is widely accepted for the learning and teaching of communication skills. The theoretical frameworks discussed in several papers which were reviewed for the purpose of this chapter listed psychology and counselling theory, communication and learning theory (SCIE, 2004), social theories, communication theory, psychological theories and biological theories (SCIE, 2008), and systems theory (Day, 1977). Nash, Munford, and O'Donaghue (2005) present four theoretical approaches – ecological systems, community development, attachment theories, and strengths-based approaches. These theories are illustrated with case studies by social work academics and practitioners showing how culturally sensitive social work interventions are carried out using these approaches. Another theoretical approach is relational or cultural theory (Edwards & Richards, 2002).

For the purpose of this chapter, the author would like to elaborate on three theories – social theories, psychological theories, and communication theory. Social theories focus on social and cultural factors; structural inequalities; and different languages, signs, and signals used by people from different backgrounds. They demonstrate how these factors influence the socialization of people and in turn affect communication patterns and skills.

Psychological theories emphasize conscious and unconscious thoughts and feelings that shape the behaviour of individuals, their perception about situations and events, and how this further influences their communication. In addition, an individual's development and self-concept is critical for communication skills which is influenced by social and psychological wellbeing. Attitudes, feelings, and values have profound influence on communication. Also pertinent is understanding how defence mechanisms and self-esteem can impact communication.

Communication theory identifies a range of concepts to describe how people, groups, and organizations exchange information and highlights the complexity of the meaning and messages conveyed and received (SCIE, 2008). It describes the importance of both verbal and non-verbal communication in social work practice. Trevithick (2005) provides the concept of transferability in communication theory. This means that communication, to make sense, must be adapted to the relevant context and situations. Any communication must be relevant to the specific socio-cultural context of the client and social worker in order to be meaningful.

Research and publications need to be undertaken on the learning and teaching of specific communication skills associated with specific theoretical approaches, as most of the papers reviewed did not present a firm theoretical framework. The social worker deals with all types of clients who may be mentally ill, violent, in custodial settings, disabled, or in any group like children, adolescents, youth, older person, men, or women. Therefore, usage of specific communication skills as per the requirement of the client group is of utmost importance. The theories mentioned here shape the understanding, behaviour, reactions, and responses of individuals.

Conclusion

Communication is a complex process, and communication skills are shaped based on several factors, like context; societal structure; culture; and the social worker's inter-personal experiences, perceptions, capacities, and experiences, to name a few. There is a dearth of literature on learning and teaching of communication skills in India. Though the social work curriculum in India has been designed to develop professional competence and enhance helping skills, hardly any attempts have been made to focus specifically on teaching communication skills systematically. Because most of the papers published on social work is by academics, there is also a need to develop literature on communication skills by social work practitioners and students who are working directly with people. They can contribute their critical perspectives to the knowledge base of social work and the essence of communication skills in practice settings. Communication skill training is still not an accepted part of the social work curriculum in India, but the social work discipline and faculty members have a responsibility to promote communication skill development, including speaking, listening, and writing, through the classes and fieldwork training. Social work students should be able to engage in critical thinking and gain communication skills during their BSW or MSW programme, as it has a vital impact on the outcome of social work interventions. At the same time, we have to be careful to promote reflection and critical thinking and not place too much emphasis on a clinical and technological approach to teaching communication skills.

References

Cartney, P. (2006). Using video interviewing in the assessment of social work communication skills. *The British Journal of Social Work*, 36(5), 827–844. Retrieved September 22, 2017, from www.jstor.org/stable/23721259.

Cross, C. P. (1974). *Interviewing and communication in social work*. London and Boston: Routledge & Kegan Paul.

Day, P. R. (1977). *Methods of learning communication skills*. Oxford: Pergamon Press.

Edwards, J. B., & Richards, A. (2002). Relational teaching: A view of relational teaching in social work education. *Journal of Teaching in Social Work*, 22(½), 33–48.

Lee, T. (1968). *Communication and communication systems: In organizations, management and interpersonal relations* (2nd ed.). IL: Richard D. Irwin Inc.

Lewis, J., & Gibson, F. (1977). The teaching of some social work skills: Towards a skills laboratory. *The British Journal of Social Work*, 7(2), 189–209. Retrieved September 2, 2017, from www.jstor.org/stable/23696773.

Lindon, J., & Lindon, L. (2000). *Mastering counselling skills: Information, help and advice in caring services*. London: Macmillan Press Ltd.

MacLennan, N. (1996). *Counselling for managers*. Aldershot: Gower.

Mayo, M. H. (1979). Teaching communication/interviewing skills to Urban undergraduate social work students. *Journal of Education for Social Work*, 15(1), 66–71.

Nash, M., Munford, R., & O'Donaghue (Eds.). (2005). *Social work theories in action*. London: Jessica Kingsley.

Pierson, J., & Thomas, M. (2002). *Dictionary of social work* (2nd ed.). Glasgow: HarperCollins.

Rossiter, A. B. (1995). Teaching social work skills from a critical perspective. *Canadian Social Work Review, 12*(1), 9–27.

Seabury, B. A. (1980). Communication problems in social work practice. *Social Work, 25*(1), 40–44.

Sheafor, B. W., & Horejsi, C. R. (2003). *Techniques and guidelines for social work practice* (6th ed.). New York, NY: Allyn and Bacon.

Social Care Institute for Excellence (SCIE). (2004). *Teaching and learning communication skills in social work education.* Retrieved September 16, 2017, from www.scie.org.uk/publications/knowledgereviews/kr06.asp

Social Care Institute for Excellence. (2008). *Overview of communication skills in social work.* Retrieved September 16, 2017, from www.scie.org.uk/assets/elearning/communicationskills/cs01/resource/underpinningKnowledge.pdf?res=true

Toseland, R., & Spielberg, G. (1982). The development of helping skills in undergraduate social work education: Model and evaluation. *Journal of Education for Social Work, 18*(1), 66–73.

Trevithick, P. (2005). *Social work skills: A practice handbook* (2nd ed.). Maidenhead: Open University Press.

Trevithick, P. (2008). Revisiting the knowledge base of social work: A framework for practice. *British Journal of Social Work, 38,* 1212–1237. doi:10.1093/bjsw/bcm026

INDEX

Note: Page numbers in *italics* denote figures, and page numbers in **bold** denote tables.

Abramson, J. 151
academic discipline 1
accommodator style 52
active listening 63–64
adult learning 50
adult participants' personalities 51
agencies 12
agency supervisors 118
Agnimitra, N. 107, 118, 119, 123
Aldamigh, S. 231
Allison, H. 153
andragogy 50
Andresen, L. W. 107
Anthony, A. 15
Argyris, C. 48
assessment and evaluation, fieldwork 103–120; block placement/block fieldwork training 113–114; components of 108–114; concurrent fieldwork 109–110; educational camp 112–113; essential guidelines 116–120; fieldwork, supervision 114–115; group conference 111–112; individual conference 110–111; nature and purpose of 106–108; orientation programme and observation visit/exposure visit 109; rural camp 112–113; skill development workshops 113; in social work and importance 104–106

Baer, B. L. 5
Barker, R. L. 221
Barnes, John 127

Bist, S. 117
block placement 10
Bloom, B. S. 49
Boesen, J. K. 124
Bogo, M. 88
Bolzan, N. 162
Bombay Association of Trained Social Workers (BATSW) 2
Bourdieu, Pierre 200
Brown, T. 15

camp committees 82–83; cultural committee 83; discipline committee 83; food committee 82; people participation committee 83; programme committee 82; *shramadhan* committee 83; stage committee 82
Cannell, C. F. 64
case studies, fieldwork 24–35; course goals 24–25; field placement goals 30–34
Chartier 243
Clapton, G. 160
classroom learning 10
climate-setting skills 225
communication skills 222–223; characteristics of 241–243; essence, fieldwork 238–249; helping relationship, developing 222; helping skills 223; non-verbal communication skills 223, 240–241; patterns of 243–245; structuring pedagogy 245–247; theories of 247–248; verbal

251

INDEX

communication skills 222–223, 239–240; writing skills 241
community-based fieldwork 204–209
Community Worker Programme 29, 30, 32
competencies, supervision 92–94; administration competencies 94; education competencies 93; evaluation competencies 94; professional practice competencies 93; relationship competencies 94; supervision competencies 93–94
components, fieldwork 201–204; block placement 203; concurrent placement 203; innovative aspects 203–204; orientation 202; rural camp 202; study tour 203; summer/winter internships 203
concurrent fieldwork 232
conscientization 76
contemporary field-level needs 124
contemporary social work education 2
Cosgriff, T. 15
Coulshed, V. 161
Council on Social Work Education (CSWE) 105, 106, 140, 235
Cross, C. P. 240
cultural committee 73, 83

Dash, B. M. 59, 104, 106, 143
Davies, H. 126
Day, P. R. 246
Delgado, M. 204
Dhemba, J. 152
DiBartola, L. M. 15
Dictionary of Sociology and Related Sciences 151
discipline committee 83
Doel, M. 38, 117, 154
Dolhi, C. 16
Dorothy, L. 214
double-loop learning 48–49

effective communication 240
entrepreneurial social worker 195
essential skills: communication skills 222–223; documentation skills 225–226; fieldwork practice, social work 221–228; interviewing skills 224–225; meaning of skills, social work practice 221–222; observation skills 223–224;

research skills 226–227; stress management skills 227–228; types of skills 222
essential strategies 124–135; advocacy 128–130; evidence-based practice 125–127; innovation 128; multicultural approach 130–131; rights-based approach 124–125; risk and resilience perspective 131–132; social network analysis 127; social policy perspective 132–134
ethical idealism 214
existential casework 63
experiential learning 29, 33, 48, 58

Federico, R. 5
field-based learning 10
field contacts 23–24
field education 87, 138–149, 199; functional issues 146–147; Indian context 140–143; in Nepal 147; in Pakistan 143–145; Socratic method 148–149; structural issues 145–146; teaching, dialogue method 148–149
field placement agencies 179–181
field practice education 59
field practicum 58
field supervision 138
field training 44
fieldwork practice, defined 152
fieldwork report: active listening 63–64; activities by trainee 62; ethical dilemmas 66; evaluation 66–67; future plan 67; home visits 64; interviewing 64; observation 64, 65; plan of day 61–62; pragmatic exercise 58–69; pragmatic learning experience 65–66; preamble 60–67; quality of reports improvement, guidelines 67–68; rapport building 63; report writing format 59; theory(ies) applied 63; tools, techniques, and methods applied 63–64
fieldwork self-assessment report 115
fieldwork supervision 87–101; administration/organization of 90–91; brief history 88–89; competencies, supervision 92–94; concept of 88; definition of 88; guidelines framework for 89–100;

INDEX

objectives of 89; outcome of 101; school–agency interface for 88; supervision functions 97–99; supervision process 95–97; supervisors preparation 91–92; supervisor–supervisee relationship 99–100; supervisory behaviours 100

fieldwork training: agency supervisors, qualified and competent 163–164; Americanism, burden 161; challenges 158–159; concurrent fieldwork placement, suitable and appropriate agencies 164; eight decades, India 151–166; ethics content in 216; field education, uniformity lack 163; fieldwork agency, social work values and principles 165; fieldwork manuals absence 163; financial support, students 164; importance in social work education 153–155; inadequate fieldwork methods 164; in India, emerging concerns 158–159; less recognition 164–165; mushrooming schools, social work 162–163; objectives of 155–157; school supervisors, lack of visitation 161; social work educators and 162; theory and practice, linkage lack 161–162; unchanged pattern of 161

finance committee 73, 79–81

Fleming, N. 15, 17

focus group discussion (FGD) 73

focusing, guiding, and interpreting skills 224

food committee 73, 82

Forrest, S. 15

Fortune, A. E. 151

four-box model 51

Freddolino, P. P. 129

Freeman, Miriam 206

Freire, Paulo 76

French, G. 15

Gaiptman, B. 15

Gambrill, E. 125

Gardner, H. 234

Garrett, A. 123

generative learning 49

geographic community 205

George 153

Gibbs, L. 125

Gibson, F. 246

Gill, D. 132

Glaser 233

Goldstein, H. 217

Goodenough, W. H. 131

grounded theory approach: in fieldwork education 229–236; gap between theory and practice 230–232; limitations 235–236; methodology 232–233; navigating with social work 233–234; signature pedagogy and 234–235; social work education, India 229–230

group learning 12

group supervision 89

Hall, N. 10, 58, 160

Harkness, D. 117

helping professions 169

Hepworth, D. H. 59, 153

Higher Education Commission (HEC) 143, 144, 146

Hipp, J. 106

Horejsi, C. R. 244

host organizations 19, 20

Howard, D. C. 15

Howard, P. A. 15

human service professions 46

Hyduk, C. A. 129

Indian Conference of Social Work (ICSW) 140

inquiry-based learning (IBL) 199; junior students and 205–207

International Association of Schools of Social Work (IASSW) 2, 43, 103, 160

International Federation of Social Work 200

International Federation of Social Workers (IFSW) 1, 2, 43, 103, 160

invitation committee 73, 82

Jeffcoat, J. 16

Johnson, D. W. 28

Justice, C. 206

Juvenile Justice Act 47

Kahn, R. L. 64

Kasake, E. 152

Kaseke, E. 165

Katz, P. 152, 155

253

INDEX

Kaudshin, A. 117
Kirke, P. 152
knowledge base 44
Knowles, Malcolm 50
Kolb, D. A. 15, 51
Krakers, Anneke 195
Krathwohl, D. R. 49

Lacerte, J. 92
Lager, P. 99
Larsen, J. A. 59, 153
latest model curriculum 140
Layton, N. 152
learning plan 25, **26–27**
learning styles 15–19; feedback
    16–17; learning contracts 17–18;
    multi-modal 18; personal awareness
    of 18, 19; student reflections 16;
    VARK model 15
Leibold, M. L. 16
letter writing 226
Lewis, I. 162
Lewis, J. 246
Lindon, J. 244
Lindon, L. 244
listening skills 224
living-learning communities (LLC) 77
Lizzio, A. 139
logistics committee 73, 81–82
Lonergan, N. 107

Maciver, R. M. 63
MacLennan, N. 245
Mallick, A. 34, 123
Manshardt, Clifford 77
*Manual for Self-Study of Social Work
    Institutions* 141
Marshall, T. H. 132
Martin, T. 124
Masis, B. B. 49
Mccarthy, M. 151
mentor role 35
Mezirow, Jack 76
micro-planning exercises 72
Middleman, R. R. 97
mid-placement review 35
Mohit 16
Moon, J. A. 18
Moxley, D. P. 129
multi-culturalism 130, 131
Munford, R. 247
Munowenyu, E. 108

Munson, C. 106
Mupedziswa, R. 165

Nash, M. 247
National Assessment and
    Accreditation Council (NAAC) 90,
    91, 141
National Association of Social
    Workers 43
Neta, P.-O. 162
New Social Worker, The 124
NGOs 186, 191, 211, 218
non-institutional fieldwork 204–209
non-traditional fieldwork 204–209
nudge theory 213
Nutley, S. 126

observation skills 224
O'Donaghue 247
open community placements 158
orientation programme: adult learning
    principles 50–51; effectiveness
    levels, aspects 54–56; knowledge
    levels 49–50; learning, critical
    aspects of 48; learning styles
    51–53; objectives 47; pedagogy
    vs. andragogy 50; relevance and
    modalities 43–56; single-loop
    and double-loop learning 48–49;
    students' feedback 54–56; types
    and contents of 53–54
Orme, J. 161

para-professionals *see* field contacts
Pareek, Udai 76
Parker, J. 161
participatory action research (PAR)
    199; senior students and 207–209
participatory rural appraisal (PRA) 72
Parton, N. 159
pedagogy 50
"Pedagogy of oppressed" 76
peer group supervision 89
peer support 12
people participation committee 83
Perlman, H. H. 63
Pierson, J. 243
pilot committee 79
Pinker, R. 133
practice-based profession 1
practice-based professional discipline
    6, 58

254

INDEX

practice-led theory 213

pre-camp committees 78–82; finance committee 79–81; invitation committee 82; logistics committee 81–82; pilot committee 79; purchasing committee 81; resource mobilization committee 81; transportation committee 81

precise expressive and comprehensible (PEC) reports 67

procedural aspects, fieldwork 1–39; academic mentor/faculty advisor 21; briefing 11; case studies, learnings 24–25; competency expectations, meeting 37–38; curriculum 6–7; evaluation 36–37; field contacts 23–24; generalist perspective, social work 3–4; group laboratory sessions 11–12; guided process 24–35; learning styles 15–19; mid-placement review 35; partnerships and collaborations 19–20; placement/fieldwork coordinator 21–22; placements 5, 12; professionalism, social work 4–5; resolution of problems, guidelines 37–38; schools/ departments 7–9; secretariat 12–13; structure 9–12; student learning 13–15; student role 20; supervisory structure 22–23; work placement/ fieldwork supervisor 20–21

process recording 226

professional helpers 4

professionalism, social work 4–5; goals and service delivery 4–5; problems, issues, and needs 4

professional socialization process 133

programme committee 73, 82

Provident, I. 16

purchasing committee 73, 81

questioning skills 224

Raphael, F. B. 161

Ray, J. 92

Report on Curriculum Development 158

Report on Social Work Education in India 159

resilience 132

resource mobilization committee 73, 81

Rhodes, G. B. 97

Richmond, M. 71, 153

Rogers, C. 16, 63

Rooney, R. 59, 153

Rosenblum, A. F. 161

Rossiter, A. B. 246, 247

Roy, S. 59, 104, 106

Royse, D. 153

rural camps 76–77, 85

Sackett, D. L. 125

Schiff, M. 152, 155

Schneider, R. L. 129

Schon, D. A. 48

schools/departments, social work 7–9; overall attitude objectives 8; overall knowledge objectives 8; overall skill objectives 8–9

Schulz, C. D. 15

Scott, A. H. 15

Seabury, B. A. 242

Second Review Committee on Social Work Education 156

self-awareness 8, 117

self-directed learning 15

self-help groups (SHG) 31

self-scoring inventories 52

Shardlow, S. 38, 117, 154

Sheafor, B. W. 244

Sheppard, M. 231

Sherer, M. 162

shramadhan committee 73, 83

Shulman, L. S. 99, 100, 105, 234

Shulman, S. L. 234

signature pedagogy 105, 138

Sim, J. 152

Singh, R. R. 95, 114, 142, 201

Singla, P. R. 104

single-loop learning 48–49

skill base 45–46

Smith, Roger 51

social barriers 50

social entrepreneurship 195

socialization 152

social justice 133

social network 127

Social Service Worker Programme 29

social welfare agency 62

social work camps 72–76; don'ts in 85; do's in 84–85

social work field education, South Asia 139–140

255

INDEX

social work practice skills:
applicants, perspectives 173–175;
clients, expectations 188–189;
competencies, tasks 170–171;
competency traits, social worker
172–173; field placement agencies,
expectations 179–181; graduating
students, expectations 181–182;
learning 169–196; personality traits
173; practising social workers,
career path 192–194; recruiters,
expectations 182–188; skill
competency 171–172; social work
employees, career path 189–192;
social work entrepreneurs,
career path 194–195; students,
expectations 175–176; universities/
institutes, perspectives 176–179
social work practice theories:
changing workplace and workforce
218; developing 211–219;
recommendations 216; self-
exploration, training 214–215; theory
building, inductive method 217–218;
values and ethics, training 215–216
Social Work Review Committee 60
Socratic method 148–149
Spielberg, G. 242
Spitzer, W. 154
Srinivas, M. N. 151
Stage 2 Review Meeting 38
stage committee 73, 82
Stage I Review Meeting 37–38
standard budgets 84
Stokes, L. 139
Strauss 233
stress management skills 227–228;
controlling workload 228;
managing time at work 227
Subhedar, I. S. 87, 89, 105, 165, 200
supervision functions 97–99;
administering function 98; advocating
function 98–99; career socializing
functions 98; catalyzing function 97;
changing function 99; evaluating
function 98; humanizing function
97; integrative functions 97; linkage
functions 98–99; service delivery
functions 98; teaching function 98;
tension managing function 97

supervisory practices: for agency
supervisors 96–97; for faculty
supervisors 95–96

Tata Institution of Social Sciences 78
Teigiser, K. S. 153
theoretical frameworks 44
Thomas, G. 66
Thomas, M. 243
Titiloye, V. M. 15
Toseland, R. 242
Towle, Charlotte 29
transactional/relationship skills 213
transformative learning: camp
committees 82–83; camps
conducting, methodology 84;
case studies 74–76; community-
based, living-learning model
77; implications 78; in-basket
household budgeting 84;
perception change 77; pre-
camp committees 78–82;
proposed social work learning
transformation model 78; rural
camps and 76–77; in social work
education, India 71–86; social
work practice, indigenizing
77–78
transportation committee 73, 81
Trevithick, P. 248
Turpin, M. 153
Tusasiirwe, S. 106
Twikirize, J. M. 106

UGC Model Curriculum
141, 157
uniform fieldwork programme 142
University Grants Commission (UGC)
90, 123, 140, 158
University of San Diego 77

value base 45
VARK model 15
Vayda, E. 88

well-organized partnerships 7
Werner, E. E. 131
Williamson, M. 119
Wilson, K. 139
work-integrated learning 19